LIBERTY
& JUSTICE FOR
SOME

LIBERTY
& JUSTICE FOR
SOME

Defending a Free Society from the Radical Right's Holy War on Democracy

By David Bollier

Preface by the Hon. John Buchanan
Foreword by Norman Lear

People for the American Way
Washington, D.C.

Frederick Ungar Publishing Co.
New York

© 1982 PEOPLE FOR THE AMERICAN WAY
1015 18th Street, NW, Suite 300
Washington, DC 20036

People for the American Way is a project of
Citizens for Constitutional Concerns, Inc.,
a nonprofit, tax-exempt organization.

The views expressed in this book do not necessarily reflect the
views of members of the National Advisory Council of People for
the American Way.

ISBN 0-8044-6060-4
Library of Congress Catalog Card Number 82-51019
Printed in the United States of America

This book was made possible by a grant from the Mary Reynolds
Babcock Foundation of Winston-Salem, North Carolina.

Janna Diekema of Unity Christian High School in Hudsonville,
Michigan, created the cover illustration. Miss Diekema is one
of nine national award winners in PEOPLE FOR THE AMERICAN WAY's
"I Love Liberty" contest for school children. More than 35,000
young people submitted essays, poems, drawings, sculptures and
songs expressing their appreciation for traditional American
liberties. Each national award winner received a $500 U.S.
Savings Bond, a personal letter from former President Gerald R.
Ford and an award certificate signed by President Ford and Mrs.
Lyndon B. Johnson.

The article, "Books Into Ashes," by Kurt Vonnegut, originally
appeared in The New York Times, February 6, 1982. Reprinted here
by permission of the author.

The pamphlet, "Where We Stand: The Evangelical Right," was
published October 4, 1981 by the American Jewish Congress.
Reprinted here by permission of the publisher.

"The Library Bill of Rights" was adopted in June 1948 and amended
January 1980 by the American Library Association Council.
Reprinted here by permission of the American Library Association.

The article, "The Old Right in the New Eighties," was published in
April 1981 by LCA Partners. Reprinted here by permission of the
Lutheran Church of America.

CONTENTS

Preface

From time to time in our national life, leaders arise who promise to restore a past that never was and enthrone a future that never can be. Their vision of America denies some of our most cherished ideals: free expression, religious liberty, and equal rights for all. America is in the midst of such a period now. Dozens of radical right organizations are working to suspend the rules that make our political system fair, orderly, and civil. They whittle and hack away at the liberties guaranteed for all Americans by the Constitution and Bill of Rights. They want liberty and justice for some, not for all.

PEOPLE FOR THE AMERICAN WAY believes it is important for more Americans to understand the nature of the radical right and what its crusades mean to our traditional freedoms. That is why it has assembled this useful primer on the latest surge of authoritarian activities. Liberty & Justice for Some offers a timely description of the issues, leaders, and activities of the radical right.

History has shown that authoritarian movements do not just disappear. As in the past, the threat posed by this militant minority will recede only when other Americans mobilize to defend their constitutional rights and freedoms. May this book sensitize Americans to the dangers at hand and the challenges ahead.

John Buchanan
Chairman, Board of Directors
PEOPLE FOR THE AMERICAN WAY

Foreword

Three years ago, I left the half-hour television comedies with which I had been associated because I wanted to stretch myself in other directions. Fascinated with the political preachers and the preachy politicians of the New Right, I decided to write and direct a feature film satirizing this phenomenon. But after some months of research, discovering the increasing power of the Radical Right and the passivity into which the rest of America had fallen, it became evident to me that I could spend three years making one movie and perhaps, after all that time, <u>miss</u> the target. So, with the help of many respected national religious, educational, labor and business leaders, we formed PEOPLE FOR THE AMERICAN WAY.

As founders, we started with the understanding that America's promise as a nation is derived from its conviction that people can live and work together peacefully and productively despite profound differences. Through PEOPLE FOR THE AMERICAN WAY, we agreed we would do all we could to encourage others to actively celebrate the diversity of our rich cultural, religious and political differences and to oppose authoritarians of all stripes who sought to capture the tools of government to violate individual freedoms. By promoting a climate hospitable to diverse ideas and beliefs, we hope we can earn our place beside more established groups with longer histories of defending all Americans' free expression and civil liberties. How? By encouraging that passive, turned-off majority of well-intentioned citizens to turn <u>on</u> again and participate once more in America's public life.

In times of political and economic hardship, strident voices of division have always tried to replace those of reason and unity. The results have inevitably been a deterioration of free and open dialogue, a tension among races, classes and religions and the temptation to grasp at simplistic solutions to complex problems.

In our time of hardship it is the moral monopolists who
are feeding on the deep and valid concerns of the American
people. With rampant inflation, high unemployment, increasing
street crime and violence, surging drug problems and mounting
fears about foreign military adventures and thermonuclear
proliferation, our people are more frustrated, anxious and
fearful than at any other time in our recent history.

Enter the Radical Right, offering its seductively simple
solutions to our most complex problems. America's purity and
strength can be restored, they say, if only the nation submits
to the political and moral answers they see as Biblically
self-evident. They can see these "truths," they say, because
God is on their side. I would rather heed the warning of
Abraham Lincoln who, during the Civil War, warned that we
should never assume God is on our side, but should always seek,
as best we can, to be on God's side.

Every generation must deal with its own infallibles. In
the fifties, it was Joe McCarthy. If you challenged his
thinking or methods, you were tagged immediately as soft on
communism. To disagree with today's infallibles of the Radical
Right on numerous matters of morality and politics is to be
labeled a poor Christian, un-American, immoral or anti-family.

The Radical Right's leaders and supporters have every
First Amendment right to express themselves as they wish. But
if we agree that the American experiment is based on the
conviction that a healthy society is best maintained through a
free and open exchange of differing opinions, then the dogma of
the Radical Right violates the spirit of the First Amendment
and the spirit of liberty.

Crisscrossing the country as PEOPLE FOR THE AMERICAN WAY
was being formed, I came to understand why the Radical Right
has met with so much success. There is a deep spiritual void
among our people, heightened by an absence of convincing
leadership in government and our other institutions. The
Radical Right tugs at common umbilicals of the spirit: the need
for faith and hope, love and warmth, assurance, and the comfort
of belonging.

These are urgent needs, and it is no wonder that so many
Americans have fallen into the embrace of those who offer all
the answers. It is obvious, too, that we who disagree must do

more than criticize. We have to offer our own views, go public
with our own set of moral priorities. What do we believe?
It's time that each of us declared ourselves.

    Liberty & Justice for Some is PEOPLE FOR THE AMERICAN
WAY's most ambitious written declaration to date. David
Bollier has my deep respect and thanks for his impeccable
research and his enviable ability to explain complex issues
with clarity and a great deal of style. I am certain others
will share my reactions to this unique book: a new dedication
to helping America keep her promise to all citizens and an
enthusiastic commitment to protecting our Constitution and our
American dreams from attack.

    The American experiment is still new. Only 200 years ago,
our Founders jumped into unfamiliar waters, with only a Declaration of Independence and the Constitution to keep them afloat.
Today we may be only halfway across those waters to the
realization of the American dream. And we are in trouble.
Well, why not? Look at the scope of our ambition: Liberty
and Justice for All. We began in turmoil, and we are again
in turmoil, but we are still in the water, and making headway.

    Standing back there on the bank we have left behind are
the moral monopolists crying "Come back! It's safe here. We
have all the answers." Well, we can't go back. It wasn't safe
back there for our Founders, and it isn't safe for us. And
those simplistic "truths" do not address the complex realities
of our time. We'll keep swimming toward that far bank, because
ahead, not behind, lies the realization of the American dream.
All we need is the full participation of the American people.
Together we have come a very long way in a very short time.
Together we can go the distance.

                                            Norman Lear

August 1982

Introduction

Religious and political freedom is a right often taken for granted in America. Many people do not fully appreciate the remarkable guarantees that our Constitution provides: the right to free speech, the freedom to practice our religious beliefs without government interference, due process of law, and equal civil rights for all Americans. Our Constitution gives us a republic, said Benjamin Franklin, "if you can keep it."

A brief glance through a daily newspaper reveals the truth of Franklin's warning. Book banning in schools and libraries has increased three-fold since 1980. Many organizations are trying to force children in public schools to be taught sectarian religious doctrines. Others want the government to abridge the civil rights of minority groups in its social policies. In the name of religious morality, a large grassroots network diligently pursues this crusade against the political and religious rights of others.

While many Americans are understandably disturbed at these developments, it is often difficult to learn more about the threat posed by the radical right. Who are its leaders? What are their organizations and arguments? Moreover, what can Americans worried about assaults on our Constitution do to defend our rights and freedoms?

Liberty & Justice for Some hopes to probe these questions by looking at the timely, controversial issues raised by ultra-fundamentalist groups: book censorship, church/state separation, mandatory school prayer, "creationism," and the role of religion in public policy questions. This book attempts to explain the history, motives, and interconnections among these and other issues. For each topic, this manual provides useful facts, arguments, quotations, and resources.

The Plan of This Book

Liberty & Justice for Some is intended as a primer, not as a comprehensive treatise. Each of the 15 topics surveyed provides a distilled overview of the points of debate, the leading activists and their statements, and the arguments and counter-arguments. The question-and-answer format is used to make each section as accessible, succinct, and readable as possible. The goal is to give a quick, concise introduction to each issue, not sustained analysis. (Astute readers will notice that some of the questions posed in the Q&A are not really questions but statements; indulgent readers will forgive this technical inaccuracy.)

For convenience, this book is divided into three parts: Religion in American Life, Education, and Public Policy Questions. There is an unavoidable overlap of issues under each heading. Mandatory school prayer, for example, could logically be classified under the other two headings also. The three parts are meant to impose a loose order on the sprawling, interconnected political agenda of the radical right.

Liberty & Justice for Some is designed as a resource guide. The first section is an introduction to PEOPLE FOR THE AMERICAN WAY: our history, issue concerns, organizational structure, and funding. This is followed by "A Brief Guide to the Radical Right," which describes the issues, activities, and leaders of the most prominent organizations.

The remainder of Liberty & Justice for Some explores 15 different issues of major concern in American politics and religion. Since each section can acquaint readers with only the basic facts and arguments, a list of suggested readings, by both mainstream and radical right authors, is included at the end of each section. The suggested readings represent only a handful of available books, articles, transcripts, and other documents. Nonetheless, they should provide helpful guideposts to researchers, public speakers, and other inquisitive students of the radical right. Further assistance can also be obtained through the organizations listed at the end of some sections or through PEOPLE FOR THE AMERICAN WAY.

Liberty & Justice for Some is also meant to be a document of public record for the statements of leading moral authoritarian

leaders. Powerful public figures like Jerry Falwell, Phyllis
Schlafly, Pat Robertson, Tim LaHaye, Ed McAteer, James Robison,
Richard Viguerie, Paul Weyrich, Howard Phillips, and Mel and
Norma Gabler have helped shape public opinion, legislation, and
local activism. Their provocative public statements deserve a
broader audience and closer scrutiny. The text is therefore
laden with many quotations culled from a variety of sources.
Each is footnoted.

Finally, Liberty & Justice for Some is meant to spark a response. Thousands of Americans are anxious to educate their
communities about constitutional rights and the dangers to
them. For these concerned citizens, this book is meant to be
an instrument of education and inspiration. The attacks on
liberty waged by the radical right will continue unabated
unless citizens mobilize to defend our heritage of freedom.

A Word on Terminologies

The current vocabulary used to describe the political agenda
of Jerry Falwell, Phyllis Schlafly, and their colleagues is
inadequate. The term "New Right" does not properly apply to
these leaders and their groups because the New Right is a
separate, distinct -- and more secular -- brand of politics
(even though the two cooperate extensively). The term "fundamentalist" is likewise misleading because many fundamentalist
Christians abhor the political values of Falwell and his
friends. Similarly, to call these activists "conservatives"
is inaccurate, and distasteful to bona fide conservatives.

To clear up this linguistic muddle, we have coined several
terms to describe more accurately the surge of "Christian"
religious activism in American politics. "Ultra-fundamentalist" and "moral majoritarian" are essentially synonymous.
They name activists whose political views are intertwined with
a certain brand of religious belief and expressed by groups
like Moral Majority, Inc., the Christian Voice, the National
Christian Action Coalition, and the Religious Roundtable.
"Moral authoritarians" is another coinage that we use to
describe political activists who want to dictate personal
morality for all Americans through the power of government.

"Moral monopolists" and the "radical right" are other terms

that we use to name a distinct form of political activism.
Use of these terms is intended to name more precisely the
leaders and organizations who advocate certain policies,
without implicating innocent third parties now victimized by
the limited vocabulary of political discourse.

Who Belongs to the Radical Right?

Who then belongs to the radical right? The people of an
extensive national, state, and local network of groups who seek
to "reform" America to conform with their religious and political values. Each group plays a distinctive role within its
sphere of influence yet the groups also work together on an
issue-by-issue basis. It rarely matters whether a group's
focus is on censorship, creationism, sex education, TV programming, "judicial activism," or equal rights for women. The
different ultra-fundamentalist groups share the conviction that
the problems we face as a nation stem from a moral breakdown,
and that individual regeneration through their brand of religion mixed with politics is the only solution. Embracing moral
absolutes, they scorn compromise and negotiation as instruments
of their "godless" opponents.

The national media tend to focus on visible national leaders
like Jerry Falwell, Phyllis Schlafly, Howard Phillips, and
other luminaries of the moral authoritarian firmament. Although
these people deserve attention for the influence they wield, it
is also important to note that the real strength of ultra-
fundamentalists lies in their grassroots organizations.

By tapping the latent citizen power of their constituents --
often through pure demagoguery or appeals to their religious
devotion -- ultra-fundamentalist leaders have harnessed a
powerful political force. Organization and communication are
key reasons for their success. Those who probe the activities
of the radical right quickly discover the dense network of
research groups, newsletters, television and radio programs,
phone trees, training seminars, and direct mail fundraising
operations.

Paradoxically, ultra-fundamentalists exploit the democratic
process, the servant of a pluralistic society, to restrict
pluralism. Consistent with their crusade for a "Christian
America," ultra-fundamentalists want to capture public

institutions to reflect their personal religious concerns.
This impulse not only runs contrary to a cherished cultural
tradition in America -- diversity and freedom of choice -- it
threatens as well the foundations of our Constitution.

Thanks to....

I am indebted to many people who helped me prepare and revise
Liberty & Justice for Some. Marcie Rickun, research librarian
for PEOPLE FOR THE AMERICAN WAY, was a constant source of
research wizardry and moral support. This book could not have
been produced without her help. Anthony T. Podesta, executive
director of PEOPLE FOR, offered many comments and suggestions
that greatly improved the final manuscript. Jeff Risberg
helped chase down dozens of elusive facts and was exceedingly
painstaking and meticulous in the production of the manuscript.

I also received valuable advice from Frances Zwenig, Gene
Karpinski, Rev. Michael McIntyre, Helen Kissinger, Piper
Phillips, and Barbara Parker. Matthew Weinstein and Teresita
Ferrera helped keep track of many, many footnotes. Sylvia
Fernanders committed much of the book to type. PEOPLE FOR THE
AMERICAN WAY is very grateful to Carol Gerson for her design
assistance, Ray Ripper of Time-Life Books for his beautiful
cover design, and to high school student Janna Diekema for her
stunning cover illustration. Nancy Debevoise provided needed
comic relief and encouragement and shepherded the book through
many production and design thickets.

We are grateful to the Mary Reynolds Babcock Foundation of
Winston-Salem, North Carolina, for their generous financial
assistance in making this book possible.

Finally, a word of appreciation to Frederick Ungar Publishing
Co. of New York, which is co-publishing this book with us.
Frederick Ungar and his staff were helpful in making valuable
suggestions for both the text and the format of this work.

                                        David Bollier

Washington, D.C.
September 1982

People for the American Way

PEOPLE FOR THE AMERICAN WAY is a nonprofit, nonpartisan educational group founded in 1980 to promote and defend citizens' constitutional freedoms and traditional American values. We are a membership organization that uses public education programs, citizen action, training, and the media to protect traditional American liberties. We also conduct research on anti-democratic movements and serve as a resource center for journalists, researchers, activists, and other organizations.

Our Founding Chairman, TV writer-producer Norman Lear, served as a catalyst in bringing together many prominent religious and civic leaders to launch PEOPLE FOR THE AMERICAN WAY. Our founders -- now our National Advisory Council -- include such nationally respected religious leaders as the Rev. Dr. Charles Bergstrom of the Lutheran Council in the U.S.A.; Notre Dame University President Fr. Theodore Hesburgh; Rev. James Dunn of the Baptist Joint Committee on Public Affairs; Rabbi Marc Tanenbaum of the American Jewish Committee; former National Council of Churches President Rev. M. William Howard; and former Congressman John Buchanan.

Our Board also includes national leaders such as New York Public Library Chairman Andrew Heiskell; former Congresswoman Barbara Jordan; editor and author Norman Cousins; and former Warner Bros. Board Chairman Ted Ashley. (See complete list at the end of this section.) Anthony T. Podesta is PEOPLE FOR's president and executive director.

PEOPLE FOR is committed to basic American principles: the promise of liberty and justice for all; individual freedom of thought and expression; religious liberty and separation of church and state; support for family and community; and constitutional democracy -- majority rule with protection for dissenters and minorities.

The Constitution and religious faith have given Americans
strength and guidance, particularly in times of great change
and upheaval. They provide living traditions that guide our
daily lives and common values that bind us together as a
people. We look to religious leaders to help affirm values
that are sorely needed in our national life: mutual respect,
tolerance, fair play and compassion.

PEOPLE FOR THE AMERICAN WAY is committed to supporting the
non-political institutions that are crucial to our constitutional democracy. We encourage churches, synagogues, schools,
community groups, individuals and families to stand up for
traditional American principles. Our Constitution, the Bill of
Rights and the ethical guidance of our religious traditions
will serve us well if we affirm them.

By mobilizing visible public support, we can help ensure
that the rights to think, speak and worship freely belong to
all citizens, not just a network of self-proclaimed arrogant
"moral Americans." Our organization deals with three major
issue categories: 1) constitutional freedoms such as freedom
of speech, religious liberty and the separation of church and
state; 2) maintaining public schools and libraries as institutions dedicated to teaching children how to think as well as
what to think; and 3) public policies that affect Americans'
traditional values and the stability of the American family and
community. The following is a brief description of our major
programs that respond to these issues:

   Mass Media Communications. PEOPLE FOR uses television
extensively to discuss freedom of expression, religious liberty
and other constitutional issues with millions of Americans.
PEOPLE FOR's press officer maintains regular contacts with
reporters, and our monthly Bulletin alerts journalists, legislators and concerned organizations and individuals to current
threats to basic American freedoms.

   Citizen Action. PEOPLE FOR has embarked on three major
programs that involve citizens at the local level: the Schools
and Libraries Project, the Media Fairness Project, and a
Speakers' Bureau program. The Schools and Libraries Project
helps citizens maintain academic and literary freedom in their
communities. Through how-to citizen action guides and expert
advice, our staff works to inform and educate citizens about
the importance of our schools and libraries. Media Fairness

Project staff helps citizens respond to one-sided controversial political broadcasts. PEOPLE FOR members organize and participate in programming designed to expand the points of view expressed on television. Participants in PEOPLE FOR's Speakers' Bureau speak to different audiences about the importance of free expression and religious diversity.

Education and Research. PEOPLE FOR publishes a Quarterly Report and a monthly Bulletin, as well as a variety of special reports, issue papers and fact sheets. PEOPLE FOR's numerous projects depend on accurate, thorough research. We have assembled a research library that has grown to become one of the best collections of primary source material on anti-constitutional movements in America. Holdings include religious and political tracts, books, periodicals, speeches, and tapes and transcripts of television and radio programs.

ORGANIZATION, MEMBERSHIP & STAFF

PEOPLE FOR THE AMERICAN WAY is a project of Citizens for Constitutional Concerns, Inc., a nonprofit, tax-exempt organization. PEOPLE FOR's support comes from membership contributions and foundation grants. All gifts are tax-deductible and directly advance our work. PEOPLE FOR's primary concern is to serve as a catalyst for action through our educational and community outreach programs. We are not a political action committee and we do not engage in any activities on behalf of or in opposition to candidates for public office.

PEOPLE FOR is based in Washington, D.C. Branch offices are operating in New York, California, Ohio, North Carolina and Texas. Our staff of 30 includes professional media specialists, researchers, writers, policy analysts and community outreach experts. Our staff and board consult frequently with organizations that share our concern for constitutional freedoms. We work cooperatively with such groups to avoid duplication of effort.

PEOPLE FOR can be contacted at:

> People For The American Way
> 1015 18th Street, N.W., Suite 300
> Washington, D.C. 20036
>
> 202-822-9450

NATIONAL ADVISORY COUNCIL

Mr. Ted Ashley*
Former Board Chairman, Warner Bros., Inc.

Mr. James A. Autry*
Vice President & General Manager, Magazine Publishing
Meredith Corporation

Ms. Marjorie Craig Benton*
United States Representative to UNICEF

The Reverend Dr. Charles Bergstrom*
Executive Director, Office of Governmental Affairs,
Lutheran Council in the United States of America

The Reverend Philip L. Blackwell
Campus Minister, University of Chicago

The Reverend Claude Broach
Former Director, Ecumenical Institute of Wake Forest University
and Belmont Abbey College

Mr. Edgar M. Bronfman
Chairman and Chief Executive Officer,
Joseph E. Seagram & Sons, Inc.

The Honorable John Buchanan*
Former Congressman from Alabama

Mr. David Cohen*
Former President, Common Cause

The Right Reverend John Coburn
Bishop, Episcopal Diocese of Massachusetts

Sister Carol Coston
Former Executive Director, Network

Mr. Norman Cousins
Editor and Author

* Member of Board of Directors

Dr. James M. Dunn*
Executive Director, Baptist Joint Committee on Public Affairs

Ms. Marian Wright Edelman*
President, Children's Defense Fund

Ms. Mary Hatwood Futrell
Secretary-Treasurer, National Education Association

Ms. Eileen Rockefeller Growald*
President, Health Headways

Ms. LaDonna Harris
Americans for Indian Opportunity

Mr. Andrew Heiskell*
Chairman, New York Public Library

Father Theodore Hesburgh
President, University of Notre Dame

The Reverend M. William Howard*
Immediate Past President,
National Council of the Churches of Christ in the USA

Ms. Shirley Hufstedler
Beardsley, Hufstedler & Kemble

His Eminence Archbishop Iakovos, Primate of the
Greek Orthodox Church in North and South America

Ms. Luci Baines Johnson

The Honorable Barbara Jordan
LBJ Public Services Professorship, University of Texas

Mr. Lane Kirkland
President, AFL-CIO

Mr. Norman Lear*
Writer and Producer

The Honorable John V. Lindsay, Esq.
Webster and Sheffield

Professor Daniel C. Maguire
Department of Theology, Marquette University

Dr. David Mathews
Former Secretary of HEW

Bishop James K. Mathews
The United Methodist Church

Bishop Marjorie S. Matthews
The United Methodist Church

Mr. J. Irwin Miller
Chairman, Executive Committee, Cummins Engine Company

Ms. Joyce D. Miller
President, Coalition of Labor Union Women

Newton Minow, Esq.
Sidley and Austin

Ms. Bess Myerson*
Former Commissioner of Consumer Affairs, City of New York

The Reverend Mary Ann Neevel
Minister, Plymouth Church -- United Church of Christ

Mr. Frederick O'Neal
President Emeritus, Catholic Interracial Council

Dr. O. Eugene Pickett
President, Unitarian Universalist Association

Mr. Anthony T. Podesta*
President, People for the American Way

Dr. Gene Reeves
Dean, Meadville/Lombard Theological School

Ms. Ramona Ripston*
Executive Director, ACLU -- Southern California

Ms. Betty Cott Ruder*
Public Affairs Consultant

Ms. Noemi Santana
Convener -- Nosotros

Mr. Stanley K. Sheinbaum*
Economist, Regent, University of California

Rabbi Francis Barry Silberg
Senior Fellow, Center for the Study of Religion
Senior Rabbi, Congregation Emanu-El B'ne Jeshurun

Ms. Sandra Slater*
Partner, North Star Communications

Ruth Carter Stapleton
President, Behold, Inc.

Ms. Margery Tabankin*
Executive Director, Arca Foundation

Rabbi Marc H. Tanenbaum
Inter-Religious Affairs Director, American Jewish Committee

Mr. William P. Thompson
Stated Clerk,
The General Assembly of the United Presbyterian Church

Mr. William Velasquez
Executive Director, Southwest Voter Registration Project

Bethuel M. Webster, Esq.
Webster and Sheffield

Dr. Colin Williams
Senior Fellow, Aspen Institute

Ms. Edna Wolf
Executive Director, B'nai B'rith Women

A Brief Guide to the Radical Right

AMERICAN LEGISLATIVE EXCHANGE COUNCIL (ALEC)

ALEC is the only national organization of New Right state legislators in the U.S. The group has over 1,500 members and is supported by 350 corporate and association members and 73,000 individuals. Since 1973, ALEC has served as a clearinghouse of research, model bills, and legislative strategies for people involved in state legislation. ALEC spreads the New Right legislative agenda through workshops, conferences, a "source book" of model bills, and two monthly newsletters, The State Factor and First Reading. ALEC's model Textbook Content Standards Act, which requires schools to buy only books that reflect "pro-family" values, has passed as a resolution in Oklahoma and has been introduced in other states.

New Right leader Paul Weyrich gained control of ALEC from its founder, Illinois activist Juanita Bartnett, in 1974 with funding assistance from the Scaife Foundation. By moving ALEC from Illinois to Washington, D.C. and infusing it with fresh talent, Weyrich helped establish ALEC as an influential and unique New Right organization. Despite its heavy involvement in promoting legislation, ALEC is a tax-exempt, tax-deductible organization. Kathleen Teague, who has worked with Young Americans for Freedom and Phyllis Schlafly, is ALEC's executive director. Louis (Woody) Jenkins, a former ALEC national chairman (1977-78), is now executive director of the Council for National Policy.

Address: 418 C Street, N.E., Washington, D.C. 20002
Phone: 202-547-4646

AMERICAN LIFE LOBBY

The American Life Lobby is the most active and vocal anti-abortion organization in the nation. Within radical right circles, this group is the acknowledged leader on the issue. By tapping into so many emotional themes -- its slogan is "For God, for Life, for the Family, for the Nation" -- the American Life Lobby successfully resurrected an issue thought to have been settled by the Supreme Court's ruling in Roe v. Wade.

The A.L.L. boasts a well-organized network of "pro-life" activists whose work and polemics are chronicled each month in A.L.L. About Issues. The magazine features articles about exemplary "pro-life" leaders, action alerts on pending legislative votes and hearings, a calendar of "pro-life" activities, advice for activists, reports from other countries, and denunciations of "humanists," environmentalists, and the women's rights movement. The American Life Lobby also conducts a vigorous direct mail fundraising operation, resorting to hysterical, sometimes lurid, claims.

Congressional leaders on the A.L.L. board of advisors include Senator Gordon Humphrey of New Hampshire and Representatives Robert Dornan of California, Henry Hyde of Illinois, Larry McDonald of Georgia, and Jim Jeffries of Kansas. Onalee McGraw, the "pro-family" pundit of the Heritage Foundation, is also an advisor to the group.

Address: P.O. Box 490, Stafford, Virginia 22554

In Washington, D.C.: 6-B Library Court, S.E., Washington, D.C. 20003 Phone: 202-546-5550

CHRISTIAN VOICE

The Christian Voice is a California-based political lobbying group, which claims more than 328,000 members and 40,000 ministers. It is perhaps best known for its "Moral Report Cards" on U.S. senators and representatives, which rate legislators on a 0 to 100 scale on some dubious "key moral/family issues." In its 1982 Report Card, for example, the Christian Voice declared that the "key moral/family issues" included banning U.S. military aid to Zimbabwe, supporting military aid to El Salvador, and abolishing the Legal Services Corporation and the Federal Election Commission.

The Report Cards have also made some questionable judgments about the "moral" and "Christian" character of legislators. The 1982 vote chart gave a Methodist minister, Rep. Robert Edgar (D-Pa.), and practicing minister Rep. William Gray (D-Pa.) scores of zero. Evangelical leader Sen. Mark Hatfield (R-Ore.) scored only 42. As for Jewish legislators, five of the six Jewish senators and 25 of the 26 representatives failed the Christian Voice's "morality" tests in 1981. None of Congress' black members passed; 16 of 18 received zero ratings. Fourteen of 20 female members of Congress failed to make the Christian Voice's "passing grade" of 70 percent.

The Christian Voice has a political action committee, the Christian Voice Moral Government Fund, which actively supports candidates with high ratings on the Report Cards. By doling out $406,000 in the 1979-80 election cycle, the Christian Voice's Moral Government Fund stood as the seventh top-spending independent expenditure political action committee. The organization also has launched a series of television commercials, in which Efrem Zimbalist, Jr. and Buddy Ebsen promote prayer in public schools and other "moral" issues.

Rev. Robert Grant is president of the Christian Voice, and Gary L. Jarmin, a former activist in Rev. Sun Myung Moon's Unification Church and the American Conservative Union, is legislative director. The Christian Voice's Congressional Advisory Committee includes Senators Orrin Hatch of Utah, Gordon Humphrey of New Hampshire, Rep. William Dannemeyer of California, and Rep. Larry McDonald of Georgia (a member of the John Birch Society's national council), among others.

In California: 413 Forrest Ave., Pacific Grove, California
                 93950   Phone: 213-795-5412
In D.C.:   418 C Street, N.E., Washington, D.C.   20002
                 Phone: 202-544-5202

COALITION FOR BETTER TELEVISION (CBTV)

CBTV monitors television for morally "offensive" programming and organizes boycotts of the TV networks and advertisers that fail to meet its standards. Although the coalition emphasizes excessive sex, violence, and profanity on TV, its campaign against the networks is also a political crusade against "secular supremacist" programming (see "The Media" section). The political motives of CBTV are apparent from its list of primary backers: Jerry Falwell's Moral Majority, Inc.; Phyllis Schlafly's Eagle Forum; Judie Brown's American Life Lobby, the leading antiabortion group; Lottie-Beth Hobbs' Pro-Family Forum; and Beverly LaHaye's Concerned Women for America. Each of these groups is avowedly political. The Coalition for Better Television was founded by Rev. Donald Wildmon of Tupelo, Mississippi, in February 1981, when he persuaded Jerry Falwell to join the battle against TV then being waged by Wildmon's own National Federation for Decency (NFD). Wildmon is also the TV critic for Viguerie's Conservative Digest. After threatening the networks with a boycott in June 1981, and then calling it off, the coalition finally announced a boycott of NBC-TV and its parent company, RCA, in March 1982.

Address: c/o National Federation for Decency, P.O. Box 1398,
           Tupelo, Mississippi 38801
Phone: 601-844-5036

COMMITTEE FOR THE SURVIVAL OF A FREE CONGRESS (CSFC)

Paul Weyrich is the founder, inspiration, and director of this preeminent New Right group. With funding from Joseph Coors and the direct mail expertise of Richard Viguerie, Weyrich started CSFC in 1974 to recruit, train, and support New Right candidates for Congress. To help its candidates win, CSFC provides money, media and polling consultants, field support, and other campaign assistance. Unlike the political parties and most PACs, the Committee for the Survival of a Free Congress is especially active in primary elections.

CSFC has acquired a reputation as a pacesetter for New Right politics, in large part because of the powerful coalitions that operate under the umbrella project, "Coalitions for America." The separate coalitions cooperate to draft legislation, mobilize grassroots organizations, plan media strategies, exchange ideas and research, and plan tactics to support or oppose pending legislation. The different coalitions include:

o The <u>Library Court Group</u>, headed by Connaught (Connie) Marshner, is a high-powered group that meets biweekly to coordinate strategies on education and social legislation. More than 20 groups participate in the sessions, which are attended by the top political operatives of the "pro-family" movement and even by prominent senators and representatives. <u>Conservative Digest</u> has called Marshner "the pivot person in Washington, D.C. for the pro-family movement." Her book, <u>Blackboard Tyranny</u>, is widely read in those circles, as is her monthly newsletter, <u>The Family Protection Report</u>.

o The <u>Stanton Group</u> is a coalition of some 25 groups who plan strategies on defense, military spending, and foreign policy. Weyrich chairs the biweekly meetings of the Stanton Group.

o The <u>Kingston Group</u> is a similar coalition that meets weekly to plan legislative strategies, alert grassroots activists, and rally support for important congressional bills. Richard Dingman, director of the Republican Study Committee, an informal congressional caucus, chairs the Kingston Group meetings, which are attended by top business leaders and single-issue organizations. Bills that the group has rallied to defeat include the Consumer Protection Act, Labor Law Reform, and public financing of congressional elections. It has also targeted federal programs like VISTA. Kingston Group members include the Christian Voice, the Conservative Caucus, the American Conservative Union, <u>The New Right Report</u>, and <u>Conservative Digest</u>.

The agenda for the Kingston Group is set by an informal, exclusive group known as <u>Six Pack</u> -- apparently a reference to the number of original members and a pun on the business of a key member, brewer Joseph Coors. The membership of Six Pack, which meets weekly at the Heritage Foundation, includes Weyrich, Coors, Richard Dingman, Warren Richardson, former general counsel for Liberty Lobby, and Ed Feulner, president of the Heritage Foundation.

Also affiliated with the Committee for the Survival of a Free Congress is the Free Congress Research and Education Foundation, Inc. (see below).

<u>Address:</u> 721 Second Street, N.E., Washington, D.C. 20002
<u>Phone:</u>   202-546-3000

CONCERNED WOMEN FOR AMERICA (CWA)

CWA is a national women's group that considers itself a coun-
terforce to groups like the National Organization for Women,
Planned Parenthood, and the League of Women Voters. Operating
through a network of churches and ultra-fundamentalist groups,
Concerned Women for America focuses on "moral reform" and
"pro-family" issues. It opposes the Equal Rights Amendment,
the right to choose abortion, "immoral" textbooks, sex education, and the ban on government-mandated prayer in public
schools. The group claims a membership of 162,000.

Beverly LaHaye, the president of CWA, is a tireless champion of
"traditional values" in the style of Phyllis Schlafly.
LaHaye's monthly newsletter features articles about TV programming (she is a board member of the Coalition for Better Television), "secular humanism," the Equal Rights Amendment,
legislative updates, and the decline of morality ("Child VD
Linked to Porno Films"). The newsletter also provides a
regular forum for her husband, Rev. Tim LaHaye, the prolific
writer, lecturer, and ultra-fundamentalist propagandist. He is
a board member of Moral Majority, Inc., the author of The
Battle for the Mind, and founder of Christian Heritage College
in San Diego and the Institute for Creation Research. Both Tim
and Beverly LaHaye tour the country lecturing on "family"
issues through their "Family Life Seminars." They also have
their own TV show, "LaHayes on Family Life," which appears
throughout the country, mostly on Christian stations.

Address: P.O. Box 82957, San Diego, California 92138
Phone: 714-440-1267

THE CONSERVATIVE CAUCUS (TCC)

Founded in 1975 by Howard Phillips, the Conservative Caucus
boasts a vast grassroots network of more then 300,000 activists
and legislators in every congressional district in the nation.
The Caucus is one of the most active, visible groups of the New
Right. On any given issue, TCC can mobilize thousands of phone
calls and letters to Congress, the President, and other
officials in a matter of days. Its annual budget is nearly $3
million. Although the Caucus' primary focus is at the grassroots level, it also researches and monitors Congress through
its Research, Analysis and Education Foundation, which

publishes "Senate Report" and "Congressional Report." Howard
Phillips, who was chosen by President Nixon to dismantle the
Office of Economic Opportunity, in 1981 launched a TCC campaign
to eliminate the Legal Services Corporation, which provides
legal aid to the poor. Phillips works closely with Paul
Weyrich (Committee for the Survival of a Free Congress) and
Richard Viguerie (Conservative Digest and RAVCO).

Phillips' sister, Susan Phillips, is a former research director
of the Conservative Caucus Research Analysis and Education
Foundation. After publishing an article in the April 1982
Conservative Digest about federal funding to "left-leaning"
groups (which include the American Bar Association and the
National Retired Teachers Association), Phillips became a top
consultant at the Department of Education.

Address: 7777 Leesburg Pike, Falls Church, Virginia 22043
Phone: 703-893-1550

COUNCIL FOR NATIONAL POLICY

The Council for National Policy was founded in May 1981 as an
umbrella "non-political" organization of top New Right, ultra-
fundamentalist, business, and political leaders. It does not
endorse candidates, lobby for or against legislation, or take
official positions on policy issues. What it does is provide a
forum for top leaders to trade ideas, make contacts, and plan
new strategies of political action. "We share a basic commitment to moral values," said Rev. Tim LaHaye, the council's
president. The goal of the group is to make the members'
"shared values" dominant in domestic and foreign policy.
(Tom Ellis, national chairman of the Congressional Club, was
selected to succeed LaHaye as president in 1983.) Woody
Jenkins, former national chairman of the American Legislative
Exchange Council, is executive director of the council.

The membership of the Council for National Policy is a veri-
table who's who of the radical religious right and the New
Right. The council's executive committee includes Richard
Viguerie, the direct mail consultant; Howard Phillips, head of
the Conservative Caucus; and Paul Weyrich, director of the
Committee for the Survival of a Free Congress. Members of the
council's Board of Governors include Ed Feulner, head of the

Heritage Foundation; Ed McAteer, president of the Religious
Roundtable; Phyllis Schlafly of the Eagle Forum and Stop ERA;
Rev. Jerry Falwell, leader of Moral Majority, Inc.; Joseph
Coors, the wealthy radical right donor; Terry Dolan of the
National Conservative Political Action Committee; Connie
Marshner, head of Weyrich's Library Court; Congressman Larry
McDonald of Georgia; Dr. Henry M. Morris of the Institute for
Creation Research; Dr. Pat Robertson, president of the
Christian Broadcasting Network; William Rusher, publisher of
the National Review; Kathleen Teague, executive director of the
American Legislative Exchange Council; Rev. Donald Wildmon,
head of the Coalition for Better Television; Herbert and Nelson
Bunker Hunt, the millionaire industrialists; Rev. James
Robison, the televangelist; and many other powerful ultra-fun-
damentalist and New Right leaders. The Council held its first
conference in Dallas, Texas, on January 17, 1982.

Address: 732 North Blvd., Baton Rouge, Louisiana 70802
Phone: 504-381-9271

CREATION SCIENCE RESEARCH CENTER (CSRC)

The Creation Science Research Center, directed by Kelly L.
Segraves, is one of the leading promoters of "creation-
science." (See the "Creationism" section.) Nell Segraves,
CSRC's founder, was formerly associated with the anti-evolution-
ist veteran Henry Morris at his Institute of Creation Research
before a rift developed. Segraves' son, Kelly, now directs
CSRC, producing reports and model legislation for interested
"creationists." CSRC has a "science coordinator," Robert E.
Kofahl, Ph.D., and claims 12 "technical consultants" on its
letterhead whose specialties are chemistry, geology, agronomy,
biology, nuclear research, anthropology, and marine biology.

Address: P.O. Box 23195, San Diego, California 92123
Phone: 714-569-8673

THE EAGLE FORUM

The Eagle Forum is Phyllis Schlafly's self-styled "alternative
to women's lib." The 50,000-member group acts as an umbrella

organization for a range of "pro-family" issues: the Equal
Rights Amendment, the abortion controversy, the "moral" content
of textbooks, sex education, and other education and social
issues. The Eagle Forum also urges its members to "support
pro-family goals such as reducing the power of the federal
courts, building a strong national defense, lowering taxes, and
cutting unnecessary federal controls and regulations."

Schlafly is a legendary figure in the "pro-family" movement.
She is an attorney, a former Senate staffer, a prolific author
and lecturer, a syndicated columnist, and editor of a monthly
newsletter, "The Phyllis Schlafly Report." For all her accomplishments, much of Schlafly's influence derives from a large
base of committed grassroots activists, mostly women, the
Eagles. The Eagle Forum's "Stop ERA" committee almost single-
handedly stymied passage of the Equal Rights Amendment.
Schlafly has said she will soon turn her attention to textbooks
through her Stop Textbook Censorship Committee, based in South
St. Paul, Minnesota.* At the state and local level, Eagle
Forum chapters wage battles against "secular humanism" in
public schools, often with the help of the national office.
The Eagles are urged to rely upon Mel and Norma Gablers'
Educational Research Analysts and Onalee McGraw's Heritage
Foundation work.

Address: Box 618, Alton, Illinois 62002 (headquarters)
          Phone: 618-462-5415
in D.C.: 316 Pennsylvania Ave., S.E., Suite 203, Washington,
          D.C. 20003   Phone: 202-544-0353

* 820 Second Avenue South, South St. Paul, Minnesota 55075
  612-451-2698

EDUCATIONAL RESEARCH ANALYSTS

This national textbook review group is a prime source of
censorship lists for more than 16,000 activists around the
nation. The organization was founded by Mel and Norma Gabler,
a retired couple living in Longview, Texas, to "review" textbooks and other educational materials for "objectionable"
content. The Gablers have been exceedingly successful in
persuading public school and state textbook commissions to ban
many textbooks and even dictionaries whose definitions did not

meet their approval. Since Texas constitutes 8 percent of the
national textbook market, publishers have been known to modify
their textbooks in order to placate the Gablers, thus affecting
the entire nation's textbooks. The Gablers' "reviews" are
published in "The Educational Research Analysts Newsletter" and
occasional handbooks that instruct parents how to purge books
from local classrooms and libraries. The Gablers' materials
are the primary research and polemical tool for grassroots
censorship activists of Falwell's Moral Majority and Schlafly's
Eagle Forum.

Address: P.O. Box 7518, Longview, Texas   75607
Phone: 214-753-5993

THE FREE CONGRESS RESEARCH AND EDUCATION FOUNDATION, INC.

Founded by Paul Weyrich in 1978, the Free Congress Research and
Education Foundation is an influential think tank and educational group with a $1 million budget. Its mission is to
spread New Right research to the public and key decisionmakers
through newsletters, monographs, reports, media appearances,
seminars, and conferences.   Much of the foundation's research
is focused on so-called family issues and campaign laws and
financing, reapportionment issues, and other electoral activities. The foundation's chief publications include "The
Political Report," a weekly newsletter on the political scene;
"The Family Protection Report," which reports on social issues
like education, abortion, drug abuse, and pornography; and "The
Initiative and Referendum Report," which keeps track of
citizen-initiated ballot measures around the country.

Perhaps the foundation's most ambitious effort is its "Judicial
Reform Project" launched in 1981. This special crusade will
try to curb the power of the federal courts through a variety
of "reforms," even through legislation of questionable constitutionality (see "The Courts" section). The theoretical manifesto for this campaign to alter the nature of the U.S. government is A Blueprint for Judicial Reform, a collection of essays
by prominent critics of the courts. Paul Weyrich is president
of the Free Congress Research and Education Foundation.

Address: 721 Second Street, N.E., Washington, D.C.   20002
Phone: 202-546-3004

THE FREEDOM COUNCIL

The Freedom Council was founded by Rev. Pat Robertson in October 1981 "to restore our religious freedoms." The group intends to promote legislation at the state and national level to bolster the "Christian" position on issues like creationism, prayer in public schools, and abortion. It also seeks to elect officials who will "advance religious freedom and Christianity." Membership in the Freedom Council is restricted to "born again Christians" so that it will not fall into "the hands of the enemy," according to National Director Ted Panteleo. Panteleo organized the "Washington for Jesus" rally that drew a crowd of more than 200,000 in April 1980.

Rev. Robertson, founder of the Christian Broadcasting Network (CBN), sometimes uses his "700 Club" broadcasts to call attention to the Freedom Council, its supporters, and its issues. Ted Panteleo, national director of the council, appeared on Robertson's show in January 1982 to warn, "[E]verywhere that humanists or others reach out to touch our religious freedoms we'll be there and we'll stop it. We will take whatever action is necessary to shine the light on this attack on religious freedom." On the same broadcast, three Congressmen -- Mark Siljander of Michigan, Christopher Smith of New Jersey, and Robert Dornan of California -- endorsed the Freedom Council. Said Dornan: "I think the Freedom Council is an organization that can bring a focus at the federal level on the moral decay in our country...."

Although the Freedom Council does not even mention the word "Christian" in its brochure, its theocratic goals are no secret. Panteleo has compared the group to the wandering tribes of Israel seeking the Promised Land. In keeping with the book of Exodus, which says that God sent hornets to clear the Promised Land for the Israelites, Panteleo sees the Freedom Council as a swarm of Christian "hornets" preparing the way for a Christian political republic.

Address: P.O. Box 64323, Virginia Beach, Virginia 23464
Phone: 804-420-0773

THE HERITAGE FOUNDATION

The Heritage Foundation is one of the most influential and
respected New Right think tanks in the country. It produces
sophisticated, intellectual studies on a range of public policy
issues -- "everything from energy and fiscal policy to international terrorism and East-West relations," according to one of
its brochures. Indeed, the Heritage Foundation turned out more
than 100 policy papers in 1981 that are used by politicians and
their staff, regulators, journalists, and the public. In
addition to its sizable staff of analysts, the Heritage Foundation sponsors a "distinguished scholars program" for scholars
around the country.

Begun in 1974 by Paul Weyrich with the help of Joseph Coors,
the Heritage Foundation has gradually become more of a mainstream political institution. Its reputation was greatly
enhanced in 1981 when its detailed 3,000-page report, Mandate
for Leadership, became the blueprint for the new administration. Since then, it has positioned itself as the "ideological
gyroscope" of the Reagan Administration, in the words of one
observer. Edwin Feulner, president of the Heritage Foundation,
works as a dollar-a-year advisor to the White House's Chief of
Staff Edwin Meese. Feulner advises primarily on domestic and
social issues. Feulner also serves on the Board of Governors
of the Council for National Policy.

Another Heritage Foundation luminary, Onalee McGraw, is
extremely influential in the "pro-family" and education
movement. McGraw is the editor of the quarterly "Education
Update," a "parent-action newsletter," and the author of
numerous scholarly, if misleading, monographs on education
policy. She has extensive contacts throughout the network of
New Right education "reformers" -- including Mel and Norma
Gabler, the Texas textbook "reviewers," whose work has appeared
in her newsletter.

Address: 513 C Street, N.E., Washington, D.C. 20002
Phone: 202-546-4400

INSTITUTE FOR CREATION RESEARCH (ICR)

The ICR is perhaps the most effective of the "creation-science" groups. It is dedicated to refuting the theory of evolution and developing a scientific basis for the biblical account of creation. It is part of Christian Heritage College, founded by Rev. Tim LaHaye, and conducts research, writing, and teaching on a hefty $650,000 annual budget. Henry Morris began ICR in 1972, and directs it with the assistance of Duane Gish, the research director. The two men are responsible for a number of polemical tracts like Evolution? The Fossils Say No! and The Remarkable Birth of the Planet Earth. ICR produces two "creationist" textbooks: a "General Edition" for Christian schools, which uses biblical citations to explain the creation theory; and a "Public School Edition" that deletes all religious references from its explanation of "creation-science." Since 1975, ICR has been promoting a model "resolution" for adoption by state legislatures calling for "balanced treatment" of evolution and "special creation."

Address: 2100 Greenfield Drive, El Cajon, California 92021
Phone: 714-440-2443

JAMES ROBISON EVANGELISTIC ASSOCIATION

James Robison is the "angry young man" of the "electronic church." He is best known for his relentless attacks against homosexuals, television programming, pornography, and the moral state of America. Robison's weekly television program, "James Robison: Man With a Message," is the flagship enterprise for his $13 million (1979) ultra-fundamentalist empire of prime-time specials, crusades, rallies, conferences, retreats, publications, and direct mail fundraising.

All of these projects give Robison's religio-political message a broad reach. His TV program is seen on 68 stations in the country and has an estimated viewership of nearly 400,000, according to A. C. Nielson in 1982. The prayer and counseling hotline affiliated with Robison's program receives some 30,000 calls each month, providing names for direct mail letters on political issues. Robison's monthly magazine, Life's Answer, dispenses religious inspiration, advice, and political commentary on a variety of topics. Periodic prime-time specials, such as the "Attack on the Family," try to mobilize viewers against the "humanist" threat. Through these projects and his numerous public appearances, Robison has become a powerful

leader in the crusade to "Christianize" government. Robison
also pursues this mission as vice-president of the Religious
Roundtable and as a member of the Board of Governors of the
Council for National Policy.

Address: P.O. Box 18489, Fort Worth, Texas 76118
Phone: 817-267-4211

KINGSTON GROUP

See COMMITTEE FOR THE SURVIVAL OF A FREE CONGRESS

LIBERTY LOBBY

The Liberty Lobby is one of the most successful and visible
anti-Semitic groups in the country. It is reportedly financed
by Willis A. Carto, a reclusive figure who also founded such
groups as the National Alliance of White Americans and Americans for National Security. Based in Washington, D.C., the
Liberty Lobby claims 30,000 members and 336,000 subscribers to
its weekly tabloid, The Spotlight. The newspaper consistently
attacks Israel, Jews, and the "myth" of the Holocaust. For
example, it has challenged the authenticity of Anne Frank's
diary and the "anti-German" bias of the NBC documentary-drama,
"Holocaust."

The Spotlight seeks respectability by running interviews with
members of Congress and by trying to ingratiate itself with
mainstream conservatism. The Liberty Lobby's former general
counsel, Warren Richardson, had been proposed to be nominated
assistant secretary of the U.S. Department of Health and Human
Services in 1981, but his name was withdrawn when several
groups pointed out the anti-Semitic nature of the Liberty
Lobby. Richardson has since worked with Paul Weyrich at the
Committee for the Survival of a Free Congress, writing a
grassroots lobbying manual. He is a member of the exclusive
"Six Pack" inner council that sets the agenda for the Kingston
Group.

The Liberty Lobby looks favorably upon the activities of the
Institute for Historical Review, another overtly anti-Semitic

organization. Based in Torrance, California, IHR sponsors conferences, publishes a quarterly journal, and distributes several books that glorify Nazism and dispute the atrocities of the Nazi Holocaust.

Address: 300 Independence Avenue, S.E., Washington, D.C.
           20003
Phone: 202-546-5611

LIBRARY COURT

See COMMITTEE FOR THE SURVIVAL OF A FREE CONGRESS

MORAL MAJORITY, INC.

Moral Majority, Inc. is perhaps the most renowned of ultra-fundamentalist political groups. Since bursting on the scene in the late 1970s, Moral Majority, Inc., has set the tone and pace for much of the ultra-fundamentalist political activism. The man most responsible for the direction of the organization, of course, is Rev. Jerry Falwell. Falwell is the pastor of the Thomas Road Baptist Church in Lynchburg, Virginia, and cele-brated preacher of the TV program, "The Old-Time Gospel Hour." Falwell has been a pioneer of preaching, fundraising, and ultra-fundamentalist political activism. Through its national office and state chapters, Moral Majority, Inc., is active on a wide range of "pro-family" and "moral" issues.

Moral Majority, Inc., is something of a flagship for the ultra-fundamentalist movement because of its size, wealth, and charismatic leader. In 1981, the organization doubled its revenues over the previous year, with $5.77 million in contri-butions, making it one of the wealthiest religiously motivated political lobbies in the nation. Falwell's combined ministries -- the Old-Time Gospel Hour, Moral Majority, Inc., Liberty Baptist College, and other enterprises -- brought in $70 million in 1981, up from $56 million in 1980.

Moral Majority, Inc., takes pains to stress it is a political organization, not a religious group. Its brochure, for example, points out that its membership includes "millions of

Americans, including 72,000 ministers, priests, and rabbis, who are deeply concerned about the moral decline of our nation...." Despite this ecumenical veneer, Moral Majority, Inc., and its leaders frequently urge legislators to impose "Christian" (i.e., ultra-fundamentalist) values on other Americans.

The membership of Moral Majority comprises an aggressive grass-roots network ready to contact federal legislators when a critical vote approaches. A realistic estimate of the group's size is 400,000, which includes 150,000 new members added in 1981. In addition to periodic legislative alerts, members receive the group's monthly tabloid, Moral Majority Report. Board members include Rev. Tim LaHaye of San Diego, Rev. Greg Dixon of Indianapolis, and Rev. Charles Stanley of Atlanta. Cal Thomas, a former TV newsman, is the adept, sharp-tongued communications director.

Address: 205 6th Street, Lynchburg, Virginia 24504
Phone: 804-528-0070
In D.C.: 499 South Capitol Street S.W., Suite 101, Washington, D.C. 20003   .
Phone: 202-484-7511

NATIONAL CHRISTIAN ACTION COALITION

The National Christian Action Coalition lobbies Congress and monitors legislation of "educational, moral, and spiritual con-cern" on behalf of 1,200 churches, Christian schools, and Christian associations. The group is dedicated to "protecting, preserving and promoting the Christian home, school and church in America." As part of its overall effort to mobilize the "Christian" grassroots, the Coalition publishes a monthly newsletter, "ALERT," and produces numerous manuals, publica-tions, and films. Like the Christian Voice, the Coalition compiles a "Congressional Scorecard" of legislators' voting records.

The Coalition's affiliated political action committee (PAC), the Christian Voters' Victory Fund, also compiles a voting chart, "Family Issues Voting Index," and makes independent expenditures during electoral campaigns. The 1982 vote chart, which claims to assess "pro-family" values and "a sensitivity to biblical values," flunked every black Member of Congress. Twenty-eight of 32 Jewish legislators of Congress also failed.

The National Christian Action Coalition was founded by Rev. Robert Billings, who later became the first executive director of Moral Majority, Inc. Billings now works as the chief liaison officer for the Department of Education's ten regional offices. Billings spearheaded the drive protesting a proposed 1978 IRS regulation that would have taxed private schools, an issue that galvanized the religious right into existence. Now in charge of the Coalition is Billings' son, William, who formerly worked for the NCPAC and Phyllis Schlafly's Stop ERA.

Address: Capitol 1, 5515 Cherokee Avenue, Suite 306,
                    Alexandria, Virginia 22312
Mailing address: Box 1745, Washington, D.C.   20013
Phone: 703-941-8962

THE NATIONAL CONGRESSIONAL CLUB

The Congressional Club, founded by Senator Jesse Helms of North Carolina, is the wealthiest independent political action committee in the country. Originally started in 1973 as a way to pay off Helms' 1972 campaign debt, the Club quickly became a major direct mail fundraising group that now claims about 350,000 contributors.

In its ability to raise money, assist candidates, and shape issues, the Congressional Club resembles a small political party. Its power stems from its remarkable wealth. For Helms' 1978 re-election bid, the Congressional Club spent $7.5 million, making it the most expensive Senate race in history. A year later, the group went national and began giving gener- ously to other New Right candidates. It became the richest independent PAC in the nation during the 1979-80 election season, when it raised $7.6 million.

Some $2.5 million of that money went to help Senate candidates like Jeremiah Denton of Alabama and John East of North Carolina (who is now honorary co-chairman of the Congressional Club with Helms). The group also spent $4.5 million to support the Reagan candidacy in 1980. From January 1981 to March 1982, the Congressional Club raised an awesome $6.7 million, again surpassing all other independent PACs.

The Congressional Club is so wealthy because of the vast grass-roots support that Jesse Helms commands nationwide. It is a power that he has mobilized on issues of concern to him, such as cutting the food stamp program, fighting the Panama Canal treaties, and permitting mandatory prayer in public schools. Tom Ellis, chairman of the Congressional Club, explained that the group seeks "to counterbalance the political activities of the union bosses, the ERA crowd and the other far-left polit-ical campaigns." Ellis will succeed Rev. Tim LaHaye as chairman of the Council for National Policy in 1983.

Most of the Congressional Club's actual direct mail fundraising and other functions are handled by Jefferson Marketing, an incorporated business sharing the same address and phone number as the Congressional Club. As a business, Jefferson Marketing can perform campaign-related work on a commercial basis, thereby avoiding the $10,000 legal limit on contributions that a PAC can make to candidates.

In North Carolina: P.O. Box 18848, Raleigh, N.C.   27619
Phone: 919-781-5220
In D.C.:   311 First Street, N.W., 7th Floor,
                     Washington, D.C.   20001
Phone: 202-783-6729

NATIONAL CONSERVATIVE POLITICAL ACTION COMMITTEE (NCPAC)

NCPAC (pronounced Nik-pak) is the well-financed political action committee that has pioneered negative campaign tactics since 1975. Instead of supporting candidates it favors, NCPAC targets incumbents in Congress and tries to defeat them. NCPAC raised $7.6 million in 1980, making it the second-richest independent PAC behind Jesse Helms' National Congressional Club. NCPAC spent $3.2 million of its war chest in 1980 to defeat Senators Culver (Iowa), Church (Idaho), McGovern (South Dakota), Bayh (Indiana), and Nelson (Wisconsin) in their re-election bids. It has targeted several Republican senators for defeat in 1982: John Chafee of Rhode Island, Lowell Weicker of Connecticut, and Robert Stafford of Vermont.

In recent years, NCPAC's tactics have provoked something of a backlash against the group. For example, when NCPAC launched a $400,000 advertising blitz against Senator Paul Sarbanes of

Maryland 20 months before the 1982 election, Sarbanes suddenly
attracted a groundswell of new support and contributions.

Under the 1974 election financing laws, NCPAC remains accountable to no one. "A group like ours could lie through its teeth
and the candidate it helps stays clean," boasted John T.
(Terry) Dolan, the chairman of NCPAC. NCPAC is also one of the
prized clients of Richard Viguerie's sprawling fundraising
empire, RAVCO.

Address: 1500 N. Wilson Blvd., Suite 513, Arlington, VA   22209
Phone: 703-522-2800

THE PLYMOUTH ROCK FOUNDATION

Founded in 1970, the Plymouth Rock Foundation is a small
"research" and education group that labors to "restore" a
Christian American republic. In its publications, newsletters,
and curricular materials, the group affects the style of a
serious think tank, but it frequently makes slipshod, eccentric
analyses of issues that have little to do with the Bible as
usually understood. The Foundation claims the Bible holds
specific answers for such contemporary phenomena as inflation,
value-added taxation, and federal funding and regulation of
test tube baby experiments. The group's dual purposes are to
"(a) advance Biblical principles of self- and civil government,
and (b) emphasize the facts concerning America's Christian
origins and heritage."

Rus Walton is the executive director of the Plymouth Rock
Foundation and one of the earliest proponents of the "Christian
nation" movement. Walton is best known for his Christian
curriculum, Fundamentals for American Christians (FACS),
which is used in hundreds of Christian schools throughout the
country. FACS is a series of 26 lessons that sketch a comprehensive "Christian" ideology of government: "the source &
nature of govt., sovereignty of God, comparative political
systems, individuality vs humanism, the property of conscience." Walton also publishes two monthly newsletters,
"Letter from Plymouth Rock" and "FAC-Sheet," which provide
scriptural analyses of current events.

Much of the "original research" used by the Foundation, acknowledges Walton, comes from the Foundation for American Christian
Education (FACE, P.O. Box 27035, San Francisco, CA 94127).
FACE has published several "Christian histories" of America and
even a facsimile edition of Noah Webster's 1828 dictionary --
"the first and only American Christian dictionary!"

Address: P.O. Box 425, Marlborough, New Hampshire 03455
Phone: 603-876-4685

THE PRO-FAMILY FORUM

The Pro-Family Forum is a national organization that fosters
the radical right perspective on education and family issues.
Begun in 1975 by Lottie-Beth Hobbs, this Texas-based group has
approximately 30,000 members and chapters in all 50 states.
The Pro-Family Forum has actively lobbied against "secular
humanism" in textbooks and public schools and serves as a
clearinghouse of radical right publications. One of the
group's most widely circulated publications, "Is Humanism
Molesting Your Child?" is a tract that denounces the ERA, sex
education, abortion, federal social programs, and evolution --
all Pro-Family Forum concerns. Mrs. Hobbs is described by
Conservative Digest as a "pro-family powerhouse." She is a
former vice-president of Phyllis Schlafly's Eagle Forum and
currently serves on the boards of the Council for National
Policy and the Coalition for Better Television.

Address: P.O. Box 8907, Fort Worth, Texas 76112
Phone: 817-531-3605

THE RELIGIOUS ROUNDTABLE

The Religious Roundtable was founded by Howard Phillips, Jerry
Falwell, and Paul Weyrich in September 1979 to educate and pub-
licize the "Christian" perspective on a wide range of public
policy issues: creationism, prayer in public schools, and
assorted "family" policies. Leadership training of ministers
and lay activists is also a major function that the Religious
Roundtable performs through periodic seminars.

The president of the group is Ed McAteer, a former marketing
manager for Colgate-Palmolive and former national field
director for the Conservative Caucus. Televangelist James
Robison is vice-president of the Religious Roundtable. Serving
on the group's "Council of 56" are Congressman Larry McDonald
of Georgia, Senator Jesse Helms of North Carolina, Woody
Jenkins of the Council for National Policy, and several board
members of Moral Majority, Inc. -- Rev. Jerry Falwell, Rev. Tim
LaHaye, and Rev. Charles Stanley.

Address: P.O. Box 11647, 3295 Poplar Ave., Memphis, Tennessee
          38111
Phone: 901-458-3795

THE RICHARD A. VIGUERIE COMPANY (RAVCO)

Richard Viguerie sits at the center of many New Right networks
through his computerized fundraising firm, RAVCO. Viguerie's
early, innovative use of direct mail solicitations and computerized mailing lists is largely responsible for the financial
success of the New Right, and has since become an entirely new
medium of political education and fundraising in America. Five
RAVCO sub-companies carry out diverse tasks for Viguerie's
radical right clients: Diversified Mailing Co. prints letter
inserts; Mail House stuffs, stamps, and mails items for RAVCO;
American Mailing List Co. rents out RAVCO-compiled mailing
lists; Prospect House publishes and distributes books; and
Viguerie Communications publishes Conservative Digest and The
New Right Report. It is difficult to know just how lucrative
Viguerie's business is, but in 1977, Business Week said RAVCO
grossed $15 million a year. That figure has undoubtedly grown
since then.

In addition to his huge fundraising activities, Viguerie's
primacy in New Right politics is also guaranteed through his
magazine, Conservative Digest, a widely circulated monthly
publication of commentary and news. The magazine features
regular columns by Paul Weyrich (Committee for the Survival of
a Free Congress) and Rev. Donald Wildmon (Coalition for Better
Television), along with excerpted articles and speeches from
many other New Right and ultra-fundamentalist leaders.
Viguerie also publishes The New Right Report, a monthly
bulletin of New Right activities.

<u>Address:</u> 7777 Leesburg Pike, Falls Church, VA   22043
<u>Phone:</u>   703-893-1411

FURTHER READING: A BRIEF GUIDE TO THE RADICAL RIGHT

Conway, Flo and Jim Siegelman, Holy Terror (Garden City, N.Y.:
    Doubleday and Company, 1982).

Crawford, Alan, Thunder on the Right: The "New Right" and the
    Politics of Resentment (New York: Pantheon, 1980).

Drew, Elizabeth, "A Reporter at Large: Senator Helms," The
    New Yorker, July 20, 1981, pp. 78-94.

Ericson, Edward, L., American Freedom and the Radical Right
    (New York: Frederick Ungar Publishing Co., 1982).

FitzGerald, Frances, "A Reporter At Large: A Disciplined,
    Charging Army" [profile of Jerry Falwell], The New
    Yorker, May 18, 1981, pp. 53-141.

Hadden, Jeffrey and Charles E. Swann, Prime-Time Preachers: The
    Rising Power of Televangelism (Reading, Massachu-
    setts: Addison-Wesley, 1981).

Hill, Samuel S. and Dennis E. Owen, The New Religious Political
    Right in America (Nashville, Tennessee: Abingdon,
    1982).

Hofstadter, Richard, The Paranoid Style in American Politics
    (New York: Alfred A. Knopf, 1965).

Lamont, Corliss, The Philosophy of Humanism, sixth edition (New
    York: Frederick Ungar Publishing Co., 1982).

Maguire, Daniel C., The New Subversives: Anti-Americanism of
    the Radical Right (New York: Continuum, 1982).

McIntyre, Thomas J., The Fear Brokers (New York: The Pilgrim
    Press, 1979).

Rifkin, Jeremy, with Ted Howard, The Emerging Order: God in the
    Age of Scarcity (New York: Putnam, 1979).

Vetter, Herbert, editor, Speak Out: Against the New Right
        (Boston: Beacon Press, 1982).

Webber, Robert, The Moral Majority -- Right or Wrong? (West-
        chester, Illinois: Cornerstone Books, 1981).

Young, Perry Deane, God's Bullies: Power Politics and Religious
        Tyranny (Holt, Rinehart & Winston, 1982).

BY RADICAL RIGHT AUTHORS

Falwell, Jerry, Listen, America! (Garden City, N.Y.: Doubleday
        and Company, 1980).

Hetley, James C., Are Textbooks Harming Your Children?
        (Milford, Michigan: Mott Media, 1979).

LaHaye, Tim, The Battle for the Family (Old Tappan, N.J.:
        Fleming H. Revell Co., 1982).

    ------ , The Battle for the Mind (Old Tappan, N.J.: Fleming
        H. Revell Co., 1980).

Viguerie, Richard A., The New Right: We're Ready to Lead (Falls
        Church, Virginia: The Viguerie Company, 1980).

Walton, Rus, FACS! Fundamentals for American Christians
        (Nyack, N.Y.: Parson Publishing, 1979).

Whitaker, Robert, editor, The New Right Papers (New York: St.
        Martin's Press, 1982).

Religion in
American Life

Religion has always played a profound role in the life of the
American people. Religious freedom has flourished here unlike
anywhere else in the world. What many citizens do not realize,
however, is the role that our Constitution plays in ensuring
religious freedom for everyone. The First Amendment limits
government authority over matters of religion, providing
Americans with the best guarantee of freedom to worship according to their conscience. This political tradition has come to
be called the separation of church and state.

It is not easy to draw the line that separates religious
influence from religious interference in one or another sphere
of American life. Thomas Jefferson tried to clear up some of
the confusion by suggesting the metaphor, "a wall of separation
between church and state." The image is appropriate even if
the wall has become, in the words of one latter-day historian,
"as winding as the famous serpentine wall" that Jefferson
designed for the University of Virginia. Church historian
Martin Marty therefore argues for a different metaphor
altogether -- a zone of separation between church and state,
not a wall, because "distinctions here are not and cannot ever
become neat."

We should consider the issues of religion in American life and
politics with this in mind: the limits of acceptable religious
influence in government are not easily defined. However,
consistent with their constitutional function, the courts have
delineated how far the state can go in touching the religious
life of its citizens.

What makes the emergence of the radical right so disturbing to
the American tradition of separation of church and state is its
determination to bypass the Constitution. Ultra-fundamentalists make no secret of their desire to "Christianize" America

and capture the tools of government for their narrow, allegedly religious purposes. Their disregard for the political rights and cultural diversity of Americans is frankly acknowledged by Gary Potter, head of Catholics for Christian Political Action: "After the Christian majority takes control, pluralism will be seen as immoral and evil, and the state will not permit anybody the right to practice evil."

Part I will briefly consider several areas of American life where moral monopolists are challenging constitutional precedent, our pluralistic traditions, and simple civility in public life. These areas include:

- o Church/State Separation. This precious constitutional guarantee is the best protection Americans have of religious liberty.

- o Theological Disputes. Ultra-fundamentalists often claim a monopoly on Christian belief. Other denominations have different ideas of what constitutes Christian behavior in politics.

- o Religious Intolerance. The radical right frequently displays gross insensitivity to people who hold other religious beliefs, especially Jews.

- o "Secular Humanism". The radical right blames this bogeyman for all sorts of problems in American society, especially in public education.

- o The "Electronic Church". By pioneering TV religion, ultra-fundamentalists have captured a vast TV congregation, huge revenues, and great political power.

Religious liberty, as construed by the framers of the Constitution, was meant to be far-reaching. But, as with any freedom, there are responsible limits -- in some cases, constitutional limits. When some groups insist on a radical re-definition of church/state relations at the expense of the liberties of other Americans, an equally forceful political response is needed. "It is proper," advised James Madison, an author of the First Amendment, "to take alarm at the first experiment on our liberties."

CHURCH/STATE SEPARATION

Q. The separation of church and state is just a creation of liberal courts. The framers of the Constitution never intended to prohibit government from helping religion.

A. The First Amendment is explicit in its intention, as are the historical documents written by Jefferson, Madison, et al. In order to assure religious freedom for everyone, the First Amendment specifies two limitations on government authority -- the "Free Exercise Clause" and the "Establishment Clause." The passage reads: "Congress shall make no law respecting an establishment of religion, or prohibiting the free exercise thereof...."

Because the doctrine of church/state separation restrains religious authoritarians in their effort to "Christianize" America, they must resort to some twisted explanations for why the "wall of separation" should fall. They blame "liberal courts" for misinterpreting the Constitution and dispute the meaning of tracts by the framers of the Constitution. They also portray the First Amendment as an oppressive restriction on their religious liberty. Televangelist Pat Robertson, for example, argues that Christians are in danger of becoming a government-persecuted minority, so a constitutional amendment "over and above the First Amendment" is needed. Such extreme action is necessary, says Robertson, because the "unelected tyrants" of the Supreme Court are making "a deliberate attempt to bring the United States into line with the Constitution, not of the U. S., but of the U.S.S.R."[1]

This is a recurrent charge made by ultra-fundamentalists against church/state separation. They claim that just as the Soviet Union has purged religion from government and enthroned atheism, so too the United States is starting down the road to secular humanism and atheistic communism by prohibiting sectarian religious devotion from government activities. In addition, ultra-fundamentalists claim that church/state separation is a departure from the early history of our country. As the following pages demonstrate, this is patently untrue. But rather than admit the clear intention of the First Amendment, they blame scapegoats: liberals, atheists, mythical secular humanists, the courts, and so forth.

Q. What exactly is the doctrine of "separation of church and state," and why is it so important?

A. The doctrine known as "separation of church and state" is a precious constitutional guarantee of religious freedom. Without it, our government could try to prevent citizens from worshiping according to their consciences. The government could also force Americans, against their consciences, to provide financial and legal support to official state-sanctioned religions. Finally, legislatures could require that all candidates for public office meet certain religious criteria.

Over the years, the federal courts have developed three standards for judging whether a law violates the Establishment Clause. First, the Act must reflect a secular legislative purpose. Second, its primary effect cannot be to advance or inhibit religion. Third, the administration of the Act cannot foster excessive government entanglement with religion.

In addition to the "Establishment Clause" and "Free Exercise Clause" of the First Amendment, the Constitution in Article VI prohibits any compulsory religious tests for public office: "No religious test shall ever be required as a qualification to any office or public trust in the United States." The principles for maintaining "a wall of separation between church and state" were included in this country's founding documents because they are considered basic rights of citizens, beyond the power of legislatures, presidents, or temporary political majorities to revoke.

Q. What are the most controversial church/state disputes right now?

A. The most enduring church/state controversies involve the government's authority to:

o permit or require religious devotions in public
   schools;

o provide tuition tax credits to private and parochial
   schools;

o tax religious organizations;

o require the teaching of creationism as science in
   public schools;

o grant tax exemptions to private segregated schools.

But there are also a wide variety of relatively unexplored
issues. How can religious broadcasters be regulated by the FCC
without infringing on their right to the free exercise of their
religion? May the government refer needy individuals to religious social welfare agencies? Is church missionary work
violated by the CIA's use of ministers and missionaries?
The breadth of church/state issues is more extensive than most
Americans realize.[2]

Q. America was founded as a Christian nation. Our problems will
   continue to afflict us until we put the Bible back into
   politics.

A. The moral principles of the major religions have helped to
   build the character of our nation, but no religious creed has
   ever been officially enshrined as a constitutional principle.
   This is a core misunderstanding that motivates so many radical
   right campaigns: school prayer, creationism, and anti-feminism
   are all regarded as part of the crusade to "Christianize"
   America. The informal, ceremonial use of Christian beliefs,
   symbols, and rituals in American politics is a well-established
   tradition (as, for example, in presidential inaugurations,
   political campaigns, and the civil rights movement).[3] But
   this voluntary use of religion is different from government-
   sponsored laws that favor one religion or church body.
   Christian values may influence our lives and morality, but
   explicit sectarian religious doctrines may not be written into
   law. That represents an abuse of government power and an
   infringement of religious liberty. Religious liberty, if it is
   to have any meaning at all, must belong to all Americans and
   not just one group of Christians.

Q. Jefferson, Madison and the colonial statesmen wrote the Constitution as an expression of Christian values.

A. Many ultra-fundamentalists argue that our political system represents the "Christian ideal of government" and that Jefferson, Hamilton, Madison, et al., were simply expressing their Christian values in writing the Constitution.[4] Although many of the colonial statesmen were in fact Christians, their political beliefs derived largely from "humanist" philosophers like Locke and Rousseau. It was Jefferson who coined the metaphor "a wall of separation between church and state" and who collaborated with Madison in opposing a proposed tax to support Christian churches in Virginia. Jefferson wrote in an 1801 letter to the Danbury (Conn.) Baptist Association:

> Believing with you that religion is a matter which lies solely between man and his God, that he owes account to none other for his faith or his worship, that the legis- lative powers of government reach actions only, and not opinions, I contemplate with sovereign reverence that act of the whole American people...building a wall of sepa- ration between Church & State.[5]

For his part, Madison was perhaps the most adamant defender of religious liberty. He played a major role in writing the First Amendment, enacting the Virginia statute for religious freedom, and drafting several of the Federalist Papers.

George Washington also resisted efforts to enshrine particular religions in the Constitution. One of his first official statements about church/state relations was made in a treaty signed with Tripoli in 1796:

> As the Government of the United States of America is not in any sense founded on the Christian Religion; as it has in itself no character of enmity against the laws, religion, or tranquility of Musselmen; and as the said States never have entered into any war or act of hostility against any Mehomitan nation, it is declared by the parties, that no pretext arising from religious opinions shall ever produce an interruption of the harmony existing between the two countries.[6]

It is perhaps also worth noting that in 1800, probably no more than 10 percent of the U.S. population belonged to churches, according to church historian Dr. Robert R. Handy. Another historian, Dr. William Warren Sweet, finds that "the great majority of Americans in the eighteenth century were outside any church, and there was an overwhelming indifference to religion."[7]

Q. But the First Amendment forbids only Congress from making any law "respecting an establishment of religion...." It says nothing about state legislatures.

A. Yes, but constitutional history and simple justice have made it applicable to all states. First, the notion of a United States is meaningless if one state is permitted to suspend rights intended for all Americans. Some states had established religions when the Constitution was adopted, but by 1833 all states had revoked official recognition to any organized religion.[8]

The Bill of Rights (and the Establishment Clause) did not formally apply to the states until 1868, when the 14th Amendment was added to the Constitution. The 14th Amendment states, "No state shall make or enforce any law which shall abridge the privileges or immunities of citizens of the United States, nor shall deprive any person of life, liberty or property without due process of law...." Although the 14th Amendment was meant to extend the religious liberty clause to the states, the Supreme Court did not formally decide this question until 1947 when it ruled in Everson v. Board of Education that the Establishment Clause does in fact apply to the states.[9] (The Free Exercise Clause had been applied to the states much earlier.) This ratified the principle that no state should be allowed to abridge the fundamental political rights guaranteed to all Americans.

Q. Christians have every right to be active in politics no matter what the First Amendment says about separation of church and state.

A. The Establishment Clause was never intended to exclude Christians or any religious group from political activity. Nor was it intended to insulate government policymaking from moral or religious principles. But the radical right deliberately misinterprets the separation of church and state doctrine

as a ban on their political activism. Televangelists like
James Robison use it as a convenient foil:

> I tire of hearing the doctrine of separation of church
> and state interpreted to mean that those who attend
> church or believe in God can have no influence in polit-
> ical activity or public policymaking....I'm tired of
> hearing about radicals, perverts, liberals, leftists
> and Communists coming out of the closet. It's time for
> God's people to come out of the closet and the churches
> to influence positive change in America.[10] (original
> emphasis)

American public policy over the past two centuries has been
deeply affected by religious groups. Some of these campaigns
now seem quaint (such as the ban against dueling) while others
are generally regarded as proud accomplishments (the civil
rights movement and the abolition of slavery). Although some
people may disagree with the policies that some religious
groups advocate, religious activists cannot be faulted for
exercising a "social witness" to their faith. In secular
terms, it simply amounts to concerned citizenship. (See
"Theological Disputes" section for more on this debate.)

Q. What makes the religious activism of ultra-fundamentalists so
   different from that of mainline church groups? How is Jerry
   Falwell different from Martin Luther King?

A. Two key differences separate ultra-fundamentalist and mainline
   churches: how they view constitutional rights and how they
   participate in politics. Ultra-fundamentalists are generally
   hostile to equal protection of the law for all Americans.
   Women, blacks, non-Christians, and "sinners" are not entitled
   to full constitutional protection, according to the radical
   right. In order to exclude these groups from their full
   rights, ultra-fundamentalists support several constitutional
   amendments, restrictive bills and legislation that would strip
   federal courts of the authority to rule on certain issues (see
   "The Courts" section). The radical right opposes equal civil
   rights for women, gays and minorities. It seeks government
   mandated school prayer even though it would violate the religious rights of other Americans.

   This activism is a sharp contrast to that of Rev. Martin Luther
   King and the civil rights movement. King and mainline churches

wanted stronger enforcement of existing provisions of the
Constitution in an effort to expand constitutional rights.
They supported equality for all Americans. In addition, they
supported the federal courts in their right to interpret and
enforce the Constitution. Martin Luther King did not want to
revamp the Constitution in order to deprive other Americans of
their rights; he wanted the government to live up to the
promise of the Constitution as written.

Ultra-fundamentalists also differ from mainline churches in the
style and tone of their activism. Rev. King tried to appeal to
Americans' better impulses and idealism. He did not try to
exploit people's fears and resentments. Nor did Rev. King
stoop to demagoguery or name-calling in order to advance the
civil rights movement. Many ultra-fundamentalist leaders,
however, enthusiastically promote their political program with
negative, hate-filled appeals. They distort facts, exploit
people's anxieties and animosities, and dehumanize their opponents. Some examples:

o Edward E. McAteer, president of the Religious Roundtable, solicits contributions in his direct mail letters
  with rhetoric like, "It's time to take stock in America
  and take power away from the homosexuals, abortionists,
  porn kings, and radical liberals."[11]

o Dean Wycoff, former head of the Santa Clara (Calif.)
  Moral Majority, Inc., advocates death for homosexuals:
  "I agree with capital punishment, and I believe that
  homosexuality is one of those that could be coupled with
  murder and other sins....it would be the government that
  sits upon this land who would be executing the homosexuals."[12]

o Jerry Falwell, founder and head of Moral Majority, Inc.,
  attacked the American Civil Liberties Union as "the
  single most destructive threat to our traditional American way of life," and accused the group of having
  extensive Communist ties.[13]

McAteer defends his manipulative approach to politics this way:
"I use shocking letters -- stimulating letters. I'm appealing
to instincts. There's nothing wrong with instincts."[14]
Journalist Bill Moyers takes a dim view of these cynical political tactics. He notes that many believers are "being

misled...by manipulators of politics masquerading as messengers of
heaven, and their hearts will be broken by false gods who, having
taken the coin of their vote or purse, will move on to work the
next crowd."[15] In the Christian "witness" that ultra-
fundamentalist leaders preach, resentment and hatred seem to play
a more influential role than Christian love and charity. It is
this negative campaign approach, political extremism, moral absolutism, and mean-spirited style that set ultra-fundamentalists
apart from their mainline Christian companions.

Q. What do mainline churches and other religious bodies say about
   political activism?

A. There is a general agreement among mainline Christian denominations in the U.S. that church bodies have every right to
   speak out and influence public affairs. This was explicitly
   addressed in the joint statement, "Christian Theological
   Observations on the Religious Right."[16] Among the points of
   agreement with ultra-fundamentalists:

        o Christians ought to be actively engaged in politics
          and influenced in their political judgments by their
          faith in God and loyalty to God's cause;

        o Church bodies and other groups of Christians have both
          the right and the responsibility to make their views
          known on public policy issues.

   Senator Mark Hatfield of Oregon, who is both a practicing
   politician and evangelical leader, offers a similar viewpoint:
   "The Church can never make a true peace with the State and
   still preserve the wholeness of The Gospel by promising to
   leave politics alone and speak only about faith. Proclaiming
   the whole Gospel of Jesus Christ as Lord has inherent political
   consequences, as the early church quickly discovered."[17]

   In an essay, "Religious Responsibility in a Free Society," the
   late Rabbi Morris Adler of Detroit made a similar observation:
   "Religion has no technical competence in the fields of politics,
   economy, and social need. But it does possess the qualities
   without which no adequate solution of the problem in these
   areas of our national life can ever be achieved, namely, large
   humane goals and a passion for justice and righteousness."[18]
   Needless to say, the spectrum of theological opinion on what
   constitutes humane and just policies is great.

Mainline religious groups acknowledge the legitimacy of secular political authority and accept the consequences of violating its laws. The more zealous ultra-fundamentalists, however, deny the legitimacy of _any_ secular political authority. Tele-vangelist Pat Robertson, for example, considers church/state separation a totalitarian doctrine: "The government has come to think that really the church exists at the leisure of the government. In other words, the Supreme Court says churches exist because of a benevolent neutrality. That's a totali-tarian statement."[19] Many in the radical religious right cannot understand that a benevolent neutrality is precisely what guarantees religious freedom for Americans with vastly differing religious faiths.

Not surprisingly, the moderate Christian denominations are dismayed at the selective and self-serving interpretations of the Bible that ultra-fundamentalists make. In their October 1980 statement, the 15 major church bodies quote theologian Reinhold Niebuhr: "The sad experiences of Christian history show how human pride and spiritual arrogance rise to new heights precisely at the point where the claims of sanctity are made without due qualification."[20]

Republican Senator Robert Packwood shares the consternation of his mainline church colleagues: "God did not speak to any of us and say, 'You are right and those who disagree with you are wrong.' If any of us thinks God has ordained us to speak for Him, we are wrong. Worse, if we are in positions of power and believe we speak for God, we become dangerous."[21]

Q. How do ultra-fundamentalists deny the pluralistic tradition of American life?

A. From the very beginning of the Republic, America's founders recognized the profound differences among the nation's citizens. Diversity of religion, ethnic heritage, race, political belief, and countless other differences have been the hallmark of American life. Our nation's original motto proclaimed this pluralistic commitment: "E Pluribus Unum" -- out of many, one. Baptist minister C. Welton Gaddy explained the logic of this motto: "Unity without diversity could mean tyranny. Diversity without unity could mean anarchy. We needed both unity and diversity. Thus, we committed ourselves to the maintenance of a healthy tension between those two."[22]

Moral monopolists deny this pluralistic tradition primarily by insisting that government abandon its commitment to church/ state separation. There are some 1,200 distinct religious groups in the United States, and several major religious tradi- tions.[23] Yet ultra-fundamentalists want to use government to promote their own sectarian doctrines, to the exclusion of others. Fortunately, the framers of the Constitution foresaw the dangers of religious extremism and the value of pluralism and republican government in checking it. James Madison wrote in Federalist No. 10, "A religious sect may degenerate into a political faction in a part of the Confederacy; but the variety of sects dispersed over the entire face of it must secure the national councils against any dangers from that source."[24] Thus pluralism is not simply a philosophical, cultural tradi- tion but a shrewd principle for sound government.

Q. How do ultra-fundamentalists deny basic premises of our polit- ical system?

A. Our pluralistic political system is based on negotiation, debate, and compromise. "Among these people," observes C. Welton Gaddy, "no longer do investigation, dialogue, and compromise have credibility in the political process. Individuals are either right or wrong, religious or irreli- gious. Society has been divided into saints and sinners."[25] Former Senator Thomas McIntyre of New Hampshire explains why ultra-fundamentalist activism in political affairs is so disruptive:

> Politics is inescapably the realm of contingencies and
> ambiguities, of difficult choices among unsatisfactory
> alternatives, of melding into workable consensus and
> conflicting values within a pluralistic society. Citi-
> zens are cruelly deceived when they are led to believe
> that it is possible, on the basis of some higher reve-
> lation as interpreted by adamantly righteous religious
> leaders, to transcend the need for study and reasoned
> debate about political issues, or to invest their polit-
> ical judgments with the same passionate certitude they
> may have about the nature of God and the ultimate destiny
> of human kind.[26]

The ultra-fundamentalist who insists upon absolute policies, without compromise, based solely on biblical revelation, denies the very essence of American politics. Many Christian denomi-

nations and church groups have profound theological disagreements with the ultra-fundamentalists as well. (See
"Theological Disputes" section.)

Q. Do the religious beliefs of Senators and Representatives
   determine how they vote?

A. Religious beliefs and values do have a profound impact on the
   voting behavior of federal legislators, according to a survey
   of 80 members of the 96th Congress (1979-80). But denominational affiliations have less influence on legislative decisions, say researchers Peter L. Benson and Merton P. Strommen,
   than "religious value systems," which they identified.[27]
   Legislators who expressed an orthodox or traditional religious
   faith -- a plurality of 44 percent -- tended to favor higher
   military spending, so-called "pro-family" positions, and an
   unregulated market economy, while opposing government action to
   help minorities, the poor, and the hungry.

   Roughly one-fifth (19 percent) of the legislators subscribed to
   a "people concerned" or "nontraditional" religious value system.
   This group tended to favor civil liberties, hunger relief,
   foreign aid, free choice on abortion, human welfare programs,
   and lower military spending. Other categories -- "integrated
   religionists," who expressed a concern for people and traditional theology, and "nominal religionists" -- did not exhibit
   any clear voting pattern. Three out of four of the evangelicals in Congress are "extremely conservative politically," say
   Benson and Strommen, yet the remainder often have extremely
   liberal voting records. All of this bolsters a central conclusion of the report, that "religion is richer and more complex
   than most people imagine and the link between religion and
   politics is even more complicated."

Q. Candidates for public office should answer a questionnaire on
   moral issues to show their biblical commitment.

A. Any citizen or group has the right to ask whatever it wants of
   political candidates. But a litmus test of religious "accept-
   ability" is an offensive idea that violates our nation's code
   of public life.

   Politically and culturally, Americans are committed to diversity of opinion and religious tolerance. Article VI of the

Constitution even prohibits the government from requiring any
religious tests for public office. Voters are entitled to know
where a candidate stands on issues of public concern but personal religious beliefs are a matter of individual conscience
and should be respected.

None of this deterred several state chapters of Moral Majority,
Inc., from asking political candidates to answer "morality
questionnaires." The New York State chapter of Moral Majority,
Inc., issued a 43-item questionnaire for candidates in 1981
which included questions like:

o "Do you think that any form of government should have
   authority over any legitimate, Biblical ministry of
   God?"   (#19)

o "Are you a church member?" "Where?" "Do you attend
   church regularly?" "How often?"   (#32-35)

o "Have you ever been born again?"   (#42)

o "If you died today do you know you would go to Heaven?"
   (#43) [28]

Moral Majority, Inc., in Ohio peppered candidates with a series
of loaded questions like "Do you believe pornography is a
problem in Stark County?" and "Do you favor equal rights for
homosexuals?"[29] Moral Majority chapters in Indiana, Idaho,
Washington, and Nebraska have also assembled religious tests
that violate the spirit of Article VI of the Constitution.

The Christian Voice, which claims to be the largest Christian
political action committee, broke new frontiers in deceptive,
negative campaigning when it started issuing "moral report
cards" for members of Congress. Their 1980 vote chart identified eight "key moral issues" including a balanced federal
budget, school busing, tuition tax credits, and a federal
grants program for behavioral research (which had given a small
grant for researching into "homosexual couple formation.") [30]
Rep. Bob Kastenmeier (D-Wisc.), singled out for voting against
Christian Voice morality 97 percent of the time, was baffled
and angry: "I fail to understand what a balanced budget has to
do with morality. If that is the case, Ronald Reagan is very
immoral indeed...."[31] The Voice demonstrated its peculiar
definition of morality in its 1982 vote chart by giving Rep.

Robert Edgar and Rep. William Gray, both ordained ministers,
ratings of zero.[32]

It is a truism that government needs good and honest public
servants. But it is highly dubious that "morality questionnaires" will improve the administration of government or the
morality of its decisions. The public business should not be
consumed by censorship and by regulating private behavior or
religious practice, but by problems of public administration,
economics, and social equity. In short, the criteria for
entrance to Heaven (as decreed by one religious group) will not
necessarily make for a good mayor, legislator, judge, or dog-
catcher. Bill Moyers put it astutely in one of his broadcasts:

> It is not that the evangelicals are taking politics
> seriously that bothers me. It is the lie they're being
> told by the demagogues who flatter them into believing
> they can achieve politically the certitude they have
> embraced theologically. The world doesn't work that way.
> There is no heaven on earth.[33]

QUOTABLE QUOTES

"The role of government is to minister justice and to protect
the rights of its citizens by being a terror to evildoers
within and without the nation."

> -- Rev. Jerry Falwell,
> Listen, America!

"The idea that religion and politics don't mix was invented by
the Devil to keep Christians from running their own country."

> -- Rev. Jerry Falwell, July 4,
> 1976, as reported in Jerry
> Falwell: An Unauthorized
> Profile

"In His infinite wisdom, mercy and justice, God gave man the
pattern for right civil govt.: the theocratic republic. It was
this form of civil govt. He ordained for the Hebrews; it was
this form of govt. that was in large part the matrix for this
republic, as constructed by our founding fathers."

> -- Rus Walton, FAC-Sheet #19,
> "Justice & the Courts"

"Neither our founding fathers nor Jesus Christ initiated the
current god-less interpretation of the doctrine of church-state
separation....We must commit ourselves to the principles of
God, then demand that both parties and politicians uphold those
eternal biblical values or be voted out."

> -- Rev. James Robison,
> Life's Answer, October 1980

"The sad experiences of Christian history show how human pride
and spiritual arrogance rise to new heights precisely at the
point where the claims of sanctity are made without due
qualification."

> -- Reinhold Neibuhr

"God does not speak to any of us and say, 'You are right and those who disagree with you are wrong.' If any of us thinks God has ordained us to speak for Him, we are wrong. Worse, if we are in positions of power and believe we speak for God, we become dangerous."

> -- Senator Robert Packwood,
> Portland Oregonian,
> August 19, 1981

"Rulers who wished to subvert the public liberty may have found an established clergy convenient auxiliaries. A just government, instituted to secure and perpetuate it, needs them not. Such a government will be best supported by protecting every citizen in the enjoyment of his religion, by neither invading the equal rights of any sect, nor suffering any sect to invade those of another."

"[T]he same authority which could establish Christianity in exclusion of all other religions could establish any particular sect of Christians in exclusion of all other sects."

> -- James Madison, "Memorial and
> Remonstrance Against Religious
> Assessment," 1785 (response to
> Virginia House of Delegates'
> proposal to levy a tax to
> benefit religious groups)

"The Senators and Representatives before mentioned, and the Members of the several State Legislatures, and all executive and judicial Officers, both of the United States and of the several States, shall be bound by Oath or Affirmation, to support this Constitution; but no religious Test shall ever be required as a Qualification to any Office or Public Trust under the United States."

> -- Article VI, The Constitution
> of the United States

THOMAS JEFFERSON ON RELIGION, POLITICS, AND GOVERNMENT

"We have no right to prejudice another in his <u>civil</u> enjoyments because he is of another church. If any man errs from the right way it is his own misfortune, no injury to thee; nor therefore art thou to punish him in the things of this life because thou supposeth he will be miserable in that which is to come -- on the contrary, according to the spirit of the gospel, charity, bounty, liberality is due to him."

"Every church is to itself orthodox; to <u>others</u> erroneous or heretical."

                              -- <u>Notes on Religion</u>, October
                                 1776

"The legitimate powers of government extend to such acts only as they are injurious to others. But it does me no injury for my neighbor to say there are 20 gods, or no God. It neither picks my pocket nor breaks my leg."

"Is uniformity attainable? Millions of innocent men, women, and children, since the introduction of Christianity, have been burnt, tortured, fined, imprisoned, yet we have not advanced one inch toward uniformity."

                         -- <u>Notes on Virginia</u>, Query 17

"The clergy, by getting themselves established by law and ingrafted into the machinery of government, have been a very formidable engine against the civil and religious rights of man."

                              -- Letter to J. Moor, 1800

"As usual, those whose dogmas are the most unintelligible are the most angry."

                              -- Letter to S. Hales, 1818

NOTES: CHURCH/STATE SEPARATION

1. Editorial "Taking a 'Club' to the First Amendment," Church
    & State, November 1981, p. 195.

2. See John M. Swomley, Jr., "The Decade Ahead in Church-
    State Issues," The Christian Century, February 25, 1981,
    p. 199.

3. See, e.g., Robert N. Bellah and Phillip E. Hammond,
    Varieties of Civil Religion (San Francisco, California:
    Harper and Row, 1980).

4. See, e.g., Rus Walton, One Nation Under God (Washington,
    D.C.: Third Century Publishers, 1975) and Peter Marshall
    and David Manuel, The Light and the Glory, (Old Tappan,
    N.J.: Fleming H.Revell Co., 1977).

5. H. A. Washington, editor, The Writings of Thomas Jefferson
    (U.S. Congress, 1854), Vol. 8, p. 113.

6. Treaty with Tripoli, 1796, Article XI, in Hunter Miller,
    Treaties and Other International Acts of the United States
    of America (U.S. Government Printing Office, 1931), p. 365.

7. Robert T. Handy, History of the Churches in U.S. and
    Canada (New York: Oxford University Press, 1977). Also,
    William W. Sweet, Revivalism in America (Magnolia, Massa-
    chusetts: Peter Smith, 1944).

    See also: Ashley Montagu and Edward Darling, The Ignorance
    of Certainty, "The United States is a Christian Nation?"
    (New York: Harper and Row, 1980). Also, Franklin Hamlin
    Littell, From State Church to Pluralism: A Protestant
    Interpretation of Religion in American History (New York:
    Macmillan Co., 1971).

8. John M. Swomley, Jr., "Has the Supreme Court Eroded the
    First Amendment?" Church & State, December 1981, p. 252.

9. Everson v. Board of Education, 370 U.S. 1 (1947).

10. James Robison, "Commit to: Bible Principles -- Not Polit-
    ical Promises," Life's Answer, October 1980, p. 2.

11. Edward E. McAteer, direct mail solicitation letter for
     "Dedicated Christians for the Family Protection Act,"
     a project of the Religious Roundtable, October 1981.

12. The Advocate, March 19, 1981.

13. Jerry Falwell, direct mail solicitation letter for Moral
     Majority Foundation, with enclosure, "Confidential!
     Expose on ACLU," 1981.

14. "'Roundtable' President to Correct Mail Campaign Errors,"
     The United Methodist Reporter, February 27, 1981.

15. Bill Moyers Journal, television transcript, Campaign
     Report #3, Show #603, Public Broadcasting Service, air
     date, September 26, 1980.

16. "Christian Theological Observations on the Religious
     Right," statement issued by 15 major church bodies in
     Washington, D.C., October 20, 1980. Groups signing
     include: United Methodist Church, Lutheran Council in the
     U.S.A.; American Baptist Churches in the U.S.A.; Evan-
     gelical Covenant Church in America; Moravian Church,
     Northern Province; Christian Methodist Episcopal Church;
     Progressive National Baptist Convention, Inc.; Friends
     General Conference; Church of the Brethren; United Church
     of Christ; Baptist Joint Committee on Public Affairs;
     Christian Church (Disciples of Christ); Presbyterian
     Church in the U.S.; and United Presbyterian Church in the
     U.S.A.

17. Mark Hatfield, Between a Rock and a Hard Place (Waco,
     Texas: Word Books, 1977).

18. Morris Adler, "Religious Responsibility in a Free Soci-
     ety," excerpted from May I Have a Word With You? (Crown
     Publishers, 1967), in Face to Face, An Interreligious
     Bulletin (Anti-Defamation League of B'nai B'rith), Vol.
     VIII, Winter 1981.

19. Rev. Pat Robertson, "700 Club" special broadcast, "Seven
     Days Ablaze", October 1981.

20. "Christian Theological Observations..." op. cit.

21. Robert Packwood, Watch on the Right (Des Moines, Iowa, newsletter), June 1981. Also, Portland Oregonian, August 19, 1981.

22. C. Welton Gaddy, "This Land is Our Land," Church & State, November 1981, p. 227.

23. J. Gordon Melton, Encyclopedia of American Religions, 2 vols. (Wilmington, N.C.: McGrath Publishers, 1978).

24. James Madison, Federalist No. 10.

25. C. Welton Gaddy, op. cit., p. 226.

26. Thomas McIntyre with John C. Obert, The Fear Brokers (New York: The Pilgrim Press, 1979).

27. The conclusions of this survey, conducted by Peter L. Benson and Merton P. Strommen for the Search Institute of Minneapolis, will be expanded into a book, Religion on Capitol Hill, scheduled for release by Harper & Row in September 1982. The article about their research appeared in "How Religion and Politics Mix on Capitol Hill," Church & State, February 1982, p. 36.

28. "Moral Majority Candidate Questionnaire," Moral Majority Report of New York State, July 1981, p. 9.

29. "Morality 'Tests' Poor Way to Judge Public Servants," Akron (Ohio) Beacon Journal, October 11, 1981.

30. Rob Fixmer, "Christian Voice Targets Kastenmeier," Madison (Wisc.) Capital Times, November 7, 1981.

31. Ibid.

32. William Billings, "Family Issues Voting Index," Christian Voters' Victory Fund, 1980.

33. Bill Moyers Journal, op. cit.

FURTHER READING: CHURCH/STATE SEPARATION

Bellah, Robert N. and Phillip E. Hammond, Varieties of Civil
        Religion (New York: Harper and Row, 1980).

Church & State, monthly magazine (Available from Americans
        United for Separation of Church and State, 8120
        Fenton Street, Silver Spring, Maryland 20910).

Dawson, Joseph Martin, America's Way in Church, State, and
        Society (New York: Macmillan Co., 1953).

Ericson, Edward L., American Freedom and the Radical Right (New
        York: Frederick Ungar Publishing Co., 1982).

Giamatti, A. Bartlett, "A Liberal Education and the New Coer-
        cion," Freshman Address, Yale University, August 31,
        1981.

Hatfield, Mark O., Conflict and Conscience (Waco, Texas: Word
        Books, 1971).

Liberty, bimonthly magazine (Available from Review and Herald
        Publishing Association, 6856 Eastern Avenue, N.W.,
        Washington, D.C. 20012).

Marty, Martin, Church-State Separation in America: the Tradition Nobody Knows, a discussion paper, 1982 (Available from PEOPLE FOR THE AMERICAN WAY).

Richey, Russell E. and Donald G. Jones, editors, American Civil
        Religion (New York: Harper and Row, 1974).

Shriver, Peggy L., The Bible Vote (New York: The Pilgrim Press,
        1981).

RADICAL RIGHT LITERATURE

Falwell, Jerry, Listen, America! (Garden City, N.Y.: Doubleday
        and Co., 1980).

Falwell, Jerry, editor, The Fundamentalist Phenomenon: The
     Resurgence of Conservative Christianity (Garden City,
     N.Y.: Doubleday-Galilee, 1981).

LaHaye, Tim, The Battle for the Mind (Old Tappan, N.J.: Fleming
     H. Revell Company, 1980).

Marshall, Peter and David Manuel, The Light and the Glory (Old
     Tappan, N.J.: Fleming H. Revell Company, 1977).

Walton, Rus, One Nation Under God (Washington, D.C.: Third
     Century Publishers, 1975).

Wood, James E., Jr., et al., Church and State in Scripture,
     History, and Constitutional Law (Waco, Texas: Baylor
     University Press, 1958).

THEOLOGICAL DISPUTES

Q. Are ultra-fundamentalists typical of Christian evangelicals?

A. No. Evangelicals are an exceedingly diverse group. They
   include, for example, Mennonites and Quakers, who are paci-
   fists; the Churches of Christ, whose 2.5 million members have
   little interest in apocalyptic, showy televangelism; the
   Southern Baptist Convention, itself a diverse mix of congregations and a strong defender of church/state separation; black
   fundamentalist churches, which constitute a large segment of
   evangelicals in America; and many smaller denominations like
   the Nazarenes, the Salvation Army, and Wesleyan groups who
   minister to the poor and helpless.[1]

   Amidst this eclectic group of evangelicals, there are fundamentalists, who hold certain religious doctrines that other
   Christian groups do not. And among the fundamentalists, there
   is a small but well-organized group of vocal, partisan political activists. We call them ultra-fundamentalists. When
   groups like Moral Majority, Inc., the National Christian Action
   Coalition, and the Religious Roundtable burst onto the
   political scene in the late 1970s, many Americans came to see
   them as typical of fundamentalists or even evangelicals.

   There are important differences between evangelicals, fundamentalists, and ultra-fundamentalists. Some evangelicals are
   fundamentalist in their theology, and some fundamentalists are
   ultra-fundamentalist in their political views. Most fundamentalists do not approve of biblical criticism or "humanist"
   ideas. They typically believe in "creation-science," an
   impending Apocalypse, and exclusive Christian righteousness.
   Evangelicals do not generally insist that these are essential
   Christian beliefs. Whatever theological differences that
   people may have, it is important to remember that a person's
   interpretation of the Bible does not necessarily imply a particular brand of political behavior.

63

Q. Who are the evangelicals in America, what do they believe?

A. Estimates of the number of evangelical Christians in America
range from 30 to 50 million.[2]   As might be expected, the
variety of doctrinal beliefs found in a group this large is
immense. In a September 1980 survey, pollster George Gallup
learned that certain people are more likely than others to be
evangelical Christians: "women, non-whites, persons with less
than a college education, Southerners, older people, Protestants, rural residents, and the less well-to-do." Roughly
one-fifth (19 percent) of Gallup's respondents -- or an
estimated 30 million Americans -- said they:

>   o believed in or had experienced a "born again" conversion
>   to Jesus Christ (Jesus taught, "...Except a man be born
>   again, he cannot see the kingdom of God." John 3:3);

>   o encouraged other people to accept Jesus Christ as
>   their savior;

>   o interpreted the Bible literally and accepted it as
>   their supreme authority in life.[3]

Although Americans tend to divide Christian faith and order
into two major categories -- Protestant and Roman Catholic --
evangelicals comprise a distinct force in both branches of
American Christianity.

Q. Are evangelicals necessarily conservative in their politics?

A. Evangelicals are not a monolithic political group. It is true,
as George Gallup notes, that evangelicals tend to be more
conservative ideologically and more Democratic, but that char-
acterization cannot support easy stereotypes. For example,
53 percent of all evangelicals support the ERA (compared to
66 percent support among non-evangelicals). Evangelicals and
non-evangelicals have similar attitudes in favor of gun registration (57 to 58 percent, respectively), the death penalty (51
and 53 percent), and government social programs (54 and 52
percent).[4]

Some evangelicals, such as those who support Sojourners
magazine (circulation, 50,000), consider themselves among the
political left. "The Bible is much more radical than Marx
ever was," says Sojourner editor Jim Wallis.[5]

History shows that theological conservatism need not produce
political conservatism. William Jennings Bryan, the three-time
presidential candidate, was a devout fundamentalist yet a committed political progressive. Members of Churches of Christ in
Oklahoma, although theologically conservative, voted in large
numbers for socialist candidate Eugene Debs in the early
1900s.[6] Nowadays, Senator Mark Hatfield defies the
evangelical stereotype held by the American public. Hatfield
demonstrates that an evangelical can, without contradiction,
oppose mandatory school prayer, the Vietnam War (e.g., the
McGovern-Hatfield Amendment), and nuclear proliferation and
weapons.

Q. Why do ultra-fundamentalists so bitterly condemn the theology
of mainline churches? Why are these disputes important?

A. The primary dispute centers on how to interpret the Bible
correctly, which, for ultra-fundamentalists, is important for
determining who is faithful to Christian belief. This controversy is about the "inerrancy," or absolute and unquestionable
accuracy, of Scripture as it stands. Most biblical scholars
accept the idea that the biblical texts reflect their authors'
historical and cultural point of view. Many of them also
believe in the doctrine of progressive revelation, in which God
is revealed to man over time, culminating in the coming of
Jesus Christ.

Ultra-fundamentalists often reject this kind of interpretation,
and condemn as unbelievers Christian denominations that use
historical-critical methods or believe in progressive revelation. "I have never learned what liberal churchmen believe
in," said Jerry Falwell. "I've always wondered why they don't
get an honest job and go out and earn money under proper
pretenses, not false pretenses."[7] "The reason the focus is
on inerrancy," explains ultra-fundamentalist Rev. Paige
Patterson, "is that there must be an agreed source of ultimate
authority or else we end up in anarchy."[8]

Mainline religious leaders and scholars do regard the Bible as
a sacred book, but also as an amalgam of historical documents
that reflect the peculiarities of the original culture,
authors, and subsequent translators. They believe that certain
parables, for example, should be understood within their
historical and cultural context. Mainline scholars also say
that different translations and translators make a literal

reading of the Bible perilous. Says Dr. Robert Bratcher, a
Southern Baptist translator: "To invest the Bible with the
qualities of inerrancy and infallibility is to idolatrize it,
to transform it into a false God."[9]   For mainline church
bodies, the fundamentalist critique of the Bible is ahistor-
ical, legalistic, and highly selective in the themes it
stresses. Tempting as it may be for secular groups to dismiss
these issues as obscure theological disputes, ultra-fundamentalists' understanding of the Bible is the mainspring for their
political behavior. "The basic tenet of...fundamentalist
Christianity, is that we have one document on which we predicate everything we believe," says Rev. Jerry Falwell, "our
faith, our practice, our life-style, our homes, etc., government -- is the inerrancy of scripture, not only in matters of
theology, but science, geography, history, etc. -- totally and
entirely, the very word of God."[10]

The "Christian attitudes" that moral majoritarians idealize,
however, often derive from interpretations of the Bible that
are more speculative than literal. Consider:

> o Rev. Pat Robertson: "I knew that Iran was going to fall,
>   and that when it did, it would fall into the Soviet
>   orbit....It says so in the Bible."[11]
>
> o Rev. Greg Dixon, national secretary of Moral Majority,
>   Inc.: "I am advocating whipping [children]. That's a
>   Bible doctrine with fundamentalists."[12]
>
> o Rev. Jerry Falwell: "Nowhere in the Bible is there a
>   rebuke for the bearing of armaments....A political
>   leader, as a minister of God, is a revenger to execute
>   wrath upon those who do evil."[13]   [Cf. Matthew 5:9]
>
> o Rev. James Robison: "...unilateral disarmament...goes
>   directly against the Bible...."[14]

Centrist religious groups completely reject this "literal"
reading of the Bible. "We use the Bible for guidance, not for
rules," says the Rev. Dr. Charles Bergstrom of the Lutheran
Council in the U.S.A. "You don't find in Scripture how to vote
on the Panama Canal or SALT II."[15] Mainline groups consider
the Bible a "signpost" for Christian life rather than a
"hitching post," in the words of Rev. William Sloane Coffin,
Jr. "[T]he fundamentalists are making the colossal error, not

made in the Bible, of putting purity of dogma ahead of integrity of love. [But] the Bible consistently says dogma is a signpost, always pointing ahead, and the hitching post is love...."[16]

Q. How do ultra-fundamentalists interpret the Bible with regard to political activism?

A. Historically, ultra-fundamentalists have not considered political activism a doctrinal necessity. In fact, many of them considered it a waste of time that detracted from preaching the gospel. In response to the civil rights movement, Rev. Jerry Falwell delivered a sermon in 1965, "Ministers and Marchers," in which he denounced racial integration, Martin Luther King, Jr., and attempts to mix religion and politics. He told his faithful:

> Believing the Bible as I do, I would find it impossible to stop preaching the pure saving gospel of Jesus Christ and begin doing anything else -- including fighting communism or participating in civil rights reforms....I believe that if we spent enough effort trying to clean up our churches, rather than trying to clean up state and national governments, we would do well.[17]

Falwell also advised, "Nowhere are we commissioned to reform the externals. We are not told to wage wars against bootleggers, liquor stores, gamblers, murderers, prostitutes, racketeers, prejudiced persons or institutions, or any other existing evil. If church leaders feel that the church should take part in school reforms, then I am forced to ask why the church is not concerned about the alcoholism problem in America. There are almost as many alcoholics as there are Negroes."[18]

Ultra-fundamentalists have, of course, dramatically reversed their attitude toward political activism in recent years. Falwell helped engineer this theological turnabout through a contorted interpretation of Mark 12:13-17. "The Bible says 'Render unto Caesar that which is Caesar's.' That means register to vote," said Falwell in 1981.[19] At another gathering, he warned any apathetic citizens, "If there is one person in this room who is not registered repent of it. It is a sin."[20] Televangelist James Robison agrees: "Not voting is a sin against God....Perverts, radicals, leftists, Communists, liberals, and humanists have taken over the country because Christians didn't want to dirty their hands in politics."[21] By making involvement in elections and grassroots politics a Christian duty, the radical religious right has been exceedingly effective in advancing their political program.

Q. What's wrong with trying to bear a Christian witness to God's word?

A. Nothing! That is a Christian mandate, to spread the Gospel. What is objectionable is claiming to speak for God or know God's will. Rev. Jerry Falwell often invokes God as an ally in his partisan political campaigns: "God has called me to take action. I have a divine mandate to go right into the halls of Congress and fight for laws that will save America."[22] Not only does this smack of false prophecy (which Jesus condemns in Matthew 7:15 and Mark 13:22), it accuses anyone who opposes Falwell's politics of being against God. Thus "liberals" become "godless liberals."[23]

By wrapping their political judgments in a "divine mandate," ultra-fundamentalists suggest that they have achieved political as well as religious certitude. Opponents are not only branded as politically "incorrect" but theologically "incorrect"...or evil. This in turn "justifies" extreme measures -- moral absolutism, vilification of opponents, censorship, and disregard for constitutional law.

The ultra-fundamentalist confusion about the boundaries of religion and politics can also lead to some questionable theology. Richard Zone, former executive director of the Christian Voice, credits his political success to his Christian righteousness: "There are offices in Congress, the first time I walked in, you know, I had to sit in the back...and I had to stand up like this and say 'yes sir, yes sir,' when they were talking to me -- 'yes sir, yes sir'. And now they just roll out the red carpet for me when I walk in because I represent Jesus' people."[24]

Mainline churches reject this boastful attitude toward Christianity. Most would agree with Bishop James Armstrong of the United Methodist Church and President, National Council of Churches, who characterizes Falwell's "social gospel" as "unbiblical, a denial of the spirit of Christ; a gospel that mocks a true evangelicalism and an authentic New Testament

evangelism." He adds that Falwell's "sexism and rigid legalism
dehumanize the very persons for whom Christ lived and
died."[25]

For comments like these, Rev. Greg Dixon, head of the Indiana
chapter of the Moral Majority, Inc., has blasted Bishop Armstrong as a "student of Communism" and the "anti-Christ."[26]
Dixon said, "He [Armstrong] is a socialist, collectivist, relativist, humanist, evolutionist, and modernist. It is hard for
me to believe that he is not a dedicated Communist." Dixon
also questioned Armstrong's patriotism: "I think the day will
come when Armstrong's name will go [down] in history as infamous
as Benedict Arnold who sold America to her enemies."[27]

Q. America was founded on Christian principles. Good Christians
   are patriotic Americans, and vice-versa.

A. Most theologians and church bodies deplore this practice of
   melding Christian and American values, known as "civil
   religion." In the past two decades, theologians and sociol-
   ogists have generated a considerable literature on the phenomenon of American civil religion. While moral majoritarians
   are comfortable with civil religion, many other Christians are
   not. The Chicago Declaration of 1973, representing the views
   of 50 evangelicals of varied persuasions, warned: "We must
   resist the temptation to make the nation and its institutions
   objects of near-religious loyalty."[28] Church bodies are
   critical of civil religion not only for the way that political
   leaders exploit the legitimacy of religion, but also for the
   harm it does to Christian belief itself. As theologian
   Robert E. Webber of Wheaton College writes:

        Although civil religion has been part of the warp and woof
        of American society from the beginning, it is not true
        Christianity....It is a blending of the Christian faith
        with national goals and destiny which blurs the distinc-
        tion between the church and the nation and shifts faith
        toward a religion of nationalism. In the end this makes
        the church apostate and creates a counterfeit reli-
        gion....What the Moral Majority is calling for, perhaps
        unknowingly, is a restoration of civil religion.[29]

QUOTABLE QUOTES

"There are offices in Congress, the first time I walked in, you know, I had to sit in the back...and I had to stand up like this and say 'yes sir, yes sir,' when they were talking to me -- 'yes sir, yes sir'. And now they just roll out the red carpet for me when I walk in because I represent Jesus' people."

                    -- Richard Zone,
                       former executive director
                       of the Christian Voice,
                       "Sixty Minutes" broadcast,
                       September 21, 1980

[Bishop James Armstrong, president of the National Council of Churches] "is a socialist, collectivist, relativist, humanist, evolutionist, and modernist. It is hard for me to believe that he is not a dedicated Communist....I think the day will come when Armstrong's name will go [down] in history as infamous as Benedict Arnold who sold America to her enemies."

                    -- Rev. Greg Dixon, head of
                       Indiana chapter of Moral
                       Majority, Inc., Franklin
                       (Indiana) Daily Journal,
                       January 23, 1982

"Not voting is a sin against God....Perverts, radicals, leftists, Communists, liberals, and humanists have taken over the country because Christians didn't want to dirty their hands in politics."

                    -- Rev. James Robison,
                       The Washington Post,
                       August 24, 1980

Rev. Jerry Falwell and the Gospel

"I have never learned what liberal churchmen believe in....I've always wondered why they don't get an honest job and go out and earn money under proper pretenses, not false pretenses."

-- "Old-Time Gospel Hour,"
November 1, 1981

"Nowhere in the Bible is there a rebuke for the bearing of armaments....A political leader, as a minister of God, is a revenger to execute wrath upon those who do evil."

-- Listen, America!, p. 98

"Believing in the Bible as I do, I would find it impossible to stop preaching the pure saving gospel of Jesus Christ and begin doing anything else -- including fighting communism or participating in civil rights reforms....I believe that if we spent enough effort trying to clean up our churches, rather than trying to clean up state and national governments, we would do well."

-- "Ministers and Marchers,"
1965 sermon

"The Bible says 'Render unto Caesar that which is Caesar's.' That means register to vote."

-- Atlanta Journal,
November 3, 1981

"The basic tenet of...fundamentalist Christianity is that we have one document on which we predicate everything we believe, our faith, our practice, our lifestyle, our homes, etc., government -- is the inerrancy of scripture, not only in matters of theology, but science, geography, history, etc. -- totally and entirely, the very word of God."

-- Penthouse, March 1981

NOTES: THEOLOGICAL DISPUTES

1. Timothy L. Smith, Revivalism and Social Reform Amid 19th
    Century America (Baltimore: Johns Hopkins Press, 1980), cited
    in Peggy L. Shriver, The Bible Vote: Religion and the New
    Right (New York: The Pilgrim Press, 1981), p. 35.

2. See, e.g., The Gallup Poll, September 7-8, 1980, and Neil
    Jumonville, "Diversity Among Evangelicals," The New York
    Times, May 12, 1981.

3. George Gallup, "Carter Holds Lead Over Reagan Among Evangel-
    icals," and "Evangelicals Not Monolithic in Views on Key
    Voter Issues," The Gallup Poll, September 7-8, 1980.

4. George Gallup, op. cit.

5. Curt Suplee, "Power and the Glory in the New Senate: A
    Growing Congregation of Born-Again Believers," The Washington
    Post, December 20, 1981.

6. Leo P. Ribuffo, "Fundamentalism Revisited: Liberals and That
    Old-Time Religion," The Nation, November 29, 1980, p. 570.

7. Jerry Falwell, "No Small Stir," Old-Time Gospel Hour,
    November 1, 1981.

8. Kenneth A. Briggs, "Drift Away from Fundamentalism Splits
    Ranks of Southern Baptists," The New York Times, March 27,
    1981.

9. Ibid.

10. "Penthouse Interview: Reverend Falwell," Penthouse, March
     1981.

11. Jane Mayer, "Baptist TV Network Says It Will Offer 'Whole-
     some Shows,'" Wall Street Journal, September 11, 1981.

12. Michael Disend, "Have You Whipped Your Child Today?"
     Penthouse, February 1982.

13. Jerry Falwell, Listen, America! (Garden City, N.Y.: Doubleday and Company, 1980), p. 98.

14. Harry Cook, "Is the Country Doomed?" Detroit (Michigan) Free Press, October 24, 1981.

15. "Lutheran Leader Says Jerry Falwell 'Dangerous,'" Madison (Wisconsin) Times, May 16, 1981.

16. John S. Workman, "Dr. William Sloane Coffin: Theologian Adds to Discussion on Moral Majority," Arkansas (Little Rock) Gazette, May 24, 1981.

17. Jerry Falwell, "Ministers and Marchers" (sermon), cited in The Bergen (Hackensack, N.J.) Record, June 21, 1981.

18. Ibid.

19. Atlanta Journal, November 3, 1981.

20. Lisa Myers, "Falwell Strives for Role as Political Kingmaker," The Washington Star, July 3, 1980.

21. Kathy Sawyer, "Linking Religion and Politics," The Washington Post, August 24, 1980.

22. Lisa Myers, "Falwell Strives for Role as Political Kingmaker," The Washington Star, July 3, 1980.

23. See, e.g., Jerry Falwell's Introduction to Richard Viguerie, The New Right: We're Ready to Lead, op. cit.

24. Richard Zone, as seen on "Sixty Minutes" broadcast, September 21, 1980.

25. Rev. James Armstrong, "Pastoral Letter #2: Evangelism, Jerry Falwell, the Moral Majority and Persons," September 15, 1981.

26. Bill Heineke, "Moral Majority Head Repeats Barrage," Franklin (Indiana) Daily Journal, January 23, 1982.

27. Ibid.

28.   "The Chicago Declaration, 1973," cited in Robert E.
      Webber, The Moral Majority: Right or Wrong? (Westchester,
      Ill.: Crossway Books, 1981), p. 159.

39.   Robert E. Webber, The Moral Majority: Right or Wrong?
      (Westchester, Ill.: Crossway Books, 1981), pp. 38-9.

FURTHER READING: THEOLOGICAL DISPUTES

Bellah, Robert N. The Broken Covenant (New York: Seabury, 1975).

Bellah, Robert N. and Phillip E. Hammond, Varieties of Civil Religion (New York: Harper and Row, 1980).

The Christian Century, weekly periodical (Available from 407 S. Dearborn St., Chicago, Illinois 60605).

Democracy, "Religion and Democracy" issue, April 1982.

Ericson, Edward L., American Freedom and the Radical Right (New York: Frederick Ungar Publishing Co., 1982).

Evangelical Review, quarterly magazine (Available from Cross Roads Publications, 4814 Highway 78, Lilburn, Georgia 30247).

Radical Religion, quarterly journal (Available from P.O. Box 9164, Berkeley, California 94709).

Hill, Samuel S. and Dennis E. Owen, The New Religious Political Right in America (Nashville, Tennessee: Abingdon, 1982).

Richey, Russell E. and Donald G. Jones, American Civil Religion (New York: Harper and Row, 1974).

Sojourners, monthly magazine (Available from 1309 L Street, N.W., Washington, D.C. 20005).

RADICAL RIGHT LITERATURE

Falwell, Jerry, The Fundamentalist Phenomenon: The Resurgence of Conservative Christianity (Garden City, N.Y.: Doubleday and Company, 1981).

Life's Answer, monthly magazine (Available from James Robison Evangelistic Association, 1801 W. Euless Blvd., Euless, Texas 76039).

Walton, Rus, FACS! Fundamentals for American Christians (Nyack, N.Y.: Parson Publishing, 1979).

RELIGIOUS INTOLERANCE

Q. What attitudes do ultra-fundamentalists show toward other religions?

A. In general: suspicion, hostility, and intolerance. Ultra-fundamentalists take pride in their theological certitude and their
self-imposed barriers from the secular world. But in affirming
their own religious beliefs, ultra-fundamentalists frequently
lash out against other "false" religions. "Liberal" churches,
Unitarianism, Catholicism, Judaism, and other religions are
often regarded not only as theologically wrong, but as menacing
threats. Religious intolerance is a frequent result.

Because ultra-fundamentalists live in a bipolar world, in which
a person either belongs or doesn't belong to the separate
community of "true" Christians, non-believers are frequently
objects of scorn and condescension. Consider these public
statements by prominent ultra-fundamentalist leaders:

   o Rev. Jerry Falwell: "If a person is not a Christian,
     he is inherently a failure..."[1]

   o Rev. James Robison, regarding dating: "Two nonbelievers
     can't share about how God is dealing with them, because
     they can't know or understand such dealings. Spiritual
     sharing can't take place if one is a Christian and
     another is not. The non-Christian can't understand
     spiritual things."[2]

   o Rev. Pat Robertson, regarding CBN's evangelical crusade
     in Japan: "The public of Japan, clinging to the
     tradition of their forefathers, worshipping gods that
     don't exist and idols that give no comfort.[sic] To the
     great majority, these old gods are giving way to a new,
     powerful god, the god of technology. The emptiness and
     materialism is taking hold and robbing them of true

happiness. Can we reach them with the Gospel of Jesus
Christ?"[3]

In their determination to establish their separatist identity,
some ultra-fundamentalist groups have even assembled a
"Christian Yellow Pages," an alternative telephone directory
that lists only merchants with "acceptable" religious
beliefs.[4] It is certainly a consumer's right to "buy
Christian," but the desire to discriminate against the
"non-Christian" world is "an act of aggression against a
pluralistic society," notes columnist George Will. The
economic impact of "Christian Yellow Pages" is less important
than their impact on public life. As Will astutely points out,
"Discrimination condoned -- indeed, incited -- in commerce
will not be confined to commerce."[5] There are many signs,
in fact, that it extends to the political sphere as well.
Rev. Pat Robertson claims a Christian monopoly on our
nation's founding charter:

> The Constitution of the United States, for instance, is
> a marvelous document for self-government by Christian
> people. But the minute you turn the document into the
> hands of non-Christian people and atheist people they
> can use it to destroy the very foundation of our society.
> And that's what's been happening.[6]

Q. Ultra-fundamentalists do in fact work closely with other
   religious groups. There is ecumenical cooperation.

A. Since entering the media spotlight, many religious authoritarians have toned down their attacks on other religious
   groups and have even made ecumenical overtures. Officials
   of Moral Majority, Inc., tout the fact that its leadership
   includes Mormons, Catholics, and Jews. (All members of the
   Board of Directors are, however, ultra-fundamentalists.)
   Falwell has tried to forge an alliance with American Jewish
   groups. On selected issues, ultra-fundamentalist leaders have
   in fact found it politically advantageous to work with other
   religious groups.

   But interfaith cooperation is a stern test of ultra-fundamentalist belief and its creed of strict separatism and rigid
   theo-politics. As Frances FitzGerald has pointed out, "The
   price of ecumenical politics was apparently the renunciation of
   a fundamental tenet of faith. Alternatively, it was the

maintenance of two separate audiences."[7]   In order to be
acceptable to mainstream audiences, ultra-fundamentalist
leaders like Falwell have learned to cloak themselves in a
mantle of ecumenical tolerance. But in their mailings and
sermons to faithful believers, they revert to the strident
"we-they" vernacular that condemns other religious viewpoints.

Those moral authoritarians more removed from mainstream
politics do not trouble themselves with two sets of rhetoric.
The Liberty Lobby and the Institute for Historical Review, for
example, are brazenly anti-Semitic. They make little attempt
to hide their contempt for other religious traditions.

Q. What attitudes do ultra-fundamentalists have toward Israel and
the American Jewish community?

A. Most ultra-fundamentalist leaders profess an enthusiastic
concern for the welfare of Israel and Jews, and in recent years
have tried to cultivate an alliance with American Jewish
organizations -- with little success. Their support for
Israel, while apparently genuine, seems to be based on self-
serving theological and nationalistic motives.

The radical religious right has strong political reasons for
sympathizing with Israel. The spectrum of ideologies in
Israeli politics resembles that of the United States, and the
two nations share similar attitudes toward the Soviet Union.
Besides periodic statements of support for Israel, the radical
religious right has developed close ties with Prime Minister
Begin; promoted friendly U.S. relations with Israel; founded
the "International Christian Embassy in Jerusalem" (ICEJ) to
serve as a Middle East outpost for ultra-fundamentalist
activism; and launched numerous Holy Land tours for pro-Israeli
ultra-fundamentalists.[8]

Q. What are the biblical reasons for ultra-fundamentalist support
of Israel?

A. Based on their reading of the Bible, especially the Book of
Revelation and Daniel, ultra-fundamentalists expect human
history to end fairly soon. They say the beginning of the end
will be marked by the appearance of the Anti-Christ, a false
prophet who will have the support of apostate churches. His
rise to power will supposedly precede a period of tribulation
for the world and a fiery battle of Armageddon initiated by the

Soviet Union. (See "Foreign and Military Policy" section.)
The great tumult will be followed by a 1,000-year reign of
Christ on earth.

In this scenario, Israel is cast as the instrument of God
against satanic aggressors. Jerry Falwell advises the United
States to remain steadfast in its support for Israel because
"to stand against Israel is to stand against God."[9] Or,
again: "God's word settles the question of whose land [it is];
it is Israel's. We believe that God very clearly promised
Abraham a blessing for those who bless Israel and a curse for
those who curse Israel."[10]

What disturbs many American Jews is the role that ultra-
fundamentalists insist Jews must play to fulfill biblical
prophecy. Most ultra-fundamentalists believe that all Jews
must return to Israel as part of the predestined "ingathering,"
and convert to Christ. In his ultra-fundamentalist manifesto,
Listen, America!, Falwell tries to pay homage to Judaism in a
chapter entitled, "The Miracle of Israel." But it is actually
a very insulting tribute:

> The Jews are returning to their land of unbelief. They
> are spiritually blind and desperately in need of their
> Messiah and Savior. Yet they are God's people, and in
> the world today Bible-believing Christians in America
> are the best friends the nation Israel has. We must
> remain so.[11]

Q. Do ultra-fundamentalists bear any hostility toward Jews?

A. They vigorously deny any antagonism toward Jews or Israel.
Ultra-fundamentalist leaders like Jerry Falwell insist,
"There is not one anti-Semite in a Bible-believing church in
America."[12] Yet ultra-fundamentalists do insist, as part of
their religious doctrine, that Jews must return to Israel and
convert to Christ before the Second Coming. And prominent
leaders like Falwell, Robison, Bailey Smith and others have
made numerous anti-Semitic remarks in recent years. The more
publicized statements include:

> o Rev. Jerry Falwell: "A few of you don't like Jews and
> I know why. He [sic] can make more money accidentally
> than you can make on purpose."[13]

o Televangelist James Robison: He said that a "Rabbi Antleman" (who cannot be located) told him that an anti-Semite is one who "hates Jews more than he is supposed to."[14]

o Rev. Bailey Smith, then-president of the Southern Baptist Convention: "It's interesting at great political rallies how you have a Protestant to pray, a Catholic to pray and then you have a Jew to pray. With all due respect to those dear people, my friends, God Almighty does not hear the prayer of a Jew. For how in the world can God hear the prayer of a man who says that Jesus Christ is not the true Messiah. That is blasphemy."[15]

and in an apology for that remark, Smith said, "I don't know why God chose the Jew. They have such funny noses."[16]

o Rev. Dan Fore, then-chairman of Moral Majority, Inc., in New York State: "I love the Jewish people deeply. God has given them talents He has not given others. They are his chosen people. Jews have a God-given ability to make money....They control the media, they control this city."[17]

It remains to be seen whether slurs like these reflect attitudes that are anti-Semitic. Indeed, each of the men making these remarks apologized profusely when called to account. Yet these crude public comments do suggest a gross insensitivity to the historical persecution of Jews. Many Jewish leaders, understandably disturbed by the remarks, may wonder how stable Jewish/moral majoritarian relations can be under the circumstances.

This was vividly demonstrated in October 1981, as the Senate debated the sale of high-technology AWAC military planes to Saudi Arabia. The ultra-fundamentalist senators who had pledged to oppose the sale quite suddenly reversed themselves. And leaders like Falwell who had presented themselves as staunch allies of Israel and who could raise a national clamor over lesser issues, were conspicuously silent as the AWACs debate reached its climax. Some observers speculate that ultra-fundamentalists conceded their support on the AWACs deal in return for Administration support on their domestic social agenda. In any case, the AWACs episode showed that the ultra-

fundamentalist commitment to Israel is less than whole-
hearted.[18]

Q. How have some leaders of the organized Jewish community
   responded to the overtures of support by moral majoritarians?

A. There has been a wide range of reactions. Many segments of the
   American Jewish community oppose the domestic social agenda of
   ultra-fundamentalists. They are especially concerned about the
   erosion of constitutional protections and attacks on church/
   state separation issues. The drive to reinstate mandatory
   prayer in public schools, for example, is very alarming. Other
   Jews dislike ultra-fundamentalist opposition to equal rights
   for women, social programs, human rights activism in U.S.
   diplomacy, and similar policies.

   Rabbi Alexander M. Schindler, president of the Union of
   American Hebrew Congregations, has been one of the most outspoken foes of an alliance with moral majoritarians. He called
   it "madness and suicide if Jews honor for their support of
   Israel right-wing evangelists who constitute a danger to the
   Jews of the United States."[19]   In a speech to the UAHC board
   of trustees, Schindler linked moral majoritarians to the rising
   tide of anti-Semitism:

>   When the head of the Moral Majority demands a Christian
>   Bill of Rights, when the president of the Southern Baptist
>   Convention tells the Religious Roundtable that 'God
>   Almighty does not hear the prayer of a Jew,' there should
>   be no surprise at reports of synagogues destroyed by arson
>   and Jewish families terrorized in their homes.[20]

   Schindler also warned that "[in Falwell's] exclusivist emphasis
   on a Christian America and the tools he chooses to build it, he
   and his associates are creating a climate of opinion which is
   hostile to religious tolerance. Such a climate, in my
   judgment, is bad for civil liberties, human rights, social
   justice, interfaith understanding, and mutual respect among
   Americans. Therefore, it is bad for Jews."[21]

Q. Can American Jews make common cause with ultra-fundamentalists
   on the issue of mutual concern -- Israel?

A. Cooperation is possible, say many Jews, without endorsing the
   distasteful aspects of the moral majoritarian political agenda.

The American Jewish Congress issued a formal statement in
October 1981, "Where We Stand," which states, "We acknowledge
the New Right's support of Israel, but it should not affect our
assessment of the movement's domestic programs. The damage
done by their efforts to curtail domestic freedom is not made
less by the soundness of their views on Israel."[22]   (For full
text of the AJC statement, see appendix.)

Rabbi Schindler, for his part, agrees that "the Jewish community cannot seek 100 percent ideological purity" with its
political allies. He noted that Jews must continue to work
with the National Council of Churches on gun control, free
choice on abortion, strategic arms limitation and other issues
despite their disagreement over Middle East policy. Similarly,
Schindler said, Jews must work with Roman Catholic bishops
despite their differences on abortion and birth control.
Finally, Jewish disagreement with blacks over racial quotas
should not rule out cooperation on social welfare programs like
national health insurance, youth employment, and decent
housing, he said.[23]

Q. What are the Liberty Lobby and the Institute for Historical
   Review?

A. These two organizations are probably the leading anti-Semitic
   propagandists in the United States. Both try to persuade the
   public that the Nazi Holocaust did not take place and that Jews
   play a malevolent role in current events. Both are reportedly
   financed by the reclusive Willis A. Carto, who has also founded
   such groups as the National Alliance of White People and
   Americans for National Security.[24]

   The Liberty Lobby, based in Washington, D.C., claims 30,000
   members and 336,000 subscribers to its weekly tabloid, The
   Spotlight. The Spotlight consistently attacks Israel, Jews,
   and the "myth" of the Holocaust. A typical article: "Anne
   Frank Fable Losing Credibility; Establishment Continues to Push
   'Diary' as 'True Story' Despite Contradictions."[25]   Another
   article offered a sympathetic report on a group that accused
   the "Holocaust" docu-drama on NBC of anti-German bias. The
   group was seeking broadcast time under the FCC's Fairness
   Doctrine in order to respond.[26]

   The Spotlight seeks respectability by running interviews with
   members of Congress and by trying to ingratiate itself with

mainstream conservatism. The Liberty Lobby's general counsel from 1969-1973, Warren Richardson, was even proposed to be nominated to become assistant secretary of the U.S. Department of Health and Human Services in 1981, but his name was withdrawn when several groups pointed out the anti-Semitic, racist nature of the Liberty Lobby.[27] Richardson has worked closely with Paul Weyrich on the exclusive caucus of radical right strategists, the Six Pack group. He also has written a lobbying pamphlet (1981) for Weyrich's Free Congress Research and Education Foundation.

The Institute for Historical Review (IHR) is another prolific source of anti-Semitic propaganda. Based in Torrance, California, IHR sponsors conferences, publishes a quarterly journal, and distributes several books published by Carto's Noontide Press. (The Six Million Reconsidered argues that the Holocaust never happened, and Imperium: The Philosophy of History and Politics, by the late Francis Parker Yockey, is a paean to Nazism.)[28]

The organization recently gained national notoriety when it offered a $50,000 bounty to anyone who could prove that "even one Jew was gassed in a Nazi concentration camp, as part of an extermination program."[29] When Long Beach businessman Mel Mermelstein, a survivor of Auschwitz, tried to put an end to the vile contest by offering proof and collecting the reward, IHR refused to pay. Mermelstein sued for breach of contract and finally won his case. The court declared, "This court does take judicial notice of the fact that Jews were gassed to death at Auschwitz."[30]

Q. How do ultra-fundamentalist leaders regard other Christian churches?

A. The "liberal" churches, represented by the National Council of Churches (NCC), are a favorite target of ultra-fundamentalists. They bitterly condemn the NCC and its leaders as agents of international communism, domestic subversion, and anti-Christian doctrines. They point specifically to the NCC's support for military disarmament, human rights in international diplomacy, and greater economic equality for Third World nations.

Rev. Greg Dixon, national secretary of Moral Majority, Inc., has blasted the NCC as having "goals parallel to that of the

Communist Party -- to subject the entire world to slavery and
tyranny." Dixon also accused NCC President James Armstrong, a
United Methodist bishop, of being a "socialist" and the "anti-
Christ."[31] Other ultra-fundamentalists, while more
restrained in their public denunciations, essentially share
Dixon's contempt for the NCC. They also vent their spleen on
the World Council of Churches, an international, inter-
denominational church body.

Q. What have some leaders of the radical religious right said
   about Catholicism, Islam, and Unitarianism?

A. For many ultra-fundamentalist leaders, Catholicism is viewed
   with suspicion and distaste. Rev. Tim LaHaye, a board member
   of Moral Majority, Inc., in his book on the end of the world,
   worries about "pagan ecumenicity," and predicts that the
   Catholic Church will play a critical role in establishing "a
   one-world idolatrous religion" in cooperation with the National
   Council of Churches. For this alleged role, the Catholic
   Church is "Babylon, Mother of Harlots," according to LaHaye's
   interpretation of Revelation 17.[32] Rev. Dan Fore, when he
   was the head of the New York State chapter of Moral Majority,
   Inc., excludes Catholics from the Christian tradition. Fore
   dismissed the horrors of the Spanish Inquisition saying, "Those
   weren't Christians, they were Roman Catholics."[33] After a
   series of such remarks, Fore was asked to resign. Bob Jones,
   Jr., chancellor of Bob Jones University, said in 1982, "The
   present pope [John Paul II] is the greatest danger we face
   today." He said the pope "is doing more to spread anti-Christ
   communism than anyone around. The papacy is the religion of
   the anti-Christ and is a Satanic system."[34]

   In spite of the ecumenical image that some ultra-fundamentalists seek for their political activism, it is not a very
   serious or deep sort of interfaith cooperation. Rev. Pat
   Robertson projects his religious prejudice across international
   borders. When he announced that his Christian Broadcasting
   Network would begin its own television station in the Middle
   East, Robertson said:

       [T]he Koran and Muslim teachings don't meet the deepest
       needs of the human heart. These are times of crisis and
       Islam stands on the divided doctrine looking to communism
       or materialism for answers. Muslims are seeking truth
       today but the Christianity presented in the Koran brings

further confusion. While there are deeply ingrained
prejudices, there's a new openness to the gospel message
if only it could be available by television.[35]

Closer to home, ultra-fundamentalists often brand other denominations as promoters of "secular humanism" in the schools. The
head of the Washington State chapter of Moral Majority, Inc.,
Mike Farris, declares Unitarians to be unfit to teach in public
schools:

As a Unitarian, my opponent practices transcendental
meditation which is also practiced in schools. He
should resign from teaching because he can influence....
Why do we only teach evolution -- his religion -- in
schools?[36]

QUOTABLE QUOTES

[The National Council of Churches has] "goals parallel to that of the Communist Party -- to subject the entire world to slavery and tyranny."

> -- Rev. Greg Dixon, national
>   secretary of Moral Majority,
>   Inc., The New York Times,
>   January 22, 1982

"The present pope [John Paul II] is the greatest danger we face today....[He] is doing more to spread anti-Christ communism than anyone around. The papacy is the religion of the anti-Christ and is a Satanic system."

> -- Bob Jones, Jr., chancellor of
>   Bob Jones University, Des
>   Moines Tribune, March 27, 1982

"As a Unitarian, my opponent practices transcendental meditation which is also practiced in schools. He should resign from teaching because he can influence....Why do we only teach evolution -- his religion -- in schools?"

> -- Mike Farris, head of
>   Washington State chapter of
>   Moral Majority, Inc., Yakima
>   (Washington) Herald-Republic,
>   April 5, 1981

[By your definition a man who is Jewish but does not worship Jesus Christ is then spiritually dead?] "Yes, yes, right."

> -- Harry Vickery, head of
>   New Jersey State chapter of
>   Moral Majority, Inc.,
>   WABC radio (New York),
>   July 12, 1982

"I don't know why God chose the Jew. They have such funny
noses."

> -- Rev. Bailey Smith, The Sunday
> (Hackensack, N.J.) Record,
> June 21, 1981

"I love the Jewish people deeply. God has given them talents
He has not given others. They are His chosen people. Jews
have a God-given ability to make money, almost a supernatural
ability to make money....They control the media, they control
this city."

> -- Rev. Dan C. Fore, then-
> chairman of Moral Majority,
> Inc., in New York State,
> The New York Times,
> February 5, 1981

"I think a war with the Soviet Union is inevitable, if I read
Bible prophecy properly. The chances are that the U.S. will
come in as a defender of Israel. It looks like everything is
shaping up."

> -- Rev. Pat Robertson,
> The Washington Post,
> March 23, 1981

"We deplore their [ultra-fundamentalists'] willingness to wield
religious commitment as an instrument of political coercion,
their use of fundamentalist piety as the principal measure of
political competence, their readiness to invoke Divine authority -- and thus trivialize Divine sanction -- for every minute,
ephemeral political issue which they find of current interest."

> -- American Jewish Congress,
> "Where We Stand,"
> October 4, 1981

Rev. Jerry Falwell

"If a person is not a Christian, he is inherently a failure..."

-- <u>Listen, America!</u>, p. 62

"God's word settles the question of whose land [it is]; it is Israel's. We believe that God very clearly promised Abraham a blessing for those who bless Israel and a curse for those who curse Israel."

-- <u>The Progressive</u>, November 1981

"The Jews are returning to their land of unbelief. They are spiritually blind and desperately in need of their Messiah and Savior. Yet they are God's people, and in the world today Bible-believing Christians in America are the best friends the nation Israel has."

-- <u>Listen, America!</u>, p. 113

"A few of you don't like Jews and I know why. He [sic] can make more money accidentally than you can make on purpose."

-- <u>The Washington Star</u>,
July 3, 1980

Rev. Bailey Smith

"It's interesting at great political rallies how you have a Protestant to pray, a Catholic to pray and then you have a Jew to pray. With all due respect to those dear people, my friends, God Almighty does not hear the prayer of a Jew. For how in the world can God hear the prayer of a man who says that Jesus Christ is not the true Messiah? That is blasphemy."

-- <u>The New York Times</u>,
April 22, 1981

Rev. Pat Robertson

"The public of Japan, clinging to the tradition of their
forefathers, worshipping gods that don't exist and idols that
give no comfort. [sic] To the great majority, these old gods
are giving way to a new, powerful god, the god of technology.
The emptiness and materialism is taking hold and robbing them
of true happiness. Can we reach them with the Gospel of Jesus
Christ?"

                        -- "700 Club" broadcast,
                           December 30, 1981

"The Constitution of the United States, for instance, is a
marvelous document for self-government by Christian people.
But the minute you turn the document into the hands of non-
Christian people and atheistic people they can use it to
destroy the very foundation of our society. And that's what's
been happening."

                        -- The Washington Post,
                           March 23, 1981

"[T]he Koran and Muslim teachings don't meet the deepest needs
of the human heart. These are times of crisis and Islam stands
on the divided doctrine looking to communism or materialism for
answers. Muslims are seeking truth today but the Christianity
presented in the Koran brings further confusion. While there
are deeply ingrained prejudices, there's a new openness to the
gospel message if only it could be available for television."

                        -- Announcement on "700 Club,"
                           April 12, 1982, that the
                           Christian Broadcasting Network
                           was beginning its own tele-
                           vision station in the Middle
                           East

Rev. James Robison

"Two nonbelievers can't share about how God is dealing with
them, because they can't know or understand such dealings.
Spiritual sharing can't take place if one is a Christian and
another is not. The non-Christian can't understand spiritual
things."

-- "Here I Stand" column,
Terrel (Texas) Tribune,
December 24, 1981

[An anti-Semite is one who] "hates Jews more than he is
supposed to."

-- Allegedly told to Robison by a
"Rabbi Antleman," who cannot
be located, Life's Answer,
January 1981

NOTES: RELIGIOUS INTOLERANCE

1. Jerry Falwell, Listen, America! (Garden City, New York:
    Doubleday and Co., 1979), p. 62.

2. James Robison, "Here I Stand," Terrell (Texas) Tribune,
    December 24, 1981.

3. Pat Robertson, "700 Club" broadcast, March 16, 1982.

4. Thomas McIntyre, The Fear Brokers (New York: The Pilgrim
    Press, 1979), p. 111.

5. George Will, "Dial a Zealot," The Washington Post,
    September 29, 1977.

6. Rev. Pat Robertson, "700 Club" broadcast, December 30,
    1981.

7. Frances FitzGerald, "A Disciplined, Charging Army,"
    The New Yorker, May 18, 1981.

8. Wolf Blitzer, "The Christian Right -- Friend or Foe?"
    The National Jewish Monthly, April 1981, pp. 10-16.

9. Harry Covert, "Jerry Falwell Says America Must Support
    Israel," Moral Majority Report, March 14, 1980, p. 6.

10. Stephen Zunes, "Strange Bedfellows," The Progressive,
    November 1981, pp. 28-9.

11. Jerry Falwell, op. cit., p. 113.

12. Kenneth Briggs, "Evangelical Leaders Hail Election and Ask
    Continuation of Efforts," The New York Times, January 28,
    1981.

13. Lisa Myers, "Falwell Strives for Role as Political
    Kingmaker," The Washington Star, July 3, 1980.

14. James Robison, "Does God Hear Prayers of a Jew," Life's
    Answer, January 1981.

15. UPI dispatch, "Baptist Acts to End Dispute with Jews,"
    The New York Times, April 22, 1981.

16. Henry Goldman, "How Jerry Falwell Wants to Change U.S.,"
    The Sunday (Hackensack, N.J.) Record, June 21, 1981.

17. Joyce Purnick, "Moral Majority Establishes Beachhead in
    New York," The New York Times, February 5, 1981.

18. See Martin Tolchin, "Many in Senate Worry About Anti-
    Semitism," The New York Times, October 28, 1981; Peter
    Kihss, "U.S. Leaders Urged to Fight Bigotry," The New
    York Times, November 17, 1981; Mary McGrory, "Friends,"
    The Washington Post, October 29, 1981.

19. David K. Shipler, "Odd Friends: Israel and the Evangelical
    Protestants," The New York Times, December 1, 1981.

20. Marjorie Hyer, "Reform Jews Told to Form a 'Coalition of
    Decency' Against the Radical Right," The Washington Post,
    November 29, 1980.

21. Ibid.

22. American Jewish Congress, "Where We Stand: The Evangelical
    Right," statement drafted by Phil Baum, associate director
    of AJC, adopted as a resolution by the National Governing
    Council of the Congress on August 4, 1981.

23. Marjorie Hyer, op. cit.

24. Mark Hosenball, "Spotlight on the Hill," The New Republic,
    September 9, 1981.

25. The Spotlight, December 1, 1980.

26. John Williams, "Fairness Doctrine Urged in NBC 'Holocaust'
    Case," The Spotlight, November 23, 1981, p. 8.

27. Spencer Rich, "Knew Liberty Lobby Was Anti-Jewish,
    Richardson Says," The Washington Post, April 24, 1981.

28. Ulick Varange, pseud. (Francis Parker Yockey), <u>Imperium:</u>
    <u>The Philosophy of History and Politics</u> (Sausalito,
    California: The Noontide Press, 1969). Also, William
    Grimstad, ed., Committee for Truth in History, <u>The Six</u>
    <u>Million Reconsidered</u> (Sausalito, California: The Noontide
    Press, 1979).

29. Jay Mathews, "California Group's Attempt to Deny Holocaust
    Stirs Anxieties," <u>The Washington Post</u>, April 11, 1981.

30. Melinda Beck, "Footnote to the Holocaust," <u>Newsweek</u>,
    October 19, 1981.

31. UPI dispatch, "Moral Majority Aide Denounces President of
    Church Council," <u>The New York Times</u>, January 22, 1982.

32. Tim LaHaye, <u>The Beginning of the End</u> (Wheaton, Illinois:
    Tyndale House Publishers, Inc., 1972), p. 148.

33. Joe Klein, "The Moral Majority's Man in New York,"
    <u>New York</u> magazine, May 18, 1981.

34. William Simbro, "'Battling' Bob Jones Wages Holy War,"
    <u>Des Moines Tribune</u>, March 27, 1982.

35. Pat Robertson, "700 Club" broadcast, April 12, 1982.

36. Charles Lamb, "Spirited Views on Moral Majority Are
    Highlight of State Convention," <u>Yakima (Wash.) Herald-</u>
    <u>Republic</u>, April 5, 1981.

FURTHER READING: RELIGIOUS INTOLERANCE

Belth, Nathan C., A Promise to Keep: The American Encounter
          with Anti-Semitism (New York: New York Times Books,
          1979).

Blitzer, Wolf, "The Christian Right -- Friend or Foe?" The
          National Jewish Monthly, April 1981.

"Concerning Evangelicals and Jews," Christianity Today, April
          24, 1981, pp. 577-80.

Dart, John, "Israel Finding Born-Again Friends in U.S.,"
          The Los Angeles Times, June 11, 1978.

Daum, Annette, Assault on the Bill of Rights: The Jewish Stake
          (Union of American Hebrew Congregations, 1982).

Dialogue, "The New Right: Implications for American Jewry,"
          Spring 1981, pp. 4-14.

Dobkowski, Dr. Michael N., The Tarnished Dream: The Basis of
          American Anti-Semitism (Westport, Connecticut:
          Greenwood Press, 1979).

Flannery, Edward H., The Anguish of the Jews (New York:
          Macmillan and Co., 1965).

Forster, Arnold and Benjamin R. Epstein, The New Anti-Semitism
          (New York: McGraw-Hill, 1974).

Glock, Charles Y. and Rodney Start, Christian Beliefs and
          Anti-Semitism (New York: Harper and Row, 1979).

Handlin, Oscar and Mary Handlin, Danger in Discord (Anti-
          Defamation League brochure).

Saperstein, Rabbi David, Commission on Social Action of Reform
          Judaism, The Challenge of the Religious Right: A
          Jewish Response, 1981 (Available for $7.75 from
          Commission on Social Action of Reform Judaism, 2027
          Massachusetts Avenue, N.W., Washington, D.C. 20036).

RADICAL RIGHT LITERATURE

Grimstead, William, editor, Committee for Truth in History,
        The Six Million Reconsidered (Sausalito, California:
        The Noontide Press, 1979).

The Spotlight (Available from the Liberty Lobby, 300 Indepen-
        dence Avenue, S.E., Washington, D.C. 20003.)

Varange, Ulick, pseud. (Francis Parker Yockey), Imperium:
        The Philosophy and History of Politics (Sausalito,
        California: The Noontide Press, 1969).

"SECULAR HUMANISM"

Q. What is "secular humanism" and why is it such an important to concept to religious authoritarians?

A. The radical right claims it is a godless religion that is responsible for nearly anything they consider anti-Christian, anti-American, anti-family, or immoral. "Humanists" are said to control the most powerful institutions in American life, which they use to corrupt the morality of the American people. The public schools, Congress, the Supreme Court, the news media, and countless other institutions allegedly promote ideas and attitudes that run counter to the "Christian" perspective.

By arguing that "secular humanism" is endorsed by government in its court decisions, laws, and school curricula, the radical right tries to show that "secular humanism" constitutes an official state religion, in violation of the Establishment Clause of the First Amendment. It is important to debunk this extravagant fiction because it serves as the linchpin for many corollary arguments against sex education, the teaching of evolution in public schools, drug abuse, the women's movement, environmentalism, unionism, the peace movement, popular music, and many other facts of modern life. If "secular humanism" is the official government religion, goes the logic, then count-less disturbing moral trends are implicitly endorsed by the government -- in violation of the Constitution's "wall of separation" between church and state.

Q. What are the tenets of "secular humanism"?

A. The theoretical foundations of "secular humanism" are fairly basic. Cal Thomas, Vice President for Communications for Moral Majority, Inc., describes it as "an incorrect view of mankind, placing the created at the center of all things, rather than the Creator. From such a presupposition flow inevitable moral and ethical consequences that I believe have proved detrimental

97

to the best interests of the human race."[1]   Although many
ultra-fundamentalists have published dense and convoluted
tracts dissecting "secular humanism," the literature on the
subject has little scholarly integrity. Nonetheless, several
tracts have become standard references within ultra-fundamentalist circles.

One such work is The Battle for the Mind, by Rev. Tim LaHaye,
a board member of Moral Majority, Inc. LaHaye rails against
"secular humanists" whose "rebellion at God, parents, and
authority" has resulted in their "tragic lack in skills,
self-worth, purpose, and happiness." In spite of their
crippled condition, "secular humanists" have somehow managed
to gain control of our country's most powerful institutions:
"Most of the evils in the world today can be traced to humanism, which has taken over our government, education, TV, and
most of the influential things in life."[2]

Q. Why is the notion of "secular humanism" so useful to the
   radical religious right?

A. Because it is a quick and easy all-purpose denunciation. It
   conjures up powerful images of evil, atheism, and degeneracy
   and offers a scapegoat. Like Joseph McCarthy's accusations
   against "Communists," no proof is ever given nor can there ever
   be: the definition of "secular humanism" is so vague that
   all sorts of activities can fall under its heading. This is in
   fact the value of the term -- it unites into one ideology
   opposition to diverse "moral" issues like feminism, the ban on
   compulsory prayer in public schools, homosexual rights, television, and liberalism. Because "humanism" is supposed to be a
   comprehensive belief system, the most innocent activities (such
   as supporting the Equal Rights Amendment) are implicated in the
   immoral "secular humanist plot."

   The term "secular humanism" thus provides a way of superim-
   posing religious beliefs onto another realm, politics. "Secular
   humanism" becomes a powerful authoritarian political ideology
   to castigate foes and affirm a "religio-political" alternative.
   As Tim LaHaye writes: "It is all very simple....We are being
   controlled by a small but very influential cadre of committed
   humanists, who are determined to turn traditionally moral-minded
   America into an amoral, humanist country. Oh, they don't call
   it humanism. They label it DEMOCRACY, but they mean humanism,
   in all its atheistic, amoral depravity."[3]

Q. Theologically, what's supposed to be so dangerous about "humanism"?

A. The idea of placing man at the center of his own universe -- instead of God, as revealed in the Bible -- is said to cause moral confusion and societal breakdown. Ultra-fundamentalists reject the idea of autonomous, independent human rationality and permit no quibbling with their conclusion: "Humanism is basically Satan's philosophy and program," writes ultra-fundamentalist economist H. Edward Rowe who was formerly the executive director of the Religious Roundtable and currently serves as acting executive director of the newly formed Coalition for Religious Liberty. "Certain features of it may sound reasonable, but it always leads to tragedy, simply because it ignores the guidance of God."[4] Or as Rev. LaHaye puts it, "Either God exists and has given man moral guidelines by which to live or God is a myth and man is left to determine his own fate."[5]

Ultra-fundamentalists distort the traditional meaning of humanism by linking it to the word "secular," implying that "secular humanists" are aggressively hostile to God or Christianity. Yet secular does not mean opposed to God. It means "pertaining to worldly things." And all Americans, including the radical right, must deal with secular institutions be they supermarkets, banks or the postal service.

Q. Do most theologians accept this understanding of humanism?

A. No! Respected mainstream theologians reject the false dichotomy that pits "humanism" against Christianity (as understood by ultra-fundamentalists). Pope John Paul II has even urged scholars in Rome to "reincarnate the values of Christian humanism,"[6] and Mark Noll of the Protestant evangelical Wheaton College in Illinois points out, "Humanistic values flow from divine creation; they attain meaning through divine redemption, and they are ordered by divine revelation."[7] Although ultra-fundamentalists consider "Christian humanism" to be a contradiction in terms, the doctrine is in fact a respected discipline in the Christian church stretching back to St. Thomas Aquinas.

Q. The Supreme Court has declared "secular humanism" an official state religion, in violation of the Constitution!

A. This is a recurrent claim made by ultra-fundamentalists based on a false reading of several Supreme Court decisions. The apparent source of this specious argument is a 1978 article in the Texas Tech Law Review by John W. Whitehead (now general counsel for Moral Majority, Inc.) and former Representative John Conlan.[8]

Supposedly the Supreme Court's first recognition of "secular humanism" as a religion was in the 1961 case, Torcaso v. Watkins. In an obscure footnote, the Court wrote, "Among religions in this country which do not teach what would generally be considered a belief in the existence of God are Buddhism, Taoism, Ethical Culture, Secular Humanism and others."[9] The reference to "secular humanism" is an apparent reference to an actual church in California that calls itself "Secular Humanist." From these sorts of passing references, ultra-fundamentalists spin a conspiracy theory that the Supreme Court, the U.S. Government, the public schools, and others in positions of power in America are actively promoting the anti-religion of "secular humanism."

Q. If "secular humanism" is imaginary, why is there an actual organization that is promoting "humanism"?

A. Religious authoritarians like to cite the existence of the American Humanist Association (AHA) as evidence of the "secular humanist" conspiracy. The "hard proof" they show are two "humanist manifestos" issued in 1933 and 1973.[10] The declarations wax eloquent about the possibilities of human achievement and ethics, and bear little resemblance to claims made by ultra-fundamentalists that the manifestos are sinister blueprints for a world takeover.

The AHA does seek to promote humanism (in its conventional sense) and has enlisted the support of prominent scientists like B. F. Skinner, Francis Crick, and philosopher Sidney Hook. But with 3,200 members and a headquarters in a suburb of Buffalo, New York, the organization has more modest ambitions than ultra-fundamentalists ascribe to it.

Q. Are ultra-fundamentalists like Jerry Falwell and Pat Robertson
   the only people railing against "secular humanism"?

A. No. The term has gained wide usage because it is used by many
   prominent people in many public contexts. Notable public
   figures like Sen. Jesse Helms (R-N.C.), Rep. Larry McDonald
   (D-Ga.), Phyllis Schlafly, and even William Rusher, publisher
   of the National Review, have condemned "secular humanism" and
   its alleged manifestations.[11] It is a code word of religious
   authoritarians also used by their secular allies to show
   sympathy and support.

Q. How can an accusation of being a "secular humanist" be
   answered?

A. Because humanist-haters must make a large leap of the imagination in translating fact into fantasy, critics should demand
   empirical evidence for any accusations. The existence of a
   "Humanist Manifesto" or a footnote in a Supreme Court case does
   not prove the existence of a national conspiracy. Critics
   should probe some of the implications of "secular humanist"
   logic:

   o Is Readers' Digest a humanist publication because
      it is publishing a condensed version of the Bible?
      (Rev. Daniel Fore, when chairman of the New York
      state chapter of Moral Majority, Inc., called the
      Readers' Digest project an attempt to "censor
      God.")[12]

   o Is Ronald Reagan a humanist because he appointed a
      woman to the Supreme Court? (Rus Walton, generally
      credited with "fathering" the "Christian nation"
      movement, warned that "one of the punishments God
      levied vs. the nation that disobeyed Him was to be
      ruled by women.")[13]

   o Is Billy Graham a humanist because he believes in
      stopping the arms race and helping poor countries?[14]

QUOTABLE QUOTES

Rev. Tim LaHaye on Humanism

"The truth is, the major social ills of our day, such as
the mass murder of 10 million unborn children since 1973,
a $5 billion annual porno business, rampant drug traffic,
teenage promiscuity and unwanted pregnancies, venereal
disease...the tragic breakdown of the family, and a cata-
strophic rise in crime, can all be laid directly at the door
of secular humanism theories that reject God and His moral
absolutes."

-- San Diego Union,
August 30, 1981

"Either God exists and has given man moral guidelines by which
to live or God is a myth and man is left to determine his own
fate."

-- Los Angeles Times,
July 16, 1981

"Most of the evils in the world today can be traced to humanism, which has taken over our government, the U.N., education,
TV, and most of the influential things in life."

-- The Battle for the Mind, p. 9

"It is all very simple....We are being controlled by a small
but very influential cadre of committed humanists, who are
determined to turn traditionally moral-minded America into an
amoral, humanist country. Oh, they don't call it humanism.
They label it DEMOCRACY, but they mean humanism, in all its
atheistic, amoral depravity."

-- "What Every Christian Should
Know About Humanism"

"Two years ago I didn't even know what secular humanism was.
Now I realize you can be a humanist without knowing it and that
there are humanists doing everything."

>   -- Joy Cook, president of parents
>   group in Blunt, South Dakota,
>   fighting "humanism" in public
>   schools, The New York Times,
>   May 17, 1981

"In the humanistic frame of reference, however, values are
relative and ethics are situational. Children are therefore
being taught at school that moral and social beliefs and
behavior are not necessarily based upon Judeo-Christian
principles being taught by most families at home, but should
be fashioned instead to suit the wishes and convenience of the
majority or society as a whole."

>   -- Onalee McGraw of the
>   Heritage Foundation,
>   Secular Humanism and
>   the Schools, p. 5

"Humanism is basically Satan's philosophy and program. Certain
features of it may sound reasonable, but it always leads to
tragedy, simply because it ignores the guidance of God."

>   -- H. Edward Rowe,
>   Save America

"We don't need a minority of secular humanists running our
country. We have gotten away from the moral, family-oriented
country which was started in the Judeo-Christian tradition."

>   -- Rev. Jerry Falwell,
>   Dallas Morning News,
>   August 17, 1980

"I believe that the overwhelming majority of Americans are sick and tired of the way the amoral liberals and secular humanists are trying to corrupt our nation from its commitment to freedom, democracy, traditional morality, and the free enterprise system."

> -- Rev. Jerry Falwell, fund-raising letter for Moral Majority, Inc., "Is Our Grand Old Flag Still Going Down the Drain?", June 15, 1981

"Secular humanism is an incorrect view of mankind, placing the created at the center of all things, rather than the Creator. From such a presupposition flow inevitable moral and ethical consequences that I believe have proved to be detrimental to the best interests of the human race."

> -- Cal Thomas, Vice President for Communications, Moral Majority, Inc., The New York Times, May 20, 1981

"The religious right, apparently, has chosen paranoia. It is a clever tactic. What otherwise would have been a shadowy struggle against a 500-year-old historical trend -- secularization -- is transformed into a crusade against a militant ideology controlled by a vanguard of party activists -- the humanists. A generation ago the pernicious sappers of our vital spiritual juices were called "godless Communists." Now they are "secular humanists."

> -- Charles Krauthammer, The New Republic, June 25, 1981

NOTES: "SECULAR HUMANISM"

1. Letter to The New York Times, May 20, 1981.

2. Tim LaHaye, The Battle for the Mind (Old Tappan, N.J.:
    Fleming H. Revell Company, 1980), p. 9.

3. Tim LaHaye, "What Every Christian Should Know About
    Humanism."

4. H. Edward Rowe, Save America!, cited in Russell Chandler,
    "Humanists: Target of the Moral Right," The Los Angeles
    Times, July 16, 1981.

5. The Los Angeles Times, op. cit.

6. Ibid.

7. Ibid.

8. John W. Whitehead and John Conlan, "The Establishment of
    the Religion of Secular Humanism and Its First Amendment
    Implications," Texas Tech Law Review, Vol. 10, No. 1,
    1978.

9. Torcaso v. Watkins 367 U.S. 488, 495, footnote 11.

10. American Humanist Association, Humanist Manifesto I & II.

11. See, e.g., Representative Larry McDonald, Congressional
    Record, February 24, 1981, p. E658; Representative William
    Dannemeyer, Congressional Record, October 27, 1981,
    p. H7723; William Rusher, "Helms Deserves Our Thanks for
    Battling Secular Humanism," New York (N.Y.) News-World
    (Universal Press Syndicate column), July 16, 1981.

12. Associated Press dispatch, "Bible Project Is Scored,"
    Richmond (Virginia) Times-Dispatch, September 15, 1981.

13. Rus Walton, Plymouth Rock Foundation, FAC-Sheet #16,
    "Women & 'Equal Rights'."

14. Billy Graham, "A Change of Heart," Sojourners, August
    1979, pp. 12-14.

FURTHER READING: "SECULAR HUMANISM"

Chandler, Russell, "Humanists: Targets of the Moral Right," The
        Los Angeles Times, July 16, 1981.

Hofstadter, Richard, The Paranoid Style in American Politics
        and Other Essays, (Chicago: University of Chicago
        Press, 1964).

Krauthammer, Charles, "The Humanist Revolution," The New
        Republic, July 25, 1981.

Farrell, Michael J., "The Humanist Scapegoat," The National
        Catholic Reporter, July 17, 1981.

Indiana State Teachers Association, "The Great Debate:
        Resolved: The Public Schools Are Preaching The
        Religion of Secular Humanism," transcript of debate
        between Edward B. Jenkinson, professor of English
        Education, Indiana University and Rev. Greg Dixon,
        national secretary of Moral Majority, Inc. and
        president of its Indiana chapter, October 30, 1981.

Interchange, "Will the Real Secular Humanist Please Stand Up?"
        Vol. 3, No. 6, December 1981.

Kurtz, Paul, The Humanist Alternative: Some Definitions of
        Humanism. (Buffalo: Prometheus Books, 1973).

Lamont, Corliss, The Philosopy of Humanism, Sixth edition, (New
        York, N.Y.: Frederick Ungar Publishing Co., 1982).

National Council of Teachers of English, "The Attack on Human-
        ism," October 1980.

Schwartz, Sheila, "The Attack on Humanism," SLATE (Support for
        the Learning and Teaching of English), National
        Council of Teachers of English, October 1980.

RADICAL RIGHT LITERATURE

Chambers, Claire, The SIECUS Circle (Belmont, Mass.: Western
        Islands, 1977).

Duncan, Homer, Secular Humanism: The Most Dangerous Religion in
        America (Lubbock, Texas: Christian Focus in Govern-
        ment, Inc., 1979).

------   , Humanism In the Light of Holy Scripture (Lubbock,
        Texas: Christian Focus on Government, Inc., 1981).

LaHaye, Tim, The Battle for the Family (Old Tappan, N.J.:
        Fleming H. Revell Co., 1982).

------   , The Battle for the Mind (Old Tappan, N.J.: Fleming
        H. Revell Co., 1980).

McGraw, Onalee, Secular Humanism and the Schools: The Issue
        Whose Time Has Come (Washington, D.C.: The Heritage
        Foundation, 1976).

Thomson, Rosemary, Withstanding Humanism's Challenge to
        Families: Anatomy of a White House Conference,
        1981. (Available from Traditional Publications,
        Box 112, Morton, Illinois 61550.)

THE "ELECTRONIC CHURCH"

Q. What is the "electronic church" and why is it important?

A. The "electronic church" refers to the television and radio ministries of more than 950 religious broadcasters in the United States.[1] Most of them are evangelical Christians, many are fundamentalists, and some have no formal affiliations with any denomination. The top-rated religious TV programs feature many churchly activities like prayer and preaching, but many of them also serve up flashy entertainment, political opinion, faith healing, and hard-sell appeals for money.

This new programming genre not only represents an important religious experience for millions of Americans, it is a power-ful force in national politics as well. Through their TV pulpits, some televangelists preach a hard-hitting religio-political message to millions of viewers, without interference from the networks or commercial advertisers: they are viewer-supported. Although many TV preachers do not preach politics (such as Oral Roberts, Robert Schuller, and Rex Humbard), those who do have become influential voices on the national scene. The nationally broadcast programs of men like Jerry Falwell, James Robison, Pat Robertson and Tim LaHaye have become potent forms of political education for millions of ultra-fundamental-ist viewers.

Q. Haven't there been religious TV programs since the 1950s?

A. Yes, but none of the early televangelists really had the showmanship, technology, political impact, or staggering revenues of contemporary TV preachers. Bishop Fulton J. Sheen is perhaps the most famous electronic evangelist of that era, but he was a singular presence -- not a multi-million dollar industry. Sheen was one of the first to demonstrate the power and appeal of TV religion. But unlike some of his present-day successors, Sheen did not exploit his national pulpit for financial gain, issue political harangues, or build a commercial empire around his ministry. Except for Sheen's brilliant TV presence, most religious shows of the 1950s consisted of sober mainline preaching.

Mainline churches originally took to the airwaves in the 1940s because the fledgling television industry had donated free air time to the National Council of Churches (NCC) as a public service, which the NCC then allocated to its member denominations. This left certain evangelical preachers to fend for themselves. They soon founded their own trade association, the National Religious Broadcasters (NRB), and set out to pioneer viewer-supported religious programming.

Their efforts went largely unnoticed until the early 1970s, when new telecommunications technologies like cable and satellite transmission were becoming financially feasible. Evangelical broadcasters were the first to recognize the potential of the technologies for religious programming. Through their entrepreneurial efforts, audiences for the electronic church grew from 9.8 million in 1970 to 20.8 million in 1975, before peaking at 22.5 million in 1978.[2] Membership in the NRB also skyrocketed, from 104 broadcasters in 1968 to over 950 in 1982.[3]

Q. Who are the most-watched televangelists?

A. The best-known TV preachers are not necessarily the most-watched. According to A.C. Neilsen data collected in May 1981 (the latest available figures)[4], these are the top ten TV religious programs based on the number of viewers:

Televangelist/Show	Viewers	Markets	Home Base
1. Oral Roberts "Oral Roberts and You"	2,179,000	189	Tulsa, Oklahoma
2. Robert Schuller "The Hour of Power"	2,819,000	164	Garden Grove, California
3. Rex Humbard "The Rex Humbard Ministry"	1,974,000	216	Akron, Ohio

	Televangelist/Show	Viewers	Stations	Home Base
4.	Jimmy Swaggert "The Jimmy Swaggert Crusade"	1,870,000	218	Baton Rouge, Louisiana
5.	Jerry Falwell "Old-Time Gospel Hour"	1,260,000	254	Lynchburg, Virginia
6.	Richard De Haan and Paul Van Gorder "Day of Discovery"	1,216,000	188	Grand Rapids, Michigan
7.	James Bakker "The PTL (Praise The Lord) Club"	946,000	178	Charlotte, North Carolina
8.	Pat Robertson "700 Club"	630,000	113	Portsmouth, Virginia
9.	James Robison "James Robison: A Man With A Message"	416,000	76	Fort Worth, Texas
10.	Kenneth Copeland "Believer's Voice of Victory"	408,000	124	Fort Worth, Texas

In addition to these nationally broadcast religious shows,
there are many local and regional TV preachers who are influential in their own right. Two members of the board of Moral
Majority, Inc. -- Rev. Greg Dixon (Indianapolis) and Rev.
Charles Stanley (Atlanta) -- have devoted regional followings.
A third board member, Rev. Tim LaHaye (San Diego), produces a
show that has begun national distribution. Other local televangelists have used their access to television audiences to
promote their political agenda.

Q. Many news accounts have estimated that the electronic church
has as many as 50 million or 100 million viewers. Are these
estimates trustworthy?

A. Since the electronic church was first discovered by the mainstream press in the late 1970s, audience estimates have fluc-
tuated wildly.[5] James Robison once boasted that he had some

50 to 60 million viewers; Rex Humbard's publicity materials at one time claimed he had 100 million viewers; and Bert Clendennen, one of the lesser-known radio preachers, had the audacity to crow that his message reached "one out of every two people on the face of the earth."[6] Many reporters took these figures at face value.

Several professional audience-measurement surveys in 1980 and 1981 punctured the grossly inflated audience estimates. The Television Information Office (part of the National Association of Broadcasters) issued a study based on Nielsen data showing that even the combined viewership of the top ten televangelists -- nearly 13 million people -- didn't equal the audience that Falwell claimed for himself -- 25 million viewers.[7]

Even the combined viewership for the top 66 syndicated religious programs in the U.S. totaled 20,538,000 in 1980, according to Arbitron.[8] A Harris poll showed that, if "occasional viewers" are included in the estimate, some 23 million Americans watch TV preachers.[9] Make no mistake: 20 million viewers of TV religious programming is a significant phenomenon. But the actual audiences for individual televangelists are invariably smaller than claimed.

Q. If actual viewership is so overstated, how can some TV preachers be so influential?

A. Regular media access to the public -- even if it is "only" one million viewers -- is a power that few national leaders possess. It is a power that some televangelists have chosen to exploit for its political potential. Jerry Falwell, Tim LaHaye, Pat Robertson, and James Robison are TV preachers who have done so by identifying themselves with leading political figures, by issuing demagogic warnings to their viewers, and by actively seeking media coverage for their political crusades. Their public image is itself a power that commands respect from legislators, journalists, and the public.

It is not essential to have a huge following to make an impact in American politics; a vocal, well-organized membership led by a colorful, charismatic personality can amplify a group's political clout beyond its actual numbers.

Q. How big is the "electronic church"?

A. There are four Christian television "networks," 95 nationally
   syndicated TV religious programs, and more than 950 religious
   broadcasters on radio and television.[10] Ben Armstrong,
   executive director of the National Religious Broadcasters,
   says that religious programmers spend at least $600 million a
   year for air time on commercial TV stations. When the costs of
   production, promotion, fundraising, and operating expenses are
   added in, TV religion is easily a $1 billion industry.[11]

   As the industry grows, it has begun buying its own stations and
   expanding internationally. Pat Robertson's Christian Broadcasting Network (CBN) owns broadcast TV stations in Atlanta,
   Boston, Dallas, and Norfolk-Portsmouth, Virginia. Other
   religious "networks" are beginning to acquire stations too.
   CBN recently opened up a station in Lebanon which broadcasts
   throughout the Middle East, and has produced an animated series
   on Bible stories that is aired in Japan. Religious programming
   by American televangelists is also beamed by satellite to South
   America and Europe.

   Radio broadcasting is another arm of the "electronic church."
   Some 1,500 radio stations devote more than 15 hours a week to
   religious programming, in addition to Sunday broadcasts. Six
   hundred of these offer full-time religious programming.[12]
   (There are approximately 10,000 AM and FM radio stations in the
   U.S.)

Q. What are the four Christian television networks, and how big
   are they?

A. Several televangelists have expanded beyond their own programs
   to buy local TV stations and produce their own secular programming. The Christian networks are fairly small, but they are
   beginning to compete with the major networks and cable enterprises as an alternative source of programming.

   The Christian Broadcasting Network (CBN) is by far the largest
   and most sophisticated religious TV network. Besides owning
   and operating four TV stations, CBN distributes 24-hour cable
   programming via satellite to 2,700 cable systems and 14 million
   homes, and produces several syndicated shows.[13] The corner-
   stone of the CBN's programming is the "700 Club," an evangelical "Tonight" show hosted by CBN founder Pat Robertson.

Besides showing reruns of popular 1950s sitcoms ("My Little Margie" and "I Married Joan"), CBN has started producing for syndication a Christian soap opera ("Another Life"), a news and information program for women, a 13-part documentary series on pornography, a weekend children's show, and a morning news program, "USAM," similar to the "Today" show.

Robertson's closest competitor is the PTL Network, run by his former co-host of the "700 Club," James Bakker. Bakker took the Christian talk show format to the Trinity Broadcasting Network, but after a falling out with Trinity's Paul Crouch, Bakker left to found his own network in Charlotte, North Carolina. "PTL" stands for "Praise The Lord," "People That Love," or as critics in North Carolina dubbed it after revelations of the network's financial mismanagement, "Pass The Loot."[14] The PTL initials and format are imitated around the world.

Other evangelical Christian TV networks include the Trinity Broadcasting Network based in Los Angeles, and the National Christian Network based in Cocoa Beach, Florida.[15]

Q. How much money do televangelists raise? How do they do it?

A. The top-grossing televangelists have been identified in several reports as Jerry Falwell ($70 million), Oral Roberts ($60 million), Pat Robertson ($58 million), and Jim Bakker ($51 million).[16] To bring in such huge revenues, televangelists have developed numerous marketing techniques and tearful appeals for contributions. Some televangelists sell cassettes of their sermons or scripture; others sell records and inspirational books. James Bakker once hawked the "PTL Masters' Art Collection."[17] Jimmy Swaggert has sent out a pamphlet, "The Fragrance of Frankincense and the True Spirit of Christmas," featuring a scratch-and-sniff patch.[18]

Viewers who do send money or call telephone "counseling" lines are entered into a computerized direct mail system, which sends "personalized" letters asking for additional contributions.[19] TV ministries also generate money through "memberships" ("Faith Partners" on Falwell's Old-Time Gospel Hour) and product giveaways that create a sense of obligation.

Mainline religious groups are especially offended by the glib use of the Lord in soliciting money. When 47 local TV stations

dropped James Bakker's hour-long show in August 1981 for
failing to pay its bills, Bakker issued a heartfelt appeal
for funds that carried the endorsement of God Himself. During
a prayer before showtime, Bakker said God told him, "'Jim, I
don't want you to let go of one possession that I gave you....
I want you to increase, not diminish.'"[20] "The fundamentalists prosper on TV precisely because they're not afraid to make
the sales pitch so blunt," write the authors of Prime Time
Preachers.[21]

Q. Why do televangelists make such hard-sell appeals for money?

A. Commercial air time is very expensive, and the stiff competition among TV ministries for prime-time slots and prime broadcast markets makes it even more costly. One solution is to
expand into additional markets to capture more viewers and
contributions. But this spiral of expansion must ultimately be
financed by viewer contributions.

And so, despite questions of taste and theological integrity,
many televangelists try to generate more money by using manipulative sales gimmicks and promises of spiritual peace. The
repeated pleas for money may also be related to the comfortable
lifestyle that many televangelists lead. James Bakker enjoys a
$90,000 salary with his wife Tammy, a clothing allowance, and
use of a $200,000 home.[22] Other televangelists have given
themselves bonuses like yachts, Lear jets, and $400,000
homes.[23]

While none of this is illegal, the Federal Communications
Commission has investigated charges that the PTL Club was
soliciting funds for a nonexistent foreign missionary fund, and
the Securities and Exchange Commission has investigated Jerry
Falwell's Old-Time Gospel Hour for financial irregularities.
[24] In response to these and other problems, religious
broadcasters created the Evangelists Council for Financial
Accountability in March 1979 to clean up their image and ward
off any formal government regulation.[25]

Q. How do TV preachers use their broadcasts to organize
politically?

A. On many occasions, TV preachers use their platform to alert
viewers to pending political issues and urge them to take
certain action. If a viewer contributes to a program or calls

the telephone "counseling" line, his or her name is added to
the computerized direct mail list, which is then used for
political fundraising and education. Thus viewers who send
money to support Jerry Falwell's religious activities will
later receive mailings and solicitations on political issues,
such as how Social Security supposedly violates scripture.
Many televangelists entice viewers religiously and respond to
them politically.

Richard Viguerie, the direct mail expert, explains how the
crusade against "immoral" network programming (to take one
example) is a useful way to capture new political followers:

> The networks may beat us, they may after three or
> four years still have their sex and violence on tele-
> vision; but in the meantime, Jerry Falwell and others
> may increase their list of supporters by three- or
> four- or five-fold. And we can do something the
> networks cannot do, which is get involved in political
> campaigns....You cannot get organized based on organi-
> zational technique, you have got to do it now with
> causes. [26]

Q. How do TV preachers use special broadcasts to promote political
   views?

A. Periodically, televangelists will produce TV specials on issues
   such as school prayer, church/state separation, creationism,
   and other topics of a blatantly political nature. Although
   many of these specials present themselves as "balanced" and
   "objective," they are little more than political diatribes.

   Falwell has produced a special on school prayer, advertised as
   being fair-minded, that refers to the 1962 Supreme Court ruling
   as "when God was kicked out of our schools 20 years ago...."
   James Robison's Evangelistic Association has produced an hour
   special, "Attack on the Family," that explores the alleged
   impact of "secular humanism" on the traditional family. It has
   aired on prime-time television nationwide. Robison has also
   produced "Wake Up America, We're All Hostages," which presents
   his view of a deteriorating America, our military preparedness
   and the SALT II treaty.

   A "700 Club" special, "The Dividing Line," is a frequently
   aired program that questions historic notions of church/state

separation. "Let Their Eyes Be Opened," another "700 Club"
production, purports to show how "secular humanism" has
infiltrated the U.S. government, schools, and society.
"Seven Days Ablaze," a week-long "700 Club" series, was
another video blast at the concept of church/state separation.
The program denounced the federal judicial system and charged
that government officials at all levels were interfering with
Christianity in the U.S.

Q. How do moral majoritarian broadcasts violate the so-called
Fairness Doctrine?

A. Even though most religious programming steers clear of
politics, many televangelists use their ministries to comment
on controversial political topics. That is their right, but
under the Fairness Doctrine administered by the Federal Communications Commission, viewers also have the right to hear both
sides of an issue. If only one side is presented by a TV
station in its overall programming, citizens may request
alternative programming or air time to present differing views.

Here are some typical examples of political statements made by
TV preachers and their guests:

> James Robison: "Right now we're trying to deal with the
> problem of poverty through what could be defined only
> properly as socialism of the purest and rankest form."[27]

> Pat Robertson: "The government has come to think that
> really the church exists at the leisure of the govern-
> ment. In other words, the Supreme Court says churches
> exist because of a benevolent neutrality. That's a
> totalitarian statement."[28]

> Connaught Marshner, head of the Library Court, appearing
> on the "700 Club": "There are many, many things that
> the government does by law, by policy, by program that
> interfere with the family relations and interfere
> with religious freedom."[29]

Despite these sorts of statements, the politically minded
televangelists condemn the Fairness Doctrine as an ungodly
restraint on their free speech. Falwell has even called it
"the most unfair doctrine ever created by moral men." Falwell's "95 Theses" -- his religious political platform --

specifically demands that "the Fairness Doctrine not be used as an excuse to prohibit church leaders from using the media to speak out against immorality."[30] But the people denied free speech are those Americans who are subjected to one-sided political messages over public airwaves. The Fairness Doctrine is meant to ensure free speech for all interested parties.

Q. What is PEOPLE FOR THE AMERICAN WAY doing to respond to this problem?

A. To help citizens exercise their First Amendment rights with regard to electronic media, PEOPLE FOR THE AMERICAN WAY launched the Media Fairness Project in 1982. This project encourages citizens to monitor unbalanced programming on important and controversial public issues. When one-sided programming is documented, the project helps citizens request alternative programming or air time to present different views on the issue. Local broadcasters often share citizens' concern that "religious" programs are not always balanced and welcome efforts to correct programming biases. Viewers who wish more information on the Media Fairness Project should contact PEOPLE FOR THE AMERICAN WAY.

QUOTABLE QUOTES

"The reason we take so much flak is that this competition flies
in the face of what religion is supposed to be. Churches are
supposed to be noncompetitive. We're all supposed to love each
other. That's Old World thinking."

> -- Ben Armstrong,
> executive director of
> National Religious Broad-
> casters, Forbes,
> July 7, 1980

"The use of the media to spread the gospel was foretold in the
Bible, including the use of satellite transmissions."

> -- Ben Armstrong, quoting
> Revelation 14:6, "And I saw
> another angel fly in the midst
> of heaven, having the ever-
> lasting gospel to preach upon
> them that dwell on the
> earth...," New York magazine,
> October 6, 1980

"The hard right has no interest in religion except to manipu-
late it. I told him [Falwell] to preach the gospel. That's
our calling. I want to preserve the purity of the gospel, and
the freedom of religion in America. I don't want to see
religious bigotry in any form."

> -- Billy Graham, Us magazine,
> September 1, 1981

"The most critical and sensitive spot in the ethics of mass
communications, we believe, is on the use of these media for
the manipulation of people....The sanction against manipulation, we further suggest, extends specifically to the manipulation of people for what is presumed to be their best
interests."

> -- A 1955 study by the United
> Church of Christ, Office of
> Communications

NOTES: THE "ELECTRONIC CHURCH"

1.   Beth Spring, "NRB Board Cites Progress," NRB Convention
     News, February 9, 1982, p. 6.

2.   "Syndicated Devotional Programs Lost Audiences Between May
     1980 and 1981," The Television Information Office, December
     3, 1981. Source of audience data: Nielsen Station Index,
     Report on Syndicated Programs, May 1980 and May 1981.

3.   Jeffrey K. Hadden and Charles E. Swann, Prime Time Preach-
     ers: The Rising Power of Televangelism (Reading, Massa-
     chusetts: Addison-Wesley Publishing Company, Inc., 1981),
     p. 81.

4.   "Syndicated Devotional Programs," op. cit.

5.   William Martin, "The Birth of a Media Myth," Atlantic
     Monthly, June 1981, pp. 9-16.

6.   Ibid.

7.   Nielson Station Index, op. cit.

8.   Hadden and Swann, op. cit., p. 50.

9.   William Martin, op. cit.

10. "Stars of the Cathode Church," Time, February 4, 1980,
     p. 64. Also, private conversation between Jeffrey Hadden
     and People for the American Way staff, October 19, 1981.

11. Ibid.

12. Inquiry to National Religious Broadcasters, April 1981.

13. Richard Zoglin, "Christian Network Tries Secular Field,"
     The Atlanta Constitution, January 16, 1982.

14. Hadden and Swann, op. cit., pp. 32-4.

15. Ibid., pp. 37-8.

16. Data Center, "Press Profile #4," p. 31-3. Also, James Breig, "TV Religion: The Price is Right," U.S. Catholic, August 1981, p. 13.

17. Hadden and Swann, op. cit., p. 118.

18. James Breig, op. cit.

19. Hadden and Swann, op. cit.

20. James Bakker, "The PTL Club" broadcast, July 15, 1981.

21. Hadden and Swann, op. cit., p. 103.

22. "Stars of the Cathode Church," Time, February 4, 1980.

23. James Brieg, op. cit.

24. Frances FitzGerald, "A Disciplined, Charging Army," The New Yorker, May 18, 1981.

25. "Stars of the Cathode Church," Time, February 4, 1980.

26. David Nyhan, "New Right Preparing for Battle Against Sex, Violence on TV," The Boston Globe, November 22, 1980.

27. James Robison broadcast, March 21, 1982.

28. Pat Robertson, "700 Club" special broadcast, "Seven Days Ablaze," October 1981.

29. "700 Club" broadcast, October 5, 1981.

30. Jerry Falwell, "Ninety-Five Theses for the 1980's."

FURTHER READING: THE "ELECTRONIC CHURCH"

Armstrong, Ben, The Electric Church (Nashville, Nelson, 1979).

Dabney, Dick, "God's Own Network," Harper's, August 1980.

Flake, Carol, "The Electronic Kingdom," The New Republic,
        August 1980.

Hadden, Jeffrey K. and Charles E. Swann, Prime Time Preachers:
        The Rising Power of Televangelism (Reading, Massa-
        chusetts: Addison-Wesley Publishing Company, Inc.,
        1981).

Horsefield, Peter G., "Religious Broadcasting at the Cross-
        roads," The Christian Century, January 27, 1982.

Quebedeaux, Richard, By What Authority: The Rise of Personality
        Cults in American Christianity (New York: Harper and
        Row, 1982).

Scholes, Jerry, Give Me That Prime-Time Religion (New York:
        Dutton, 1980).

Schuller, David S., Merton P. Strommen, and Milo L. Brekke,
        editors, Ministry in America (New York: Harper and
        Row, 1980).

Time, "Stars of the Cathode Church," February 4, 1980.

Warner, Gregory Dunn, "The Development of Religious Pressure
        Groups in Broadcasting," unpublished manuscript.

Education

Next to religious belief itself, education is a key concern of the radical religious right. It is not unusual for parents to want the best possible education for their children, but ultra-fundamentalists seek a wholesale transformation in the public education system. Its leaders argue that the specter of "secular humanism" has so corrupted the public schools that radical reforms are necessary. The major battlefronts include:

o Textbooks and Curricula. Censorship of teaching materials is on the rise in public schools throughout the nation, often for strictly political reasons.

o Library Policies. Moral authoritarians want to restrict access to different ideas by banning books from school and public library shelves. These efforts also are on the upswing nationwide.

o Creationism. Despite a major legal setback in Arkansas, advocates of creationism continue to push for teaching religion in science classes.

o Sex Education. Ultra-fundamentalists not only argue that sex education has a corrupting influence on young people but that it should not be an option available to other parents' teenagers.

o Prayer in Schools. Despite the Supreme Court's conclusive rulings 20 years ago, ultra-fundamentalists still wage their crusade to reinstate mandatory prayer rituals in public schools.

The radical right's hostility to the public schools has fueled the "Christian school" movement in America. Hundreds of private religious academies have sprung up in the past decade as an alternative to secular, pluralistic public schools. What

has made this trend especially disturbing to defenders of
public education are the tax privileges that ultra-fundamentalists seek. They want tax exemptions for their schools even
if they discriminate on the basis of race and they want tuition
tax credits, which would seriously weaken the public education
system.

Part II will sketch the lines of debate in each of these areas.
Although each issue has its own history and themes, some core
questions arise in each case: What are the goals of education?
What are the rights of students, parents and the community in
education? When one citizen's religious convictions clash with
another citizen's constitutional rights, how can a community
resolve the conflict? In answering these questions, we should
look toward basic principles of constitutional democracy. We
must defend intellectual freedom, the separation of church and
state, and due process in policymaking.

Q. Why does the radical right condemn the public school system?

A. The radical right has a profound distrust of many assumptions of public education. It is not convinced that all races
   and creeds should rub shoulders in the classroom; that public
   schools should be neutral toward religion; or that education
   should teach children to be independent, creative thinkers.
   Instead, the radical right sees education as a good-versus-evil
   "battle for the mind." Ultra-fundamentalists claim that two
   opposing philosophies -- amoral "secular humanism" and ultra-
   fundamentalist religious beliefs -- are vying for the alle-
   giance of American school children. Education is thus seen as
   an indoctrination process that should teach children what to
   think but not how to think.

Q. Why does the radical right consider "secular humanism" so
   dangerous?

A. It believes that "secular humanist" teachers, textbooks, and
   curricula are instilling godless values into their children.
   According to Mel and Norma Gabler, the influential leaders of
   Educational Research Analysts, a national censorship group,
   "The teaching of humanism in public schools not only defies
   Christian values and the authority of parents, but borders on
   treason and violates the U.S. Constitution by teaching a
   religion."[1] (See "Secular Humanism" section.)

As the Gablers' activities suggest, the radical right's hostility to public education is based more on <u>political</u> than
moral objections. Consider their criticisms of textbooks:[2]

<u>Textbook Passage</u>	<u>Objection</u>
"It was so false, so pointless. How could they sing of the land of the free, when there was still racial discrimination?"	"Majority of people are free. Only people in jail are not free."
"But it was always China that we were taught was home. In those days we were all <u>immigrants</u>. Whether we were born in America or not, we were all immigrants."	"This does not foster patriotism toward America and is a somewhat deroga- tory statement about our country."
Reference to UNICEF, United Nations International Children's Emergency Fund.	"UNICEF is a known Communist front."
"There was a riot on our block, and there were a lot of whites doing most of the shooting. Sometimes some blacks would come by with guns, but not often; they mostly had clubs."	"Infers [sic] that whites are bad and blacks are good. Talk about discrim- ination! There is no story in this series that depicts the reverse!"

In 1981, the Wyoming Family Rights Forum sued a school board to
suppress a history text that it considered "anti-family" (not
all women described were mothers and homemakers) and "anti-free
enterprise" (it accurately stated that the 19th-century
populist movement favored a graduated income tax).[3] As these
instances reveal, "secular humanism" often serves as a code
word for any views that the radical right finds politically or
culturally objectionable; actual moral issues are rarely at
stake.

Q. <u>Public schools do not teach moral standards.</u>

A. This is a root fallacy of the radical right's critique of
   public education. In their crusade against "secular humanism,"
   ultra-fundamentalists reject the possibility that secular
   institutions can uphold moral values. Yet public schools do
   teach the values of good citizenship and moral integrity. They

do teach honesty, fair play, decency, and so forth. No religion has an exclusive claim to these values.

But because the radical right does claim a moral monopoly, any values that fail to conform to its own values are dubbed "immoral." They condemn the public schools for not teaching their specific religious doctrines or promoting their political interpretation of the world. This is the source of their hostility. The Gablers express the resentments of many ultra-fundamentalists:

> As long as the schools continue to teach ABNORMAL ATTITUDES and ALIEN THOUGHTS, we caution parents NOT to urge their children to pursue high grades and class discussion, because the harder students work, the greater their chances of brainwashing.[4]

Rev. Tim LaHaye, a board member of Moral Majority, Inc., agrees: "Modern public education is the most dangerous single force in a child's life: religiously, sexually, economically, patriotically, and physically."[5] A book or curriculum is not "immoral" simply because it does not conform to one interpretation of the Bible. Reasonable people can disagree about education policy without being agents of Satan. Moreover, the public schools have no role endorsing the specific religious or political beliefs of any single group in our society.

The question communities must face is not which set of ideas is "better" but how disagreements over education policy can be resolved. Consistent with our Constitution, differences of opinion should be resolved through due process and open democratic participation by all segments of the community. Vigilante actions, intimidation, and pressure group politics should not be permitted to abridge other people's rights.

Q. What teaching techniques does the radical right condemn?

A. It sees conspiratorial designs in many common teaching methods, especially those that try to prod a child's intellectual creativity and critical judgment.[6] Some of the methods frequently attacked are:

   o psychological testing, because it is seen as an unwarranted intrusion of "the state" on a child's personal values and beliefs;

o "survival games," because the simulations of
life-and-death situations allegedly cause undue
emotional stress and force students to make profound
ethical decisions;

o role-playing, because it is supposedly a tool for
teaching "situational ethics," and sanctions moral
ambiguity and relativism; and

o diary-keeping, because it provides an opportunity for
"humanist" teachers to probe a child's private thoughts
and "brainwash" the child.

According to a list of 26 "Don'ts for Students" prepared by
Parents Actively Concerned, an ultra-fundamentalist group in
North Carolina, students should not discuss values in class or
exchange opinions on political or social issues. Nor are
students supposed to play "blindfolded" games or talk about
science fiction. Students are also advised to refuse to
participate in classroom discussions that begin with such
phrases as "What is your opinion of...?" "Do you think...?"
"What might happen if...?" and "Should we...?"[7] These
activities presumably could lead to moral confusion.

Teachers generally use these activities to stimulate a child's
imagination and encourage independent thinking. But ultra-
fundamentalists consider open discussions of different ideas
unnecessary and possibly heretical because they recognize only
one, absolute biblical truth. Rev. Tim LaHaye argues, "[A]ca-
demic freedom means that humanists and other atheists are free
to teach their atheistic beliefs, but Christians may not teach
theirs. Consequently atheism has become the official doctrine
of public education."[8]

Q. Who are the "humanists" supposedly corrupting public education?

A. National organizations such as the National Education Association, the American Federation of Teachers, the American Civil
Liberties Union, the United Nations, labor unions, Planned
Parenthood and the U.S. Department of Education are the most
frequently mentioned "humanists" affecting public education.
The national influence of these institutions, say critics like
Barbara M. Morris, is reshaping American schools to resemble
the Communist Chinese educational system. "Call it what you
will," says Morris, "'citizen education,'...'world order

education,' 'global perspectives,' 'peace studies' -- it's all
political indoctrination intended to train youngsters to be
'global servants' and world citizens...."[9]

Historically, say ultra-fundamentalists, the great villains of
Christian morality in public education are "humanist" educators
and psychologists like John Dewey, Jean Piaget, Carl Rogers,
Horace Mann, Lawrence Kohlberg, Abraham Maslow, and others.
These men are reviled for theories that stress human self-
reliance, self-improvement, and independent judgment.

Q. What is the "Christian school" movement?

A. It is a thriving alternative system of education that stresses
   ultra-fundamentalist religious and political beliefs. "Because
   of the vacuum in our public schools in the area of character
   building," writes Jerry Falwell, "Christian educators have
   found it necessary to begin their own schools."[10]   These
   schools are considered an essential part of ultra-fundamentalist evangelism and leadership training. Falwell describes
   the curriculum at "Christian schools":

>   In the Christian schools, education begins with
>   God. The objectives are based upon biblical prin-
>   ciples, with God as the center of every subject.
>   The philosophies taught stand as witness to society,
>   as the ultimate goal, not as a reflection of man's
>   sinful nature. In science, the student learns God's
>   laws for the universe [creationism]; in history,
>   God's plan for the ages; and in civics, God's
>   requirement of loyalty and support for the govern-
>   ment He has ordained.[11]

Because the "Christian school" movement is so decentralized, it
is difficult to make a reliable estimate of its size. However,
Jerry Falwell claimed in 1980 that there were 14,000 "conservative Christian schools" and that that number was growing by
three new schools per day.[12] A more reliable guess might be
4,500, the number of "Christian schools" that receive curricular
materials developed by Accelerated Christian Education, Inc.,
one of the major suppliers of "Christian" curricula. (Falwell
has praised ACE's founder, Rev. Donald Howard, as "the driving
force in Christian education today.")[13]   In The Battle for
the Family, Rev. Tim LaHaye claims there are 5.5 million
children attending "Christian schools."

Whatever the actual number, ultra-fundamentalists look forward
to the day when "Christian schools" will have replaced all
public schools. As Falwell puts it:

> One day, I hope in the next ten years, I trust that we
> will have more Christian day schools than there are public
> schools. I hope I live to see the day when, as in the
> early days of the country, we won't have any public
> schools. The churches will have taken them over again and
> Christians will be running them. What a happy day that
> will be![14]

Televangelist Pat Robertson has similar hopes. He predicts
that "in the next twenty years you are going to see all schools
going private."[15]

Q. Does the radical right support racial integration in its schools?

A. Its educators insist they are not racists yet they frequently
   make racist remarks or take segregationist positions. William
   Billings, the director of the National Christian Action Coalition, has said, "America is so pluralistic, with so many
   cultural backgrounds that are not Judeo-Christian, that you
   reach the lowest common denominator in trying to reach all the
   ethnic groups."[16] Janet Egan, co-founder of Parents of
   Minnesota, speaks for many ultra-fundamentalists:

> Why this idea that we have to really inculcate in the
> children a healthy respect and appreciation for these
> different cultures? Why, if it's not to neutralize?
> And that's exactly what it's for. I don't have to be
> enhanced and appreciate the different peoples. I mean,
> let them live their lives, let me live mine. I don't
> force my kids on them, don't force their kids on mine.
> Not that I'm against them playing together but the whole
> point is for interracialness. I personally like my own
> race.[17]

The radical right has usually opposed attempts to desegregate
public schools through busing, and is seeking legislation to
prohibit the courts from even ruling on school desegregation
cases (see "The Courts" section). Ultra-fundamentalists also
want to reinstate tax exemptions for private schools that
practice racial discrimination.

Q. How do ultra-fundamentalists defend tax privileges for schools
   that practice racial discrimination? What is the history of
   this issue?

A. The issue surfaced in January 1982 when the Reagan administration announced that it would revoke a 12-year policy of denying
   tax exemptions to schools that discriminate on the basis of
   race. President Reagan's announcement provoked intense criticism from civil rights groups. Within a week, administration
   officials had suspended the previous decision, saying Congress,
   not the Internal Revenue Service, should decide what tax
   exemption policy should be. However, Congress shows no sign
   of wanting to overturn the IRS policy.[18]

   This episode enraged the radical right, which argued that the
   government has no right to judge sincere religious beliefs,
   even if those beliefs include racial discrimination. "Personally, I would not practice racism and I think my record proves
   that," said Jerry Falwell. "But I would die for the right of
   other religious groups to do so for theological reasons."[19]
   Without a trace of irony, Falwell said, "The government must be
   careful not to let a religious issue become a social issue."
   [20]

   The National Christian Action Coalition called the bill pending
   in Congress to overturn the IRS policy the "Church Regulation
   Bill,"[21] and Connaught Marshner, director of the Family
   Policy Division of the Free Congress Research and Education
   Foundation, termed the bill "an open invitation to tyranny."
   [22] In the name of religious liberty, ultra-fundamentalists
   want the government to lend financial support to racial discrimination.

   The whole issue of tax exemptions for private religious schools
   has been volatile in radical right circles since August 1978,
   when the IRS tried to issue stricter guidelines for tax exemptions. The proposed regulations prompted 150,000 letters of
   protest to the IRS, the most it has ever received on a single
   issue. The regulations were never issued. "That was the spark
   that set off the powder keg," says Gary Jarmin, legislative
   director of the Christian Voice. "That was the issue that
   caused the Christian Right to come into existence."[23]

Q. Why shouldn't parents be given tuition tax credits if they send
   their children to private schools?

A. Tuition tax credits or education vouchers would undermine the
   financial base of public education. In addition, they would
   help create a dual track education system in the United States
   of elite private schools and disadvantaged public schools.
   Schemes that subsidize private schooling at the expense of the
   public schools are an attack on equal educational opportunity,
   an American tradition and basic right.

   Parents should be free to enroll their children in schools
   with special religious, political, or economic orientations,
   of course, but it should be a privately financed option. The
   federal government has no obligation to help parents pay for
   a private or religious education for their children.

   Some parents argue that the competition between public and
   private schools engendered by tuition tax credits or vouchers
   would make both school systems better. But tuition tax credits
   would only weaken public schools by siphoning away pupils and
   funding (much state money for education is allocated on a
   per-pupil basis). Public schools would find it increasingly
   difficult to compete. Pupils whose parents could not afford
   private schooling would be trapped in a deteriorating and
   underfunded public school system.

   Tuition tax credits would also break down the barriers that
   separate church and state. By accepting tax privileges for
   religious schools, ultra-fundamentalists would open the door
   for all kinds of government intrusion into religious affairs.
   Special government favors create obligations that private
   schools may not want to meet. Indeed, church groups should
   oppose any measure that would allow government to intervene
   in its activities. Senator Ernest Hollings of South Carolina
   sums up the case against tuition tax credits:

       [Tuition tax credits] would turn our nation's educational
       policy on its head, benefit the few at the expense of the
       many, proliferate substandard segregationist academies,
       add a sea of red ink to the federal deficit, violate the
       clear meaning of the First Amendment of the Constitution,
       and destroy the genius and diversity of our system of
       public education. [24]

QUOTABLE QUOTES

"Secular Humanism" in the Schools

"The teaching of humanism in public schools not only defies
Christian values and the authority of parents, but borders on
treason and violates the U.S. Constitution by teaching a
religion."

> -- Mel and Norma Gabler,
> Handbook No. 1

"The humanists literally control most of our public schools
from kindergarten through the university. (Currently, they are
after our preschoolers -- that's why they have launched their
pre-school day-care center program.)"

> -- Rev. Tim LaHaye, "What
> Every Christian Should
> Know About Humanism"

"In the humanistic frame of reference, however, values are
relative and ethics are situational. Children are therefore
being taught at school that moral and social beliefs and
behavior are not necessarily based upon Judeo-Christian
principles being taught by most families at home, but should be
fashioned instead to suit the wishes and convenience of the
majority or society as a whole."

> -- Onalee McGraw of the Heritage
> Foundation, Secular Humanism
> in the Schools, p. 5

"When a student reads in a math book that there are no
absolutes, suddenly every value he's been taught is destroyed.
And the next thing you know the student turns to crime and
drugs."

> -- Mel Gabler, quoted in The
> American School Board Journal,
> June 1979

"Inasmuch as humanistic curriculum programs and 'values clarification' and 'moral education' teaching strategies are based upon materialistic values found only in man's nature itself, they reject the spiritual and moral tradition of theistic faith and religion. Thus, many parents who subscribe to Judeo-Christian belief may oppose humanistic education in the tax-supported schools on grounds that such programs promote and advocate the religion of secular humanism in violation of the First Amendment to the U.S. Constitution."

> -- Onalee McGraw of the Heritage
>   Foundation, The Family,
>   Feminism and the Therapeutic
>   State, p. 7

"How could such complex issues of Humanism possibly be indoc-trinated into your child in elementary or high school? NOT BY ACCIDENT. Under Lenin and Stalin, Pavlov developed the technique of conditioning dogs to bring about the desired results; and from this beginning, Humanist psychologists and behavioral scientists successfully developed techniques which can GRADUALLY CHANGE YOUR CHILD'S CONSCIENCE, PERSONALITY, VALUES, AND BEHAVIOR." (original emphasis)

> -- Lottie-Beth Hobbs,
>   Pro-Family Forum pamphlet,
>   "Is Humanism Molesting Your
>   Child?"

Public Education

"Never until this decade did teachers on the public payroll demand the professional and civil right to choke down every child's throat the most disgusting, demoralizing, frightening, treasonable, blasphemous, and soul-withering facts and fancies."

> -- The Mel Gablers,
>   Handbook No. 14:
>   Censorship

"As long as the schools continue to teach ABNORMAL ATTITUDES
and ALIEN THOUGHTS, we caution parents NOT to urge their
children to pursue high grades and class discussion, because
the harder students work, the greater their chance of brain-
washing."

-- Mel and Norma Gabler,
Handbook No. 1

"Modern public education is the most dangerous single force in
a child's life: religiously, sexually, economically, patriotically, and physically."

-- Rev. Tim LaHaye,
The Battle for the Family,
p. 89

"All are pressing problems that demand attention and solution.
But those problems -- each in its own way -- stem from a
central cancer, a root evil: compulsory education."

-- Rus Walton, One Nation Under
God

"Why this idea that we have to really inculcate in the children
a healthy respect and appreciation for these different
cultures? Why, if it's not to neutralize? And that's exactly
what it's for. I don't have to be enhanced and appreciate the
different peoples. I mean, let them live their lives, let me
live mine. I don't force my kids on them, don't force their
kids on mine. Not that I'm against them playing together but
the whole point is for the interracialness. I personally like
my own race."

-- Janet Egan, co-founder of
Parents of Minnesota, in
WCCO-TV (Minneapolis)
broadcast, "One Nation Under
God," January 5, 1981

"Call it what you will, 'citizen education,'...'world order education,' 'global perspectives,' 'peace studies' -- it's all political indoctrination intended to train youngsters to be 'global servants' and world citizens...." (original emphasis)

-- Barbara Morris,
Change Agents in the Schools:
Destroy Your Children,
Betray Your Country, p. 216

"One day, I hope in the next ten years, I trust that we will have more Christian day schools than there are public schools. I hope I live to see the day when, as in the early days of our country, we won't have any public schools. The churches will have taken them over again and Christians will be running them. What a happy day that will be!"

-- Rev. Jerry Falwell,
America Can Be Saved, p. 53

"The ultimate solution is that we have to work to get the state out of the business of educating kids at the primary and secondary levels, and get that education back in the hands of parents where it belongs."

-- Rev. Pat Robertson,
"700 Club" broadcast,
October 2, 1981

"The educators have taken religion out of our schools and now they are wondering why the people are dishonest, smoke drugs, don't pay attention and are juvenile delinquents."

-- Rev. Pat Robertson,
"700 Club" broadcast,
December 2, 1981

"America is so pluralistic, with so many cultural backgrounds that are not Judeo-Christian that you reach the lowest common denominator in trying to reach all the ethnic groups."

> -- William Billings, director of the National Christian Action Coalition, Life magazine, August 1981

"The best thing that could happen to education in America would be the demise of the public schools....Parents who really care about their children will take them out of the public schools as quickly as possible."

> -- Barbara Morris, Change Agents in the Schools

"Public schools? They don't exist. But there are government schools and that's what this book is all about: the incredible hoax and ultimate tragedy -- government schools that serve as change agents for the destruction of Christian Western civilization and to establish instead, a Humanist/Socialist 'new world order.'"

> -- Barbara Morris, Change Agents in the Schools

"If you mean to circulate a rumor, don't do it on your official stationary or in the name of your group....Make sure the targeted school board member feels your opposition. Seed the candidate's forum with hostile questions....The point is not so much to change the board as it is to make a target of John Doe, thus teaching future board members a cautionary lesson....Never give the appearance of being organized...."

> -- Connaught Marshner, Blackboard Tyranny

"What about the parents' rights? See, this is what is usually
avoided because the general consensus we find among the educational establishment is that the day that that child enters the
doors of the school, the parental rights cease and the state's
rights...begin. In other words, the school is representative
of the state, and now, see, that is exactly the same philosophy
Hitler had and this is what we're getting more and more in
educational establishments. The parents' rights don't count,
and after all, the school people were hired to teach for the
parents...."

> -- Mel Gabler appearing on
> William F. Buckley's Firing
> Line, January 11, 1982

Tuition Tax Credits

"One of the great strengths of private and parochial education
is found in the freedom from government intervention. It would
be sad to see that freedom swapped for a mess of tax credit
pottage."

> -- Rev. James M. Dunn, Executive
> Director, Baptist Joint
> Committee on Public Affairs

"Government does have a fundamental responsibility to public
education, but its responsibility to private schools is to
leave them alone."

> -- Senator Ernest Hollings
> of South Carolina, American
> School Board Journal,
> September 1981

[Tuition tax credits would] "reestablish a blatant class system
in which the wealthy and middle class buy their way out and pay
just enough taxes to keep squalid public schools in the slums."

> -- Stephen Bailey,
> Professor of Education,
> Harvard University

NOTES: EDUCATION

1. Mel and Norma Gabler, Handbook No. 1 (Longview, Texas:
    Educational Research Analysts, 1981).

2. Examples of Gablers' textbooks criticisms are cited in
    Edward Jenkinson, Crisis in the Classroom: The Mind
    Benders (Carbondale, Illinois: Southern Illinois
    University Press, 1979), p. 117.

3. Greg Bean, "Group Files Motion to Ban Book," Casper
    (Wyoming) Star-Tribune, August 11, 1981.

4. Mel and Norma Gabler, Handbook No. 1 (Longview, Texas:
    Educational Research Analysts, 1981).

5. Tim LaHaye, The Battle for the Family, (Old Tappan, N.J.:
    Fleming H. Revell Co., 1982) p. 89.

6. See, e.g., Onalee McGraw, Secular Humanism in the Schools:
    The Issue Whose Time Has Come (Washington, D.C.: The
    Heritage Foundation, 1976).

7. Polly Paddock, "Robots in Our Classrooms?" Charlotte
    (North Carolina) Observer, August 3, 1981.

8. Tim LaHaye, The Battle for the Family, p. 91.

9. Barbara M. Morris, Change Agents in the Schools:
    Destroy Your Children, Betray Your Country (Upland,
    California: The Barbara M. Morris Report, 1979), p. 216.

10. Jerry Falwell, Listen, America! (Garden City, N.Y.:
    Doubleday and Company, 1980), p. 219.

11. Ibid.

12. Ibid.

13. Michael Disend, "Have You Whipped Your Child Today,"
    Penthouse, February 1982.

14. Jerry Falwell, America Can Be Saved, (Murfreesboro,
    Tennessee: Sword of the Lord Publishers, 1979), p. 53.

15.   "700 Club" broadcast, April 14, 1982.

16.   "Young Turks of the Radical Right," Life, August 1981.

17.   Janet Egan appeared on the broadcast, "One Nation Under God," produced by WCCO-TV, Minneapolis, Minnesota, January 5, 1981.

18.   Robert Timberg, "Christian Right to Fight Reagan on Segregated Schools Tax Bill," The Baltimore Sun, January 27, 1981. See also Charles R. Babcock, "Religious Right Decries Shift on Tax Exemptions," The Washington Post, January 28, 1982.

19.   "Falwell Would Back Tax Exemptions," The News & Daily Advance (Lynchburg, Virginia), January 23, 1982.

20.   Ibid.

21.   William Billings, "Reagan Sends 'Church Regulation Bill' to Congress," Alert (newsletter of National Christian Action Coalition), February 1982.

22.   Robert Timburg, op. cit.

23.   Ibid.

24.   Bill Anderson, "Public Schools Are Under Fire, But We Have Just Begun to Fight," American School Board Journal, September 1981, pp. 19-23.

FURTHER READING: EDUCATION

American Federation of Teachers, "The $5 Billion Mistake:
        Tuition Tax Credits" (Available from AFT, 11 Dupont
        Circle, N.W., Washington, D.C. 20036).

Anderson, Bill, "Public Schools Are Under Fire, But We Have
        Just Begun to Fight," American School Board Journal,
        September 1981.

Augenblick, John, "Tuition Tax Credits: Federal Legislation"
        (Denver, Colorado: Education Commission of the
        States, Issuegram, April 1981).

Bryant, Gene, "Entanglement by the New Right," Tennessee
        Teacher, April 1980.

Lester, Julius, "Moral Education," Democracy, April 1982, pp.
        28-38.

Lines, Patricia M., Religious and Moral Values in Public
        Schools: A Constitutional Analysis, 1981 (Available
        for $2 from the Law and Education Center, Education
        Commission of the States, Suite 300, 1860 Lincoln
        Street, Denver, Colorado 80295. Report LEC-1).

National Education Association, Connecticut Education
        Association, The Council on Interracial Books for
        Children, Violence, The Ku Klux Klan and the Struggle
        for Equality, 1981.

National Education Association, The Right-to-Work Revival...Far
        Right and Dead Wrong, 1981.

Park, J. Charles, "Preachers, Politics and Public Education: A
        Review of Right-Wing Pressures Against Public
        Schooling in America," Phi Beta Kappan, May 1980.

Raywid, Maryann, The Ax-Grinders, Critics of Our Public Schools
        (New York: Macmillan and Co., 1962).

"Why Public Schools Fail," Newsweek, April 20, 1981.

RADICAL RIGHT LITERATURE

Carle, Erica, The Hate Factory (Milwaukee, Wisconsin: Erica
        Carle Foundation, 1974) Available from P.O. Box
        4357, Milwaukee, Wisconsin 53210).

LaHaye, Tim, The Battle for the Family (Old Tappan, N.J.:
        Fleming H. Revell Co., 1982).

        ------ , The Battle for the Mind, (Old Tappan, N.J.: Fleming
        H. Revell Co., 1980).

Marshner, Connaught, Blackboard Tyranny (Westport, Connecticut:
        Arlington House, 1979).

McGraw, Onalee, Family Choice in Education: The New Imperative
        (Washington, D.C.: The Heritage Foundation, 1978).

        ------ , Secular Humanism and the Schools: The Issue Whose
        Time Has Come (Washington, D.C.: The Heritage
        Foundation, 1976).

Morris, Barbara M., Change Agents in the Schools: Destroy Your
        Children, Betray Your Country (Upland, California:
        The Barbara M. Morris Report, 1979).

Norris, Murray, Weep for Your Children (Available from
        Christian Family Renewal and Valley Christian
        University, Box 73, Clovis, California 93613,
        209-291-4958).

Schlafly, Phyllis, "How and Why I Taught My Children To Read,"
        The Phyllis Schlafly Report, June 1981.

        ------ , "Parents' and Pupils' Rights in Education," The
        Phyllis Schlafly Report, October 1981.

West, E. G., Critical Issues: The Economics of Education Tax
        Credits (Washington, D.C.: The Heritage Foundation,
        1981).

SCHOOL TEXTBOOKS AND CURRICULA

Q. School textbooks and curricula are polluted with "secular humanist" values that are corrupting American youth.

A. This has become a standard criticism made by the radical right as a justification for censorship of "objectionable" materials. They object to all materials that question their rigid understanding of American history, conflict with their strict interpretation of the Bible, or provide discussions of ideas not held by them. Curricular areas where "humanism" is most frequently taught, say moral monopolists, are the social sciences, history, art, communications, and health.[1]

The national attack on schoolbooks is not a simple case of parents trying to screen out nasty words or match reading materials with a child's maturity. Seemingly isolated local incidents of censorship are part of a nationally coordinated campaign to advance certain political values and exclude others. A small corps of vocal parents, armed with lists of "humanist" books drawn up by national book "reviewers," is challenging the very goal of education -- to foster independent, creative, critical minds.

Most of the attacks on textbook content are exaggerated if not entirely groundless. For example, Rev. Jerry Falwell during his "Clean Up America" campaign in 1981 declared that most public school textbooks are nothing more than "Soviet propaganda."[2] Barbara Morris, author of Change Agents in the Schools: Destroy Your Children, Betray Your Country, claims the U.S. Department of Education in the Carter years was "promoting Communist Chinese education as a model for U.S. education."[3] Other religious authoritarians want to ban dictionaries with "obscene" definitions (such as a definition of "bed" as a verb).[4]

Q. Who are the chief censorship groups in the country?

A. Most censorship activity occurs at the local level, but there
   are several national organizations that help coordinate the
   crusade against "dangerous" books. They include:

   o Educational Research Analysts is recognized by textbook
     publishers and state textbook review panels as a very
     powerful lobbying force. The group is directed by Mel and
     Norma Gabler from their home in Longview, Texas.

   o Stop Textbook Censorship Committee, based in South St.
     Paul, Minnesota, is part of Phyllis Schlafly's Eagle
     Forum. (The group says it opposes "censorship" currently
     practiced by "secular humanists.") Schlafly has said she
     intends to concentrate on school textbooks after defeating
     the Equal Rights Amendment.

   o Moral Majority, Inc., headed by Rev. Jerry Falwell, works
     through its state chapters and membership to wage censor-
     ship campaigns.

Q. How influential are the censorship groups and their local
   activists?

A. Very influential. They have succeeded in intimidating school
   boards, state textbook review commissions, publishers, booksellers, librarians and teachers to censor books and teaching
   materials. Dorothy Massie of the National Education Association reports, "Probably at no time have the pressures been more
   severe than they are just now."[5] According to a comprehensive
   national survey, one-quarter of the school administrators and
   librarians surveyed reported challenges during the 1978-80
   school years, and half of these challenges resulted in some
   form of censorship.[6] During the 1978-79 school year, there
   were more cases of attempted censorship of school materials
   reported to the American Library Association's Office of
   Intellectual Freedom than at any time during the previous 25-
   year period. Since November 1980, according to the ALA,
   reported censorship cases have skyrocketed 300 percent -- some
   900 challenges to books, textbooks, and instructional materials
   between November 1980 and April 1982.[7]

Q. Why are Mel and Normal Gabler so successful in banning books
   they dislike?

A. The Gablers' Educational Research Analysts has assembled a
   national network of activists that thrives on the lack of an
   organized opposition. As the self-styled "nation's largest
   textbook review clearing house," Educational Research Analysts
   sends 'reviews' and censorship instructions to some 16,000
   activists on its growing national mailing list.[8]   In 1981,
   the Gablers succeeded in having banned from Texas schools seven
   social studies texts that it had targeted during the Texas
   textbook commission hearings.[9] ·

   The Gablers' immense influence over textbook approval in Texas
   is felt nationwide. A textbook that doesn't sell in Texas is
   almost guaranteed to be an economic flop nationwide, since that
   state accounts for more than 8 percent of the nation's textbook
   purchases. It is economically unfeasible for publishers to
   issue more than one textbook edition, so many publishers
   willingly pre-censor their own texts to gain the approval of
   Texas textbook officials and the Gablers. "As Texas goes, so
   goes the nation," says censorship expert Edward Jenkinson.[10]

   The Association of American Publishers' school division
   acknowledged that some publishers have purged Shirley Jackson's
   classic short story, "The Lottery," from all literature anthol-
   ogies after the Texas State Textbook Committee ordered it
   deleted.[11]   Doubleday publishers have removed the word
   "evolution" from its only high school biology text, Experiences
   in Biology, because they wanted "to avoid the publicity that
   would be involved in a controversy over a textbook." (See
   "Creationism" section.)   "We'd like to sell thousands of
   copies," explained Doubleday executive Eugene Frank.[12]

   The Gablers magnify their influence by concentrating on the 22
   states where textbooks are approved on a statewide basis (the
   "adoption" states). In 1981, textbook adoptions in half of the
   22 adoption states were influenced by the Gablers, according to
   a comprehensive national study.[13]   The Gablers' successes
   inspire other moral authoritarians and intimidate school
   boards, publishers, and teachers. A concerted opposition is
   just beginning to emerge.

Q. What laws have been proposed to alter textbook content?

A. A national coalition of radical right legislators, the American
Legislative Exchange Council (ALEC), has succeeded in introduc-
ing its model bill in four states.[14]   The "Textbook Content
Standards Act" was passed as a resolution in the Oklahoma
legislature in 1981 and is now pending in several other states.
(It was defeated in Alabama in 1982.)   The bills, each contain-
ing virtually identical language, would force all public
schools in the state to use only books that preach "absolute
values of right and wrong," tout "the free market economy and
the effectiveness of the system," and reflect "the traditional
roles of men and women, boys and girls."

Nationally, book banners have placed a provision in the Family
Protection Act to cut off federal funds for any educational
materials that

> ...do not reflect a balance between the status role of men
> and women, do not reflect different ways in which women
> and men live and do not contribute to the American way of
> life as it has been historically understood.[15]

The radical right's fierce concern for states' rights melts
away when it comes to enforcing its own social concerns.   (For
more on the Family Protection Act, see "The 'Pro-Family'
Movement" section.)

Q. What constitutes censorship?   What constitutes educational
selection?

A. When a group successfully bans a book for political or religious reasons, despite its educational value, it constitutes
censorship.   Censorship occurs when school or library officials
(usually at the behest of a vocal parent or group) bans access
to an educationally worthy book or vetoes its use in the
classroom.   This usually occurs without due process, public
hearings, or community participation.

Educators obviously have to make selections of what they will
teach in class or buy for the school library.   Not all these
selections will meet every child's or every parent's approval,
and individuals with sincere objections to assigned classroom
materials might be reasonably accommodated.   But it is contrary
to the goals of education to select only those books that meet

narrow political or religious criteria. The mere use of "objectionable" books does not constitute an endorsement of everything in them.

Self-censorship by teachers and librarians is at least as dangerous as overt censorship because it occurs automatically. Fear and intimidation have a chilling effect on the very purpose of education: to teach pupils to ask questions and think critically.

The radical right likes to argue that feminists, blacks, and Jews have censored textbook materials by objecting to certain portrayals of their minority group. But such opposition to sexist, racist, or religious stereotypes is surely different from what moral monopolists have in mind. They want to impose their restrictive, rigid stereotypes on everyone else, while minority groups are usually seeking to break down derogatory stereotypes and expand materials available.

Q. What's wrong with parents trying to clean up textbooks they find objectionable?

A. All parents should take an active interest in their children's education. But no parent or small group of parents acting as vigilantes should have the authority to remove a book from a classroom or library. Official policies for parental involvement in textbook selection procedures, as well as procedures for the reconsideration of challenged materials, should be established and followed. Schools should have a written list of criteria that is used in the selection of textbooks, library books, and other curricular materials. If an individual book meets the selection criteria, it should be presumed to have educational value. The selection criteria may be targets for criticism, but individual books that meet the guidelines should not be. Parents and school boards may not seek to impose one orthodoxy in political and religious matters on the entire community.

Q. What kinds of curricular materials do ultra-fundamentalists consider "dangerous"?

A. Any material that does not reflect the ultra-fundamentalist view of the world is "questionable." This includes textbooks that acknowledge more than one interpretation of history, current events, or Christian ethics. Book banners typically oppose textbooks that discuss women's suffrage and the women's movement, slavery in America, trade unions, ecology, world hunger, American Indian experiences and the Watergate history.

Phyllis Schlafly's Eagle Forum in St. David, Arizona, successfully banned all required reading lists in the school system, which included classics by Conrad, Hawthorne, Hemingway, Homer, Poe, Steinbeck, and Twain.[16]   In North Carolina, the state chapter of Moral Majority, Inc., condemned a social studies text because it asked, "Do we really need fifty state governments plus one national government?" The objection: "The importance of federalism should be clearly taught, not questioned."[17]   Another text was criticized because students are not "emotionally or intellectually capable" of discussing food shortages, overpopulation and ecology.

The Gablers' textbook reviews illustrate how so many criticisms are based on political factors, a literal-minded reading of the text, or arbitrary fears.[18]

Textbook passages	Objection
"The title [Luther] has allusive force, recalling Martin Luther and Martin Luther King, Jr., both reformers."	"These two men should not be put in the same category. Martin Luther was a religious, non-violent man."
The People Make a Nation, pages 34-43, dealing with slavery and indentured servants.	"Why 10 pages and two pictures here, plus nearly an entire chapter later, to emphasize the horrors of slavery which has [sic] long since been eliminated. This can only serve to arouse racial tensions."
"What are some other experiences that cause fear in people? Choose one of these experiences and tell how you think you would deal with it."	"Invasion of privacy."

Textbook passages	Objection
Story entitled, "What are the doldrums?"	"This story is silly and a waste of time except for pure amusement."
Reference to UNICEF, United Nations International Children's Emergency Fund.	"UNICEF is a known Communist front."

It is from examples like these that the radical right condemns public school textbooks and sometimes succeeds in banning them. The criticisms reveal a fairly crude notion of what education should be. "Reformers" like the Gablers assume that rote/ indoctrination is the best way to teach a child. "Allowing a student to come to his own conclusions about abstract concepts creates frustration...a concept will never do anyone as much good as fact."[19] Most parents, of course, believe that proper guidance and quality education enable their children to make independent judgments. Such training is crucial to young people if they are to be prepared to participate in our demo- cratic system.

Q. Have there been actual book burnings?

A. Yes. There have been numerous public burnings of books, records, posters, and other artifacts that ultra-fundamentalist congregations consider satanic and occult. The burning rituals are intended to "drive out the demons" that allegedly inhabit the books and other materials. Some of the recent burnings include:

Wilkes-Barre, Pennsylvania, 1982. About 150 members of the First Assembly of God smashed records by Frank Sinatra and Barry Manilow and books by James Michener and Harold Robbins. Rev. Ken Kashner told his parishioners that Deuteronomy 7:25 justified the burning: "The graven images of gods shall yet burn with fire."[20]

Texas City, Texas, 1982. The scheduled bonfire was rained out but members of the First Assembly of God went to their church altar to rip and tear up books like The Omen and Snow White, and smash records like "Urban Cowboy" and destroy "Star Wars" figurines. Penny Baker, a country- western singer and self-proclaimed devil chaser, organized the rally, and has planned others.[21]

Virginia, Minnesota, 1981. A crowd of 250 people burned
an estimated $3,000 worth of books, magazines, and record
albums in what was called a "destruction celebration."
Among the items destroyed: a ceramic Buddha, children's
Halloween stories, and Beatles albums. The crowd sang "In
the Name of Jesus."[22]

Gastonia, North Carolina, 1981. Students of the Parkdale
Baptist Church's school threw records, posters, and
several copies of "The Living Bible" into a bonfire to
shouts of "Amen." Rev. Don Sessions explained that "The
Living Bible," a paraphrased translation, is one of many
that Satan used "to trick people in the last days. There
are a lot of books out there called Bibles, But we hold
the [King James] Bible in the highest esteem. We get
upset about all these translations that come out."[23]

Rev. Tim LaHaye, national board member of Moral Majority, Inc.,
endorsed the book- and record-burning campaign of the Peters
Brothers on his TV program, "LaHayes on Family Life."
Thousands of people around the country have participated in
bonfires (billed as "Public Destruction Services") organized by
the Peters Brothers. Records, tapes, comic books and novels
are torched to "renounce Satan" and "make a public commitment
to Jesus Christ."[24]

Q. What can be done to help prevent textbook censorship?

A. The best protection against censorship is vigilance by parents
and students. The principle of local control of schools should
not be confused with "vocal control," in which the loudest
minority imposes its orthodoxy on a community. In June 1982,
the Supreme Court reaffirmed First Amendment rights in this
area when it ruled, 5-to-4, that local school boards do not
have an absolute right to ban books from their libraries.

The case, Board of Education, Island Trees Union Free School
District No. 26 et al. v. Pico et al., arose when several
school board members removed from high school and junior high
school libraries nine books that they considered "anti-
American, anti-Christian, anti-Semitic and just plain filthy."
[25] The books had been on a list of "objectionable" books
that school board members had obtained at a radical right
conference.[26] The Court cleared the way for a federal trial
of the school board's book banning (thereby agreeing that

Rev. Jerry Falwell on Textbooks

"Textbooks have become absolutely obscene and vulgar. Many of them are openly attacking the integrity of the Bible. Humanism is the main thrust of the public school textbook. For our nation this is a life-and-death struggle, and the battle lines for this struggle are the textbooks."

-- Dayton (Ohio) Journal Herald,
October 5, 1981

"Our textbooks deceive our young people about pre-marital sex, about the role of the father and the mother in the home, and even about history. We should be angry with our textbooks because they push socialism and one-world government. What makes me mad is that it is our own tax money that is underwriting the destruction of the morals of our nation, our church, and the world in which our children will live."

-- Families magazine,
February 1982

"In school textbooks, pornography, obscenity, vulgarity and profanity are destroying our children's moral values in the guise of 'value clarification' and sex education. Our children are being trained to deny their 200-year-old heritage. Books that don't accurately present the American heritage must be eliminated. Rise up in arms and throw out every textbook.... [Public school textbooks are nothing more than] Soviet propaganda."

-- "Clean Up America" rally
at the U.S. Capitol,
quoted in Buffalo Evening
News, July 12, 1981

"Believing the Bible as I do, I would find it impossible to stop preaching the pure gospel of Jesus Christ and begin doing anything else -- including fighting communism or participating in civil rights reforms....I believe that if we spent enough effort trying to clean up our churches, rather than trying to clean up state and national governments, we would do well."

-- "Ministers and Marchers,"
sermon delivered in 1965

"I would think moral-minded people would object to books that are philosophically alien to what they believe. If they have books and feel like burning them, fine."

> -- Rev. George A. Zarris,
> chairman of Illinois chapter
> of Moral Majority, Inc.,
> New York Times,
> December 11, 1980

"To put a book on a shelf, or even feature it in the curriculum, is by no means to endorse it. Indeed, encouraging students to read Mein Kampf would help them understand how profoundly evil Hitler was. Similarly, skillful teachers could use the sexually explicit passages in so much modern fiction to demonstrate the heartlessness and moral bankruptcy of the authors' vision."

> -- Wall Street Journal editorial,
> January 18, 1982

"I wrote 'Tom Sawyer' and 'Huck Finn' for adults exclusively, and it always distresses me when I find that boys and girls have been allowed access to them. The mind that becomes soiled in youth can never again be washed clean. I know this by my own experience, and to this day I cherish an unappeasable bitterness against the unfaithful guardians of my young life, who not only permitted but compelled me to read an unexpurgated Bible through before I was 15 years old. None can do that and ever draw a sweet breath again...."

> -- Mark Twain in 1905, upon
> learning that his books were
> excluded from the children's
> room of the Brooklyn Public
> Library as "bad examples."
> Quoted in letter to the
> editor, The New York Times,
> June 14, 1981

"We are not afraid to entrust the American people with unpleasant facts, foreign ideas, alien philosophies, and competitive values. For a nation that is afraid to let its people judge the truth and falsehood in an open market is a nation that is afraid of its people."

> -- President John F. Kennedy
> at the 20th anniversary
> of the Voice of America,
> February 26, 1962,
> Washington, D.C.

"If they [book censors] succeed, Americans might as well get ready to gather 'round the bonfires. They'll start by incinerating the works most often found on the hit lists by the far right -- books by Ernest Hemingway, John Steinbeck, J.D. Salinger, and so on. What will really be going up in smoke, however, is the U.S. Constitution and its guarantees of freedom of thought, expression and belief."

> -- Miami Herald editorial,
> August 11, 1981

"If we're going to go back to the old moral values that made this country great, we're going to have to do it with search-and-destroy methods. First, we must burn the books -- and if that isn't enough, then we must burn the people."

> -- Art Buchwald, May 28, 1981

NOTES: SCHOOL TEXTBOOKS AND CURRICULA

1. "Guide to Humanistic Terminology," The School Bell
    (Dallas, Texas), January/February 1978.

2. Linda Roeder, "Reverberations of Moral Majority Felt in
    Area," Buffalo (N.Y.) Evening News, July 12, 1981.

3. Barbara M. Morris, Change Agents in the Schools: Destroy
    Your Children, Betray Your Country (Upland, California:
    The Barbara M. Morris Report, 1979), pp. 217-18.

4. Virginia Ellis, "Texas Bans Dictionary Textbook As
    Obscene," Dallas (Texas) Times-Herald, November 13, 1981.

5. Dorothy Massie, "Censorship in Schools: Something Old and
    Something New," Today's Educator, November/December 1980.

6. Limiting What Students Shall Read. Books and Other
    Learning Materials in Our Public Schools: How They Are
    Selected and How They Are Removed, Association of American
    Publishers, American Library Association and Association
    for Supervision and Curriculum Development, July 31, 1981.

7. UPI dispatch, "Calls for Banning of Library Books Rise
    Sharply Since Reagan Victory," in The New York Times,
    December 11, 1980.

8. Printed sheet, "The Mel Gablers' Educational Research
    Analysts," November 1977, included in a packet of
    materials that Gablers sent to a concerned parent.
    Quoted in "How the Gablers Have Put Textbooks on Trial,"
    by Edward B. Jenkinson in Dealing With Censorship, edited
    by James E. Davis (Urbana, Illinois; National Council of
    Teachers of English, 1979). See also Cheryl Ernst, "Moral
    Majority Found 'Frightening,'" Spokane (Washington)
    Spokesman-Review, August 21, 1981, and Gene I. Maeroff,
    "Texas Textbook Choices Prompt Wide Concern," The New York
    Times, August 15, 1982.

9. "The Newsletter of the Mel Gablers' Educational Research
    Analysts," November 1981.

10. Hilary DeVries, "Book Banning: Saving Morals By Giving Up Key Freedoms?" Christian Science Monitor, December 15, 1981.

11. American Library Association, "Newsletter on Intellectual Freedom," March 1979, p. 36.

12. "All Things Considered," National Public Radio broadcast, December 12, 1981.

13. Limiting What Students Shall Read, op. cit.

14. Nancy Mathis, "Educators Blast Bills on Textbooks," Tulsa (Oklahoma) World, March 26, 1982.

15. S. 1378, "The Family Protection Act," introduced by Senator Roger Jepson in the 97th Congress, 2nd Session. The section cited, "Courses of Instruction and Education Materials," is Section 440C.

16. Charles Bouden, "St. David Tries to Close Book on Censorship Flap," Tucson Citizen, November 27, 1981; Charles Bouden, "St. David's Reading List Is Optional," Tucson Citizen, February 13, 1982; Jane Ericson, "Book Review Forms Released," San Pedro Valley News-Sun, February 4, 1982.

17. Moral Majority, Inc., of North Carolina, Textbook Reviews, 1981, in response to Scholastic Book Service, Scholastic American Citizenship, Grades 10-12.

18. Examples of Gablers' textbook criticisms are cited in Edward Jenkinson, Censors in the Classroom: The Mind Benders (Carbondale, Illinois: Southern Illinois University Press, 1979), p. 117. They are contained in a letter from the Gablers to Dr. M.L. Brockette, Texas Education Agency, Capitol Station, Austin, Texas, dated August 9, 1974. A mimeographed copy of the letter was included in a packet that the Gablers mailed to a concerned parent when he requested reviews of the Ginn 360 Reading series. Other examples are cited in Edward Jenkinson, "How the Mel Gablers Have Put Textbooks on Trial," in James E. Davis, editor, Dealing with Censorship (Urbana, Illinois: National Council of Teachers of English, 1979).

19. Bill Anderson, "The Battle for Public Education," American School Board Journal, September 1981.

20. Dave Drury, "Books, Television, Records Perish in the Name of God," The Wilkes-Barre (Pa.) Times-Leader-News Record, April 26, 1982.

21. Associated Press dispatch, "'Snow White,' Music Ruined to Oust Devil," Austin (Texas) American-Statesman, May 8, 1982. See also Chuck Stevick, "Books, Toys, Records Destroyed by Church," Texas City Sun, May 7, 1982.

22. Associated Press dispatch, "Religious Group Burns Albums to Drive Out 'the Demons,'" The Washington Star, October 26, 1981.

23. Dave Baity, "Church School Burns New Bibles, Rock Music Records," The Charlotte Observer, May 9, 1981.

24. "LaHayes on Family Life" broadcast, May 23, 1982.

25. 50 U.S. Law Week 4831, Board of Education, Island Trees Union Free School District No. 26 et al. v. Pico et al., June 24, 1982.

26. Fred Barbash and Charles R. Babcock, "Court Allows Trial in Book Banning," The Washington Post, June 26, 1982.

FURTHER READING: SCHOOL TEXTBOOKS AND CURRICULA

Davis, James E., ed., Dealing With Censorship (Urbana, Illinois:
     National Council of Teachers of English, 1979).

FitzGerald, Frances, America Revised: History Schoolbooks in
     the Twentieth Century (New York: Vintage Books,
     1980).

Indiana State Teachers Association, Censorship: Professional
     Improvement Packet (150 West Market Street, Indiana-
     polis, Indiana 46204).

Jenkinson, Edward B., Censors in the Classroom: The Mind
     Benders (Carbondale, Illinois: Southern Illinois
     University Press, 1979).

PEOPLE FOR THE AMERICAN WAY, "Mind Control in the Schools,"
     special report, October 1981.

------   , Podesta, Anthony T., "Textbook Censors on the
     March," The Washington Post, April 3, 1982.

Marty, Martin E., "Politics and God's Prophets," The New York
     Times, April 29, 1982.

Norwick, Kenneth P., Lobbying for Freedom: A Citizen's Guide to
     Fighting Censorship at the State Level (New York: St.
     Martin's Press, 1975).

O'Neil, Robert O., Classrooms in the Crossfire (Bloomington,
     Indiana: Indiana University Press, 1981).

RADICAL RIGHT LITERATURE

Gabler, Mel and Norma Gabler, A Parent's Guide to Textbook
     Review and Reform, Special supplement to Education
     Update, newsletter of The Heritage Foundation,
     Washington, D.C., Winter 1978.

Hefley, James C., Textbooks on Trial (Wheaton, Illinois: Victor
     Books, 1977), distributed by the Mel Gablers, Long-
     view, Texas.

LaHaye, Tim, The Battle for the Mind (Old Tappan, N.J.: Fleming
        H. Revell Co., 1980).

Marshner, Connaught Coyne, Blackboard Tyranny (New Rochelle,
        N.Y.: Arlington House Publishers, 1978).

Morris, Barbara M., Change Agents in the Schools: Destroy Your
        Children, Betray Your Country (Upland, California:
        The Barbara M. Morris Report, 1979).

Norris, Murray, Weep for Your Children (Available from Chris-
        tian Family Renewal and Valley Christian University,
        Box 73, Clovis, California 93613, 209-291-4958).

National Organizations Concerned with Intellectual Freedom

American Association of School Administrators
1801 North Moore St.
Rosslyn, VA 22209   703-528-0700

American Association of University Women
2401 Virginia Avenue, N.W.
Washington, DC   20037   202-785-7760

American Civil Liberties Union
22 East 40th St.
New York, NY 10016   212-925-1222

American Federation of Teachers
11 Dupont Circle N.W.
Washington, DC 20036   202-797-4400

American Library Association
Office for Intellectual Freedom
50 East Huron St.
Chicago, IL 60611   312-944-6780

American Society of Journalists and Authors
1501 Broadway, Suite 1907
New York, NY   10036   212-997-0947

Association for Supervision & Curriculum Development
225 N. Washington St.
Alexandria, VA 22314   703-549-4110

Constitutional Rights Foundation
1501 Cotner Avenue
West Los Angeles, CA 90025   213-473-5091

National Association of State Boards of Education
444 N. Capitol St., N.W.
Washington, DC 20001   202-624-5845

National Coalition Against Censorship
132 West 43rd St.
New York, NY 10036   212-944-9899

National Coalition for Democracy in Education
108 Spring St.
Saratoga Springs, NY 12860   518-584-3427

National Council for the Social Studies
3615 Wisconsin Avenue, N.W.
Washington, DC 20016   202-966-7840

National Council of Jewish Women
15 East 26th St.
New York, NY 10010   212-532-1740

National Council of Teachers of English
1111 Kenyon Road
Urbana, IL 61801   217-328-3870

National Education Association
1201 16th St. N.W.
Washington, DC 20036   202-833-4000

National School Boards Association
1055 Thomas Jefferson St. N.W.
Washington, DC 20007   202-337-7666

PEOPLE FOR THE AMERICAN WAY
1015 18th St., N.W., Suite 300
Washington, DC 20036   202-822-9450

LIBRARY POLICIES

Q. How widespread are censorship attacks against libraries?

A. Complaints about library holdings are increasing rapidly. The
   American Library Association's Office for Intellectual Freedom
   in Chicago received about 100 complaints a year during the
   early 1970s. In 1981, the ALA identified nearly 1,000 cases of
   attempted or actual library censorship. Most of these incidents are not reported by news media.[1] Based on the ALA
   survey of library censorship, Robert Doyle of the Office of
   Intellectual Freedom notes, "Only 15 percent of the attacks
   against libraries are reported by the media. This means the
   public is unaware of 85 percent of the censorship efforts
   around the country."[2] Censorship consists of any attempt to
   restrict access to library materials, or alter, remove, or
   destroy them.

Q. Why is censorship in libraries so dangerous?

A. Because it is repugnant to the principles of a free and open
   democracy. Our democracy is based on the principle of free
   access to diverse ideas and the ability of citizens to come to
   their own independent judgments. In addition, censorship is
   contrary to the very goal of education -- to foster inquisitive, critical, creative minds. The radical right has a
   radically different notion of what education should be; they
   consider it a process of political and religious indoctrination. In their avowed "battle for the mind," ultra-fundamentalists consider censorship just another tool for instilling
   their rigid orthodoxy.

Q. What are the most common objections to certain library books?

A. Sex, sin, and violence are typical objections but they are by
   no means the only ones. Unfamiliar political or social attitudes are also attacked. As one commentator notes, "The

censors also condemn...unflattering portraits of American authority, criticisms of business and corporate practices, and radical political ideas."[3] Ultra-fundamentalists often say they simply want to protect their children from offensive ideas. But in their determination to eliminate books from library shelves, they also impose their narrow orthodoxy on everyone's children. Public education and public libraries have a broad, non-sectarian agenda, and should not be forced to reflect any single minority (or majority) viewpoint.

Q. What are some of the books that have been attacked in libraries across the country?

A. The materials range from classics to pulp paperbacks to popular magazines. Literary classics that have been challenged include Hemingway's A Farewell to Arms, Steinbeck's The Grapes of Wrath, Orwell's 1984, Huxley's Brave New World, Margaret Mitchell's Gone With the Wind, and Robin Hood. Popular best-sellers that have incurred the wrath of moral majoritarian censors include Judith Guest's Ordinary People, Sidney Sheldon's Rage of Angels, and books by Harold Robbins, Jacqueline Susanne, and Shere Hite. Even dictionaries, such as the American Heritage Dictionary, have been banned by school districts because they objected to certain definitions.[4]

Our Bodies, Ourselves, the acclaimed health manual for women, became the target of Moral Majority, Inc., in January 1981 when Jerry Falwell launched a major campaign to remove it from school libraries. In a fundraising letter, Falwell urged his followers:

> Examine your public schools' libraries for immoral, antifamily, and anti-American content....[I]t is so important that we remove offensive materials from classrooms immediately....Moral Majority is already working with several organizations to remove these harmful sex education materials from classrooms....[5]

The letter asks readers to check a box marked, "Yes! I will inquire in our local public libraries and let you know if Our Bodies, Ourselves and/or Life and Health is available to our young people." Despite this campaign, Falwell told a Religious Newswriters Association in June 1982 that Moral Majority was not involved in book banning or burning, and would disassociate himself from censorship activities.

Often moral authoritarians object to the political views of library books. The school board in Baileyville, Maine, voted to remove from the library a book of interviews with wounded soldiers entitled 365 Days. In one Wisconsin community, nine parents checked out 33 books from two school libraries and refused to return them. Included in the seizure was The Diary of Anne Frank, apparently because of brief passages that discuss the girl's tensions with her father. Groups like the Liberty Lobby object to the book because it "perpetuates the hoax" that the Holocaust actually occurred.

Finally, many cases of attempted censorship occur when moral authoritarians perceive great dangers in innocuous materials. Story books like Mr. & Mrs. Pig's Evening Out and The Twelve Days of Christmas have been singled out for removal. One such removal, of a book called Making It With Mademoiselle, backfired when it was discovered that the book was a how-to dressmaking book for teenagers published by Mademoiselle magazine.

Q. Why should my tax money be used to buy un-American or immoral books for publicly funded libraries?

A. Who is to judge what is un-American or immoral? Our national political life is founded on the idea of "the free marketplace of ideas"; all libraries should be committed to providing the richest diversity of ideas.[6] Would-be censors must realize that providing access to ideas is not the same as advocacy of those ideas. As the Wall Street Journal put it:

> To put a book on a shelf, or even feature it in the curriculum, is by no means to endorse it. Indeed, encouraging students to read Mein Kampf would help them understand how profoundly evil Hitler was. Similarly, skillful teachers could use the sexually explicit passages in so much modern fiction to demonstrate the heartlessness and moral bankruptcy of the authors' vision.[7]

Robert Doyle of the ALA notes that if a library "only has books that you deem good or worthy, it isn't doing its job."[8] Neither learning nor democracy is well-served by a monochromatic selection of books in libraries.

Q. Many censorship attempts are defeated, so what is there to worry about?

A. Censorship attempts, even if unsuccessful, can have a chilling effect on librarians, booksellers, publishers, and readers. "The real danger," warns one editorialist, "lies not so much in the public confrontation that results in the removal of a book from a library's shelves, however harmful that may be; it lies in the quiet removal of the same book by the librarian down the road who's sure they're coming to get her next."[9] Self-censorship by librarians is equally harmful to a community as outright book banning. When a bookseller in Abingdon, Virginia, was sued for selling "obscene" materials, his distributor discontinued sales of the magazines and books for the entire county -- even though the trial ended in a hung jury.[10]

Q. What about the confidentiality of library records?

A. In many communities, moral monopolists are trying to obtain library circulation records to see who has been reading what. The Washington State chapter of Moral Majority, Inc., sued the state library board to obtain a list of who had borrowed sex education materials.[11] An ultra-fundamentalist radio minister in Abingdon, Virginia, demanded to know the names of library patrons who had checked out certain materials.[12] In response to these attacks, many libraries are establishing formal policies that ensure the confidentiality of library circulation records. Freedom of thought is in great jeopardy if anyone, be it the government or inquisitive outsiders, is allowed to monitor the reading habits of citizens.

Q. What can be done to fight the influence of would-be censors?

A. The prescription is similar to the one against textbook censors. Concerned citizens must alert news media about censorship efforts, organize other people to publicly support academic freedom, and encourage library officials and school boards to adopt formal policy guidelines to handle complaints. Many national organizations stand ready to provide technical assistance. The American Library Association has written a "Bill of Rights" for library patrons (see appendices) and the National Education Association has numerous resources to help citizens fight library censors. PEOPLE FOR THE AMERICAN WAY can also help citizens organize their community, deal with news media, and argue the case against library censorship.

QUOTABLE QUOTES

"I would think moral-minded people might object to books that are philosophically alien to what they believe. If they have the books and feel like burning them, fine."

> -- Rev. George A. Zarris,
> chairman of Illinois chapter
> of Moral Majority, Inc.,
> The New York Times,
> December 11, 1980

"I am really mortified to be told that, in the United States of America, a fact like this [prosecution of the sale of a book on the creation of the world] can become a subject of inquiry, and of criminal inquiry too, as an offence against religion; that a question about the sale of a book can be carried before the civil magistrate. Is this then our freedom of religion? and are we to have a censor whose imprimatur shall say what books may be sold, and what we may buy? And who is thus to dogmatize religious opinions for our citizens? Whose foot is to be the measure to which ours are all to be cut or stretched?"

> -- Thomas Jefferson, letter to
> Monsieur N. G. Dufief,
> April 19, 1814

"Censorship is stupid and repugnant for two empirical reasons: censors are men no better than ourselves, their judgments no less fallible or open to dishonesty. Secondly, the thing won't work; those who really want to get hold of a book will do so somehow."

> -- George Steiner,
> Language and Silence

"As good almost kill a man as kill a good book: Who kills a man kills a reasonable creation, God's image; but he who destroys a good book kills reason itself."

> -- John Milton, Areopagitica, 1644

I wrote 'Tom Sawyer' and 'Huck Finn' for adults exclusively,
and it always distresses me when I find that boys and girls
have been allowed access to them. The mind that becomes soiled
in youth can never again be washed clean. I know this by my
own experience, and to this day I cherish an unappeasable
bitterness against the unfaithful guardians of my young life,
who not only permitted but compelled me to read an unexpurgated
Bible through before I was 15 years old. None can do that and
ever draw a sweet breath again...."

> -- Mark Twain in 1905, upon
> learning that his books were
> banned from the children's
> room of the Brooklyn Public
> Library as "bad examples."
> Quoted in letter to the editor,
> The New York Times,
> June 14, 1981

"To put a book on a shelf, or even feature it in the curriculum, is by no means to endorse it. Indeed, encouraging
students to read Mein Kampf would help them understand how
profoundly evil Hitler was. Similarly, skillful teachers could
use the sexually explicit passages in so much modern fiction to
demonstrate the heartlessness and moral bankruptcy of the
authors' vision."

> -- Wall Street Journal,
> editorial, January 18, 1982

"We are not afraid to entrust the American people with
unpleasant foreign ideas, alien philosophies, and competitive
values. For a nation that is afraid to let its people judge
the truth and falsehood in an open market is a nation that is
afraid of its people."

> -- President John F. Kennedy at
> the 20th anniversary of the
> Voice of America, February 26,
> 1962 in Washington, D.C.

NOTES: LIBRARY POLICIES

1. Colin Campbell, "Book Banning in America," The New York
    Times Book Review, December 20, 1981.

2. Ruth Seen Pearson, "Controversy on the Shelves," Elgin
    (Illinois) Courier-News, November 20, 1981.

3. Colin Campbell, op. cit.

4. Limiting What Students Shall Read: Books and Other
    Learning Materials in Our Public Schools, How They Are
    Selected and How They Are Removed, Association of American
    Publishers, American Library Association, and Association
    for Supervision and Curriculum Development, July 31, 1981.

    Articles about specific censorship cases:

    365 Days: The Washington Post, September 20,
                            1981.
    Brave New World: Des Moines (Iowa) Register,
                            July 23, 1981.
    Native Son: Boston Globe, September 1, 1981.
    Catcher in the Rye: Greensboro, (N.C.) News,
                            April 25, 1981.
    Working: The New York Times, February 3, 1982.
    Lord of the Flies: The Tucson (Ariz.) Citizen,
                            November 11, 1981.
    Of Mice and Men: The Tucson (Ariz.) Citizen,
                            November 11, 1981.
    Merriam-Webster
       Dictionary: The Dallas Times-Herald, November
                            13, 1981.
    Making It With
       Mademoiselle: Edward B. Jenkinson, Censors in the
                            Classroom (Carbondale, Illinois:
                            Southern Illinois University Press,
                            1979), p. 79.

    The Diary of
       Anne Frank: Lee A. Burress, "A Brief Report of the
                            1977 NCTE Censorship Survey," in James
                            E. Davis, Dealing with Censorship
                            (Urbana, Illinois: National Council of
                            Teachers of English, 1979).

5. Moral Majority fundraising letter, January 1, 1981.

6. Butler v. Michigan (Supreme Court decision, 1957).

7. The Wall Street Journal, January 18, 1982.

8. Ruth Seen Pearson, op. cit.

9. Peter Schrag (Editorial Pages Editor), Fresno (California) Bee, June 21, 1981.

10. Sixty Minutes broadcast, CBS, November 1, 1981.

11. Sue Fontaine, "Dismissal with Prejudice," Library Journal, June 15, 1981.

12. Sixty Minutes broadcast, op. cit.

FURTHER READING: LIBRARY POLICIES

American Library Association, "Dealing with Complaints About
        Resources," January 1981.

Association of American Publishers, American Library Associa-
        tion, and Association for Supervision and Curriculum
        Development, Limiting What Students Shall Read.
        Books and Other Learning Materials in Our Public
        Schools: How They Are Selected and How They Are
        Removed, July 31, 1981.

Blanshard, Paul, The Right to Read: The Battle Against
        Censorship (Boston: Beacon Press, 1955).

Campbell, Colin, "Book Banning in America," The New York Times
        Book Review, December 20, 1981, p. 1.

Donelson, Kenneth L., "The Student's Right to Read," National
        Council of Teachers of English brochure (Urbana,
        Illinois).

Ericson, Edward L., American Freedom and the Radical Right (New
        York: Frederick Ungar Publishing Co., 1982).

RADICAL RIGHT LITERATURE

Schlafly, Phyllis, "How to Improve Fairness in Your Library,"
        The Phyllis Schlafly Report, November 1981.

SEX EDUCATION

Q. Why do moral majoritarians so vigorously condemn sex education in public schools?

A. They claim that sex education teaches immoral sexual attitudes that violate the Bible, destroy the family, and weaken the nation's moral fiber. They also consider sex education an unwarranted intrusion of government into family life and personal privacy. Only parents and clergy, say ultra-fundamentalists, can properly explain the emotional and ethical dimensions of sexuality. Furthermore, they argue that sex education simply encourages teenagers to become sexually active and that results in more abortions, pregnancies, and emotional trauma. (Separate responses to these claims are made below.)

Q. Is sexual morality the only concern in the sex education debate?

A. No. The controversy over sex education reflects larger moral majoritarian concerns -- the rights of parents in public education, the desire for strict obedience and authority, and the broader ultra-fundamentalist political agenda. "The issue at hand," says Onalee McGraw of the Heritage Foundation, "is who should have ultimate control over the child's education, the family or the professional educators who act as agents of the state." To McGraw and her allies, sex education represents a serious infringement of the rights of parents by the "secular humanist" state.[1]

Yet the public schools became involved in sex education largely because so many parents could not or would not teach their children about their sexuality. Now that sex education is offered in many schools, parents still retain the option to keep their teenagers out of sex education programs. They also retain the opportunity to influence the nature of sex education curricula in their local schools.

Q. Sex education encourages teenage promiscuity, pregnancies, and venereal disease.

A. This is the most common objection to sex education...and the least documented. Moral majoritarians blame sex education and family planning agencies for urging teenagers to become sexually active. In the words of one commentator summarizing their objections, sex education "teaches that sexual activity among teenagers is inevitable and acceptable as long as pregnancy does not result; that contraceptives should be made available to teens at government expense to prevent pregnancy; and that if unwanted pregnancy does occur abortion is the only alternative."[2] As "proof" of these charges, moral majoritarians cite the rate of unplanned teenage pregnancies (over one million per year), abortions, venereal disease, and other sex-related problems among adolescents.

But is sex education part of the problem or part of the solution? Information is more effective in preventing unwanted pregnancies than ignorance. Teenagers will not remain chaste simply because birth control information is withheld from them or because parental consent is required to obtain contraceptives. One in five teenagers has sexual intercourse by age 13 or 14, and more than half the illegitimate births in 1980 were to teenagers, according to federal studies.[3]

When teenage girls go to Planned Parenthood for help, notes columnist William Raspberry, "most of them have been sexually active for at least a year. Refusing them contraceptive information, either directly as a matter of policy or indirectly by requiring their parents' consent, would not restore them to chastity. It would only increase the likelihood that they become pregnant."[4]

Nationally, sex education is so limited in scope that it cannot possibly cause all the teenage immorality that moral majoritarians claim it causes. Only one in ten public schools nationwide provides sex education programs, and most of these consist of only a few weeks of instruction.[5] "A 12-minute filmstrip is hardly a match for two hours of 'R'-rated films every weekend," says Scott Thomson, executive director of the National Association of Secondary School Principals.[6] Even Dr. Edward N. Brandt, Jr., Assistant Secretary of Health in the Reagan administration, agrees that knowledge about family planning and increased pregnancy are "unrelated."[7]

Q. Sex education destroys family values at taxpayer expense.

A. Sex education and family planning help reduce the number of
   unplanned teenage pregnancies. Surely this is a desirable
   goal. By assuming that teenage chastity is the only possible
   solution to the problem, moral majoritarians are rejecting
   available remedies to the high rate of out-of-wedlock births.

   The federal government sponsors the Family Planning Services
   Program, to provide medical services, counseling, education and
   training in the use of contraceptives. Every federal dollar
   invested in the program ($1.5 billion since 1970), notes Sen.
   Howard Metzenbaum (D-Ohio), "saves at least two dollars in
   government subsidized health and welfare services. In 1980,
   these savings totaled $570 million."[8] Perhaps mindful that
   unwanted pregnancies can destroy families, Dr. Edward N.
   Brandt, Jr., Assistant Secretary of Health, calls this program
   "a necessity." Yet Senator Jeremiah Denton (R-Ala.) dismisses
   it as superfluous: "I am not opposed to family planning when
   we are planning families. But unemancipated minors do not plan
   families."[9] That is precisely the problem, argue advocates
   of sex education and family planning.

Q. Sex education materials are obscene and teach perversion.

A. Most sex education material is simple and clinical. Explicit-
   ness of some degree is unavoidable. When moral majoritarians
   object to sex education materials, it is more often to the idea
   of sex education than to genuinely offensive materials. Their
   objections are often misinformed. For example, Phyllis Schlafly
   claims, "The major goal of nearly all sex education curricula
   being taught in the schools is to teach teenagers (and sometimes children) how to enjoy fornication without having a baby
   and without feeling guilty."[10] This is simply not true.
   Opinions about sex education materials will differ, and parents
   should have a right to inspect teaching materials. But sex
   education courses are not seminars in hedonism or immorality.

Q. Sex education programs violate the rights of parents to teach
   their children the "facts of life" as they see fit.

A. No sex education program denies parents this right. In fact,
   parents must provide their written consent for their children
   to participate in most programs. Parents usually have the
   opportunity to shape the curricula of sex education through

the appropriate local forum and inspect the materials that will
be used in a course. The radical right wants to prevent other
people from deciding what their own children should be taught.

Sex education courses have evolved, in part, because parents
have neglected to talk about sex and responsibility to their
teenagers. Many parents themselves are not well informed about
contraception, abortion, and related issues. It is this void
that public schools fill with their sex education programs, in
an effort to combat the myriad social problems that result from
sexually active -- and uninformed -- teenagers. Three out of
four Americans approve of schools offering sex education,
according to a 1981 survey by the Associated Press and NBC.[11]
In those cases where parents have the opportunity to keep their
children out of sex education courses, only 3 percent have done
so, according to Planned Parenthood.[12]

Q Schools are not equipped to teach the emotional and ethical
   dimensions of sexuality.

A. Public schools cannot claim to have the ethical expertise nor
   the moral authority of parents. But this should not preclude
   public schools from discussing human sexuality. The public
   schools have a legitimate interest in educating adolescents
   about their sexuality, especially when teenage sex has some
   significant public consequences (whether sex education courses
   are offered or not). Public schools must respect the equally
   legitimate concern of parents to keep their own children out of
   sex education programs. But parents do not have the right to
   bar other people's children from receiving sex education,
   especially when most segments of a community usually favor the
   option of such instruction in public schools.

   Contrary to the distortions of Phyllis Schlafly, Beverly
   LaHaye, and others, sex education does not advocate pre-marital
   sex, abortion, homosexuality, or masturbation. (The mere
   mention of a controversial issue does not constitute endorsement.) The schools, it should be remembered, have a strong
   interest in promoting a stable social fabric and family values.

Q. Who are the chief opponents of sex education and family
   planning in the schools?

A. Most controversies about sex education occur at the local
   level, where such decisions are made. There are, nonetheless,

several prominent national figures who wage the battle against
sex education. They include:

o Phyllis Schlafly, the president of the Eagle Forum and
  leader of the anti-ERA movement;

o Beverly LaHaye, who teaches "Family Life Seminars" with
  her husband, Rev. Tim LaHaye (a board member of Moral
  Majority, Inc.);

o Claire Chambers, author of The SIECUS Circle: A Humanist
  Revolution, a 445-page tract that considers sex educa-
  tion part of the "humanist" conspiracy led by the Sex
  Information and Education Council of the United States;

o Dr. Onalee McGraw, education consultant to the Heritage
  Foundation and ultra-fundamentalist theorist on "family"
  issues; and

o Connaught Marshner, "the pivot person in Washington,
  D.C., for the pro-family movement," according to
  Conservative Digest.

Sen. Jeremiah Denton (R-Ala.) has also gained some national
prominence on the issue of adolescent sexuality by his sponsor-
ship of a $30 million bill to promote teenage chastity. His
legislation, passed in 1981, seeks to promote abstinence as the
alternative to contraception or abortion. Rev. Jerry Falwell
has also been highly visible in denouncing sex education. In
January 1981, Falwell launched a massive direct mail campaign
to ban from school libraries a single book, Our Bodies,
Ourselves, the acclaimed health manual for women. "Examine
your public school libraries and textbooks for immoral,
anti-family, and anti-American content," he urged, with the
postscript, "Remember -- our children's moral values are at
stake!"

Q. What people and groups are most frequently condemned as immoral
   advocates of sex education?

A. Family planning agencies like Planned Parenthood Federation of
   America (Faye Wattleton, president) and the Sex Information and
   Education Council of the United States (Dr. Mary Calderone,
   founder and executive director) are the most reviled groups.
   Planned Parenthood is criticized for providing birth control

information, contraceptives, and abortion counseling. SIECUS
is condemned not only for its family planning activities but
for its alleged leadership of a "humanist revolution" waged by
"subversive" groups like the American Medical Association, the
YMCA and YWCA, the Council on Foreign Relations, and other
groups allegedly seeking world domination. Numerous authors
who write about family and sex-related issues are also
condemned. A partial list includes sex educator Sol Gordon,
anthropologists Margaret Mead and Ashley Montagu, pediatrician
Dr. Benjamin Spock, and family planning advocate Dr. Alan F.
Guttmacher.

QUOTABLE QUOTES

"The facts of life can be told in 15 minutes."

> -- Phyllis Schlafly, The Phyllis
> Schlafly Report, February 1981

"It is very healthy for a young girl to be deterred from promiscuity by fear of contracting a painful, incurable disease, or cervical cancer, or sterility, or the likelihood of giving birth to a dead, blind, or brain-damaged baby (even ten years later when she may be happily married)."

> -- Phyllis Schlafly, The Phyllis
> Schlafly Report, February 1981

"The major goal of nearly all sex education curricula being taught in the schools is to teach teenagers (and sometimes children) how to enjoy fornication without having a baby and without feeling guilty."

> -- Phyllis Schlafly, The Bergen
> (Hackensack, N.J.) Record,
> June 9, 1981

"One of the most devastating enemies of the family is radical sex education in the public school. It is more explicit than is necessary for the good of the child. Too much sex education too soon causes undue curiosity and obsession with sex."

> -- Beverly LaHaye, Concerned
> Women for America, April 1981

"I am not against sex education, when taught as biological science, but I am against offensive sex education materials that distort and warp our children's minds and moral values."

> -- Rev. Jerry Falwell,
> fundraising letter,
> January 1981

"A certain percentage [of the population] will have to practice contraception and birth control and certain percentages will have to commit suicide. So that's why they're teaching our little junior high school age children to commit suicide. You know why? Because they are Nazis. They believe in the survival of the fittest. And they know the fittest will not commit suicide....Now you know why they're teaching sex education in school. Now you understand why they're trying to teach your children to get an abortion. Now you understand why they teach little junior high school age kids to commit suicide. To keep from having overpopulation by the year 2000, they either have to control or kill through the schools."

> -- Rev. Greg Dixon, National Secretary of Moral Majority, Inc., in a sermon, "How Public Schools Make Communists of Your Children," reported in Education Week, March 3, 1982.

"A 12-minute filmstrip is hardly a match for two hours of 'R'-rated films every weekend."

> -- Scott Thompson, executive director, National Association of Secondary School Principals, Los Angeles Times, May 14, 1981

NOTES: SEX EDUCATION

1. Onalee McGraw, Family Choice in Education: The New
   Imperative (Washington, D.C.: The Heritage Foundation,
   1978), p. 39.

2. William Raspberry, "Ignorance Does Not Beget Abstinence,"
   The Washington Post, December 30, 1981.

3. "Americans Favor Sex Education," Terre Haute (Indiana)
   Tribune, October 8, 1981.

4. William Raspberry, op. cit.

5. Ann Landers, The Washington Post, September 28, 1981.

6. Patricia McCormack, "Schools Flunk Sex Education Test,"
   The Los Angeles Times, May 14, 1981, Part V, p. 11.

7. Bernard Weinraub, "Reagan Aide Backs Birth-Curb
   Education," The New York Times, June 24, 1981.

8. Ibid.

9. Ibid.

10. Bruce Rosen, "Schlafly Assails Sex Education," The Bergen
    (Hackensack, N.J.) Record, June 9, 1981.

11. "Americans Favor Sex Education," Terre Haute (Indiana)
    Tribune, October 8, 1981.

12. Ibid.

FURTHER READING: SEX EDUCATION

Boston Women's Health Book Collective, Our Bodies, Ourselves
     (New York: Simon & Schuster, 1973).

Council for Basic Education, A New Approach to Teach Morality,
     Bulletin for Basic Education, October 1978
     (Available from Council for Basic Education, 725 15th
     St. N.W., Washington, D.C. 20015).

Julian, C.J. et al., Modern Sex Education (New York: Holt,
     Rinehart and Winston, 1980).

Morrison, E.S., and M.V. Price, Values in Sexuality: A New
     Approach to Sex Education (New York: Hart Publishing
     Co., Inc., 1974).

Nass, Gilbert D., et al., Sexual Choices: An Introduction to
     Human Sexuality (Belmont, California: Wadsworth
     Health Sciences Division, 1981).

National Education Association, Suggestions for Defense Against
     Extremist Attack: Sex Education in the Public Schools,
     Commission on Professional Rights and
     Responsibilities.

Planned Parenthood Federation of America. (For list of
     publications, films, and materials, write to 810
     Seventh Avenue, New York, New York 10019, or call
     212-541-7800.)

Scales, Peter, "Education for Sexuality," Free Inquiry, Summer
     1981.

Sherry, Paul H., "Sex is Aweful," Journal of Current Social
     Issues, Vol. 15, No. 1, Spring 1978.

RADICAL RIGHT LITERATURE

Chambers, Claire, The SIECUS Circle: A Humanist Revolution
      (Belmont, Massachusetts: Western Islands, 1977).

Lorand, Rhoda, "The Betrayal of Youth," Education Update,
      newsletter of The Heritage Foundation, Washington,
      D.C., Summer 1979.

Otto, Herbert, The New Sex Education (Follett, 1978).

Schlafly, Phyllis, "What's Wrong with Sex Education," The
      Phyllis Schlafly Report, February 1981.

Senate Committee on Labor and Human Resources, Adolescent
      Family Life, Report No. 97-161, July 21, 1981.

CREATIONISM

Q. Why does the radical right condemn the teaching of evolution in public schools?

A. It blames the teaching of evolution for a great many woes in American society today. Radical right leaders claim that teaching evolution -- an alleged tenet of the "secular humanist" creed -- teaches children to forsake the laws of God for the selfish, immoral ways of man. Nell Segraves, founder of the Creation Science Research Center in San Diego, claims:

> So many of society's problems stem from children being taught that they evolved from other creatures rather than that they were created in God's image....If man is taught that he is of animal lineage, he is able to do as he pleases, restrained only by fluctuating value systems. If it is unconstitutional to teach of God, then it is equally unconstitutional to teach the absence of God.[1]

Another leading opponent of evolution, the Institute for Creation Research, flatly states, "Evolution is the best tool Satan can use to destroy the minds of young people."[2] Of course, ultra-fundamentalists produce no evidence proving a causal connection between teaching evolution and moral turpitude; their case rests on bald assertion.

To counter the alleged damage of teaching evolution, the radical right wants public schools to teach "creationism" (or "creation-science") as either a substitute or supplement to teaching evolution. "Creationism" is a doctrine that holds that God created the world in six days some 6,000 to 10,000 years ago and that humans did not evolve from any other species but were created by God, as described in the Book of Genesis. Even though "creationism" cannot be verified in any scientific manner, ultra-fundamentalists persist in claiming scientific (and not religious) status for it. Simultaneously, they assert that evolution is a religion -- "secular humanism."

Q. How does the teaching of creationism in public schools violate constitutional principles?

A. Under the First Amendment of the Constitution, government "shall make no law respecting an establishment of a religion, or prohibiting the free exercise thereof...." Numerous Supreme Court decisions have clarified what activities constitute unconstitutional preferential treatment for one religion or religious doctrine. "Creation-science" pretends to be a secular scientific doctrine that merely has coincident tenets with sectarian religion. But in fact, the creationist doctrine is religiously motivated and did not emerge from any secular scientific controversy.

Thus, creationist statutes are affected by the landmark 1962 Supreme Court case, Engel v. Vitale. This decision prohibits a state, through its schools, from placing "the power, prestige and financial support of government...behind a particular religious belief."[3]   Another major Supreme Court case, Epperson v. Arkansas in 1968, set a broad precedent: "There is and can be no doubt that the First Amendment does not permit the State to require that teaching and learning must be tailored to the principles or prohibitions of any religious sect or dogma...."[4]   In general, the courts use three distinct criteria to determine whether a law violates the Establishment Clause:

> First, does the Act reflect a secular legislative purpose? Second, is the primary effect of the Act to advance or inhibit religion? Third, does the administration of the Act foster an excessive government entanglement with religion?[5]

Contrary to radical right claims that the United States was founded as a "Christian nation," the Constitution and its framers always intended that there be a wall of separation between religious activities and the state. It is a doctrine that the Supreme Court continues to uphold. (See "Church/State Separation" section.)

Q. But teaching evolution exclusively is what constitutes the establishment of a state religion, "secular humanism." This is unconstitutional.

A. Creationists argue that evolution is a tenet of the "secular humanist" religion and, thus, teaching evolution exclusively represents preferential treatment of a particular religion. The State of Arkansas made this claim in defending its creationist statute, saying that teaching evolution alone gives "preference to theological liberalism, humanism, nontheistic religions, and atheism, in that these religious faiths generally include a religious belief in evolution."[6] Ultra-fundamentalists make the further assertion that since the theory of evolution is based on many inferences that cannot be "proven" beyond a doubt, that evolution is really a doctrine of faith -- religious faith.

These are clever but specious arguments. The reasoning for it collapses when it is shown that "secular humanist evolution" is not a religion, let alone the official religion of the United States. (See "Secular Humanism" section.) Furthermore, simply because a secular scientific doctrine like evolution cannot make an ironclad case ("it's only a theory") does not make it a religious faith. Science is based on provisional belief; new evidence can lead to new theories. But "creation-science" posits an absolute, eternal "theory" based on evidence no one can test scientifically. This distinction was pithily drawn by one observer: "The essence of religion is faith; the essence of science is doubt."[7]

Q. Is it possible to believe in evolution yet still be a Christian?

A. Ultra-fundamentalists say it is impossible. Since Darwin first published Origin of Species in 1859, some fundamentalists have viewed opposition to evolution as a badge of their religious identity and a test of Christian faith. "Belief in evolution is a necessary component of atheism, pantheism, and all other systems that reject a sovereign authority of an omnipotent personal God," asserts Henry M. Morris, a 20-year veteran of the creationist movement.[8]

Evolution contradicts the Bible, says Morris, because the theory claims humanity evolved over millions of years without the shaping hand of God. By contrast, creationists believe that God created man on the sixth day of Creation Week some 6,000 to 10,000 years ago. They say humanity descended directly from Adam and Eve, not from a lower species. (See Genesis 1-2.)

Mainstream Christian churches see no conflict between belief in evolution and belief in God. They do not insist on a literal reading of the Old Testament creation accounts. (Only 3 percent of the Episcopal clergy and 16 to 18 percent of Methodist and Presbyterian clergy believe that God literally created Adam and Eve.)[9] Charles Darwin himself felt a person could believe in the theory of evolution and still believe in God. "It seems to me absurd," he wrote to author John Fordyce on May 7, 1879, "to doubt that a man may be an ardent Theist and an evolutionist."[10]

Q. What have leading religious figures and churches said about creationism?

A. Pope John Paul II told the Pontifical Academy of Science in October 1981:

> The Bible itself speaks to us of the origin of the universe and its make-up, not in order to provide us with a scientific treatise but in order to state the correct relationships of man with God and with the universe. Sacred Scripture wishes simply to declare that the world was created by God, and in order to teach this truth it expresses itself in the terms of the cosmology in use at the time of the writer....Any other teaching about the origin and make-up of the universe is alien to the intentions of the Bible, which does not wish to teach how heaven was but how one goes to heaven.[11]

The United Presbyterian Church in the USA issued a six-point resolution in 1982 that pointed out "the dispute is not really over biology or faith, but is essentially about Biblical interpretation, particularly over two irreconcilable viewpoints regarding the characteristics of Biblical literature and the nature of Biblical authority."[12] Like most other mainstream Protestants, the United Presbyterian Church disputes the notion that evolution conflicts with Christian belief.

Langdon Gilkey, a prominent professor of theology at the Divinity School, University of Chicago, who has written extensively on the topic, considers creationism laws a serious threat to religious freedom:

[T]he law endangers the free practice of religion in
our society by the establishment in the public schools
of one particular tradition (Christianity) and, indeed,
one particular interpretation of the Christian religion.
It does this by presenting as "science" a particular,
even sectarian, interpretation of the Christian symbol
of the creation and so of the Book of Genesis -- thus
ruling out not only other religious and philosophical
traditions than the Christian but also other Christian
views of creation, my own included.[13]

Q. Does creationism have any scientific basis?

A. None whatsoever. Despite their claims to scientific rigor,
several leading creationists have virtually admitted the
lack of scientific evidence or procedure in "creation-science."
Henry Morris admits: "Creationism...is inaccessible to the
scientific method. It is impossible to devise a scientific
experiment to describe the creation process, or even to
ascertain whether such a process can take place."[14] Duane
Gish, also affiliated with the Institute for Creation Research,
acknowledges: "We do not know how the Creator created, what
processes He used, for He used processes which are not now
operating anywhere in the natural universe." (original
emphasis)[15]

Thus do "creation-scientists" forfeit any serious claim to the
scientific tradition of empirical observation, testing, and
hypothesizing. The plaintiffs' brief in the 1981 Arkansas
trial unmasked "creation-science" in this manner: "A system of
belief that has as its center the interruption, suspension or
nonexistence of natural laws and, in lieu thereof, the intervention of a supernatural and omnipotent Creator (God), is not
science. Even if some of its minor premises look, smell,
taste, feel and sound scientific, its major premise -- God --
is not subject to testing or to disproof and, accordingly, is
not scientific."[16]

Q. Why is creationism so profoundly incompatible with science?

A. Because creationism contradicts the basic principles of
biology, geology, nuclear physics, astronomy, and other natural
sciences -- each of which is based on mountains of empirical
evidence that cannot be summarily dismissed. Nuclear physi-
cists have gauged the age of the earth to be 4.6 billion years

by measuring the decay of radioactive materials in rocks. But
if the creationist claim that the earth is only 10,000 years
old is true, then the theories of nuclear physics must be
discarded entirely. Similarly, modern astronomy would have to
be discarded because it calculates that most stars are more
than 10,000 light-years away. The creationist "scientific"
belief in a 10,000-year-old earth also contradicts the fundamental principles of geology and paleontology.[17]

Allen Hammond and Lynn Margulis, a geophysicist and biologist
respectively, point out why "creationism" cannot meet the most
elemental requirements of science:

> Since science proceeds by the abandonment of one theory
> only when another can better explain the existing
> evidence, the creationist "theory" faces severe
> difficulties. It must not only offer a self-consistent
> explanation to account for the accumulated evidence of
> science -- it must offer a more compelling explanation to
> replace the combined (and self-consistent) edifices of
> physics, astronomy, and geology.
>
> Instead, the creationists attempt to explain away the
> evidence of an ancient universe by assuming that the
> evidence itself was created....In essence, the creationist
> must propose a deceitful Creator if their hypothesis of a
> 10,000 year old world is to deal with the evidence at
> hand. Most scientists have a more abiding faith in the
> reasonableness of the world.[18]

Hammond and Margulis also note that creationists do not
participate in serious scientific enterprises (they do not
publish in scientific journals or present papers) nor do they
even allow the possibility that their "theory" can change with
new evidence -- a rather basic scientific and intellectual
principle.

Q. Why then do ultra-fundamentalists persist in claiming a
   scientific basis for creationism?

A. It is a tactical ploy designed to evade the Establishment
   Clause of the Constitution. A straightforward demand that
   creationism be taught as a religious doctrine has been rejected
   by the courts repeatedly. By portraying creationism as scientific, ultra-fundamentalists hope to bypass these precedents

and also acquire some polemical leverage by claiming to support academic freedom and fair play. They argue that since science is based on a review of all available evidence, and since creationism is "simply another theory" about the origins of life, conscientious scientists are duty-bound to consider it as well.

By casting their argument in this way, notes science journalist John Skow, the mandatory teaching of creationism would not be seen "as an intrusion of sectarian dogma into the lives of free citizens and of religious myth into science, but as a reasonable request for fair play."[19]

Q. Why shouldn't creationists be given "equal time" for their theory?

A. Because creationism has absolutely no scientific basis and because it forces the state to endorse a sectarian religious doctrine, in violation of the Constitution. As plaintiff lawyers successfully argued in the Arkansas case: "The secular educational value of 'creation-science,' if taught as science, is nil. Without God, 'creation-science' is a motley assortment of facts and assertions bound to puzzle and confuse. With God, 'creation-science' is religious, forbidden by our Constitution to be taught in public schools."[20]

Beyond the issue of church and state is the integrity of education. Science educators cannot maintain any sense of professional integrity if forced to teach a doctrine that no reputable scientists endorse. And school children will be confused if two radically different, incompatible doctrines are both taught as science. Furthermore, a turn from the scientific principles of evolution could have serious consequences for American science. It is not coincidental that Soviet biological sciences, especially agriculture, stagnated for decades when the USSR banned the teaching of Darwin's theory in Soviet classrooms.

Finally, there is the massive expense to school systems, at a time of austerity, to help propagate a fraudulent science. Education officials in Louisiana estimate that their state statute, if not ruled unconstitutional, will cost the state $7 million.[21] The primary beneficiary of this expenditure would be the largest publisher of "creation-science" textbooks, the Institute for Creation Research.

Q. But isn't there a controversy in scientific circles about the validity of evolution theory?

A. Yes, but none of the dissenters question the basic principles of science, as creationists do. By pointing to current scientific disputes about evolution theory, moral majoritarians try to put creationism on an equal footing with other scientific alternatives to evolution; creationism presented as "just another theory" among many.

The "modern synthesis" evolution theory is the prevailing explanation for biological change, but it is under attack by some scientists as too reductionist. There are several alternative theories to traditional evolutionary theory:

o "Punctuated equilibria" claims that fossils show long periods of stability punctuated by short periods of rapid change, when new biological forms suddenly appear. The phrase was coined by paleontologists Stephen Jay Gould and Niles Eldridge.

o "Cladists" argue that the different branches of animal and plant life coincide with the splitting of the earth's continents, which led to variations in life.

o A theory of "biological fields" disputes the assumption that genes and cells are the directing agencies of life, but holds instead that they are organized by an invisible field, just as planets are affected by gravity or words by an invisible syntax.[22]

For all the controversy that these theories have provoked, none denies the root assumptions of the scientific method.

Q. Who are the most prominent creationist groups and their leaders?

A. Virtually all moral majoritarian groups support the creationist movement, but there are three organizations that are especially influential:

o The Institute for Creation Research (ICR) is probably the most effective of the "creation-science" centers. Its director is the veteran creationist, Henry M. Morris. ICR is home to two other leading creationists,

Duane T. Gish (Associate Director) and Richard Bliss
(Director of Curriculum). ICR produces most of the
"creation-science" textbooks and educational materials
used in both public and Christian schools.

o The Creation Science Research Center (CSRC) in San Diego
  can claim responsibility for many state bills and
  national publicity for creationism. Like Morris,
  Nell Segraves is a 20-year veteran of the movement.
  She runs CSRC with her son Kelly, providing a religious
  emphasis to creationist advocacy that contrasts with the
  "scientific" focus of ICR.

o Citizens for Fairness in Education was founded by Paul
  Ellwanger, a Catholic Biblical literalist who claims
  that the teaching of evolution amounts to using "our tax
  dollars...against God." He also claims that teaching
  evolution leads to many problems including "Nazism,
  racism, and abortion...." Ellwanger distributes model
  legislation and promotional materials around the
  country, both of which served as catalysts for the
  Arkansas creationist statute.[23]

Other "creation-science" organizations include the Creation
Research Society (Ann Arbor, Michigan), the Creation Social
Science and Humanist Society (Wichita, Kansas), and the Bible
Science Association (Minneapolis, Minnesota).

Q. What has the creationist movement accomplished in recent years?

A. It has built a national network of activists responsible for
   considerable publicity, changes in textbooks, and proposed
   "creation science" legislation in nearly half the states.
   The televangelists have been among the leading advocates for
   creationism, giving the issue considerable attention on their
   shows. Falwell's Old-Time Gospel Hour produced a one-hour
   TV special, "Creation Versus Evolution," that featured a debate
   between Dr. Duane Gish of the Institute for Creation Research
   and Dr. Russell Doolittle of the University of California at
   San Diego.

   Doubleday and Co. has purged the word "evolution" from its only
   high school biology text, Experiences in Biology, because of
   the controversy over creationism. Doubleday executive Eugene
   Frank explained, "The reason for self-censorship is to avoid

the publicity that would be involved in a controversy over a
textbook. We'd like to sell thousands of copies."[24]   In
1982, the New York City Board of Education took a step that may
discourage this sort of self-censorship. It rejected three
high school biology texts that inadequately treat evolution and
uncritically endorse creationism. In a letter to one of the
publishers, the Board explained, "This book does not state that
evolution is accepted by most scientists today and presents
special creation without characterizing it as a supernatural
explanation that is outside the domain of science."[25]

To date, bills mandating that creationism be taught in public
schools have been introduced in 15 states. "Creation-science"
bills in Arkansas and Louisiana were enacted into law in 1981.
The creationism movement suffered a serious setback in December
1981, however, when a U.S. District Court declared the Arkansas
statute unconstitutional. As State Senator Jim Holstead,
sponsor of the Arkansas legislation noted, "If the law is
unconstitutional, it'll be because of something in the language
that's wrong. So we'll just change the wording and try again
with another bill....We got a lot of time. Eventually we'll
get one that's constitutional."[26]

QUOTABLE QUOTES

"We object to the idea that we are the random products of chance that -- as evolutionists maintain -- there is no God, that there is no one to whom we are responsible. We are nothing more than a mechanistic product of a mindless universe. I believe this is wrong. I believe the scientific evidence is clearly in contradiction to that."

> -- Duane T. Gish, Associate Director, Institute for Creation Research

"I'm convinced that the problems we have in America, and especially in the public schools in terms of dissonance and rebellion and disobedience and juvenile delinquency, are directly related to the concept of evolution."

> -- W. Lloyd Dale, a biology teacher and pastor in Lemmon, South Dakota

"I believe that this teaching of evolution as a fact in our public schools has been largely responsible or certainly significantly responsible, for what we see in our society today: the crime, the violence, the lack of respect for parents, for teachers, and our government and everything else...."

> -- Dr. Duane Gish, Associate Director, Institute for Creation Research, appearing on "LaHayes on Family Life," April 24, 1982

"You would have to believe in more miracles, you'd have to believe in the Great Pumpkin and the Tooth Fairy to believe some of the things these folks try to unload on you as science."

> -- Rev. Pat Robertson, "700 Club" broadcast, February 8, 1982

"The chaos of the sixties is the result of teaching evolution."

> -- Rev. Tim LaHaye,
> "Creation vs. Evolution:
> Battle in the Classroom,"
> KPBS-TV, San Diego, Calif.,
> July 7, 1982

"Science begins with questions and pursues answers -- testing, proving, disproving. It is this process of reasoning that underpins all modern science. Creationism begins with answers and pursues doubts only to erase them. It is fundamentally hostile to science."

> -- Ellen Goodman,
> syndicated columnist,
> December 19, 1981

"We're more concerned with God as the creator of the world than with how he created....So long as whatever is taught in the schools allows room for that interpretation, there's no problem."

> -- Rev. Thomas Gallagher,
> secretary for education,
> U.S. Catholic Conference

[Creationism laws] "endanger the free practice of religion in our society by the establishment in the public schools of one particular tradition (Christianity) and, indeed, one particular interpretation of the Christian religion. It does this by presenting as "science" a particular, even sectarian, interpretation of the Christian symbol of the creation and so of the Book of Genesis -- thus ruling out not only other religious and philosophical traditions than the Christian but also other Christian views of creation, my own included."

> -- Langdon Gilkey,
> Professor of Theology,
> University of Chicago,
> Christianity and Crisis,
> April 26, 1982

NOTES: CREATIONISM

1. "Scientific Creationism," Issuegram (newsletter of the Education Commission of the States), October 1981.

2. Institute for Creation Research textbook, quoted in "The Crucifixion of Evolution," Mother Jones, September/October 1981.

3. Engel v. Vitale, 370 U.S. 421, 431 (1962).

4. Epperson v. Arkansas, 393 U.S. 97 (1968).

5. Tilton v. Richardson, 403 U.S. 672, 678 (1971); accord, Lemon v. Kurtzman, 403 U.S. 602, 612 (1971).

6. State of Arkansas, Act 590 of 1981, the "Balanced Treatment of Creation-Science and Evolution-Science Act," Section 6, Legislative Declaration of Purpose.

7. Philip J. Hilts, "Creation Trial: Less Circus, More Law," The Washington Post, December 21, 1981.

8. Henry M. Morris, The Remarkable Birth of Planet Earth (San Diego: Creation-Life Publishers, 1972), p. vii.

9. Martin E. Marty, "An Answer to a Creationist Who Sees Evolution as Cause of Terrorism," American Council of Evangelical Lutherans newsletter, May 1981.

10. "Belief in God and in Evolution Possible, Darwin Letter Says," The New York Times, December 27, 1981.

11. Pope John Paul II, Address to Pontifical Academy of Science, October 1981, quoted in Creation/Evolution, Winter 1982, Issue VII, p. 45.

12. Resolution adopted by the 194th General Assembly, 1982.

13. Langdon Gilkey, "Creationism: The Roots of the Conflict," Christianity and Crisis, April 26, 1982.

14. Henry M. Morris, Scientific Creationism (San Diego, Creation Life Publishers, 1974), p. 5.

15. Duane T. Gish, Evolution? The Fossils Say No!, p. 40.

16. McLean v. State of Arkansas, United States District Court, Eastern District of Arkansas, Western Division, plaintiffs' pre-trial brief, at 5.

17. Allen Hammond and Lynn Margulis, "Farewell to Newton, Einstein, Darwin...: Creationism as Science," Science 81, December 1981, pp. 55-7.

18. Ibid.

19. John Skow, "The Genesis of Equal Time: Creationism as a Social Movement," Science 81, December 1981, p. 54.

20. McLean v. State of Arkansas, op. cit., at 5-6.

21. "Creating Controversy: Louisiana Attacks Evolution," Church & State, September 1981.

22. John Davy, "What If Darwin Were Wrong?" The Washington Post, August 30, 1981, Section C, p. 1. Also, Walter Sullivan, "Creation Debate Is Not Limited to Arkansas Trial," The New York Times, February 27, 1981.

23. Ellwanger Deposition in McLean v. State of Arkansas, op. cit. Ellwanger Ex. 19 at 1237; Appendix 15. Quoted in plaintiffs' pre-trial brief.

24. National Public Radio, "All Things Considered" broadcast, December 12, 1981.

25. Gene I. Maeroff, "City Schools Bar Three Textbooks As Inadequate on Darwin," The New York Times, June 24, 1982.

26. Philip J. Hilts, "Law Requiring Teaching Creation Faces Trial Today," The Washington Post, December 7, 1981.

FURTHER READING: CREATIONISM

Creation/Evolution (quarterly journal dedicated to promoting
          evolutionary science, available for $8.00/yearly from
          P.O. Box 5, Amherst Branch, Buffalo, NY 14226).

Gilkey, Langdon, "Creationism: The Roots of the Conflict,"
          Christianity and Crisis, April 26, 1982, pp. 108-15.

Gould, Stephen Jay, Ever Since Darwin (New York: Norton Press,
          1977).

------- , Ontology and Phylogeny (Cambridge, Massachusetts:
          Harvard University Press, 1977).

Lyons, Gene, "Repealing the Enlightenment," Harper's,
          April 1982.

McLean et al. v. Arkansas Board of Education, plaintiffs'
          pre-trial brief, filed in the United States District
          Court, Eastern District of Arkansas, Western Division.

Murray, N. Patrick and Neal D. Buffaloe, Creation and Evolu-
          tion: The Real Issues (Available for $1.00 from
          The Bookmark, Inc., P.O. Box 7266, Little Rock,
          Arkansas 72217).

Skoog, Gerald, "The Textbook Battle Over Creationism," The
          Christian Century, October 15, 1980, pp. 974-76.

National Association of Biology Teachers, A Compendium of
          Information on the Theory of Evolution and the
          Evolution-Creationism Controversy, 1978 (Available
          from NABT, 11250 Bacon Drive, Reston, VA 22090).

Nelkin, Diane, Science Textbook Controversies and the Politics
          of Equal Time (Cambridge, Massachusetts: MIT Press,
          1978).

Parker, Barbara, "Creation vs. Evolution: Teaching the Origin
          of Man," The American School Board Journal, Vol.
          167, No. 3, March 1980 (Available from National
          School Boards Association, 1055 Thomas Jefferson St.
          N.W., Washington, D.C. 20007).

Viviano, Fran, "The Crucifixion of Evolution," Mother Jones, September/October 1981.

Wolfe, Alan, "Creationism's Second Coming," The Nation, March 21, 1981.

A comprehensive bibliography of creationism materials (dissertations, books, monographs, periodical articles, and daily newspaper articles) is available for $8.00 from Ernie Lazar, 495 Ellis Street, San Francisco, CA 94102.

RADICAL RIGHT LITERATURE

Creation Research Society Quarterly (Available from Creation Research Society, 2717 Cranbrook Rd., Ann Arbor, MI 48104).

Gish, Duane T., Evolution? The Fossils Say No! (San Diego: Creation Life Publishers, 1978).

Lee, Francis Nigel, The Origin and Destiny of Man (Christian Studies Center, P.O. 11110, Memphis, Tennessee 38111).

Morris, Henry, The Remarkable Birth of Planet Earth (San Diego: Creation Life Publishers, 1972).

------ , Scientific Creationism (San Diego: Creation Life Publishers, 1974).

Morris, Henry M. and H. Clark, The Bible Has the Answer (San Diego: Creation Life Publishers, 1976).

Morris, Henry M. and John C. Whitcomb, Jr., The Genesis Flood (Presbyterian and Reformed Publishing Co., distributed by Creation Life Publishers, 1961).

SCHOOL PRAYER

Q. What's wrong with voluntary prayer devotions in public schools?

A. No matter how benign the motive, school prayer violates one of the most basic premises of our Constitution -- that government should neither restrict an individual's religious freedom nor promote any particular religious doctrine. This neutrality provision is laid out in the First Amendment: "Congress shall make no law respecting an establishment of religion, or prohibiting the free exercise thereof...." (For more, see "Church/State Separation" section.)

Government-mandated prayer in public schools is also offensive to many religious groups, who consider it a bland substitute for meaningful religious devotions. As columnist George Will put it, "[T]he question is: is public school prayer apt to serve authentic religion, or is it apt to be mere attitudinizing, a thin gruel of vague religious vocabulary? Religious exercises should arise from a rich tradition, and reflect that richness. Prayer, properly understood, arises from the context of the praying person's faith."[1]

Q. Children who object to school prayer don't have to participate. It's a voluntary activity.

A. When required or even permitted by law, school prayer is not voluntary. It is in effect a mandatory religious observance. Providing children with the option not to participate does not make it truly voluntary because exercising that choice singles out individuals on the basis of their religion and carries a stigma. It is not likely that an eight-year-old child will buck peer pressures and the teacher's authority in order to exercise his or her constitutional right, yet that is the burden imposed by government-mandated school prayer.

Let's not forget that voluntary prayer in the public schools is a reality right now. Any child can individually pray at school as long as it does not disrupt the educational program. But once the state directs group prayer devotions, it ceases to be a voluntary practice.

Q. What is the Supreme Court record with respect to school prayer?

A. Two landmark Supreme Court decisions 20 years ago continue to guide the courts in their rulings on religious activity in public schools. In 1962, the Engel v. Vitale decision prohibited the recitation of a prayer approved by the New York Board of Regents. A year later, in Abington School District v. Schempp and its companion case, Murray v. Curlett, the Court told the State of Pennsylvania that it could not require readings from the Bible or recitation of the Lord's Prayer. In these and subsequent cases, the Supreme Court has consistently affirmed the principle of separation of church and state.[2]

The courts are frequently asked to strike a balance between the "Establishment Clause" and the "Free Exercise Clause" of the First Amendment. In both Vitale and Schempp, the courts restricted the government's authority under the Establishment Clause; there was no restriction on the free exercise of religion. Religious freedom is actually enhanced when the government is banned from supporting religious activity. As the Court declared in Engel v. Vitale: "When the power, prestige and financial support of government is placed behind a particular religious belief, the indirect coercive pressure upon religious minorities to conform to the prevailing officially approved religion is plain."[3] The Vitale and Schempp decisions did not ban the free exercise of religion through voluntary prayer; it did ban mandatory, state-imposed prayer.

Q. What efforts are being made to overrule the Court's decisions in order to permit prayer in public schools?

A. President Reagan proposed a constitutional amendment to the First Amendment in May 1982 that would permit so-called voluntary prayer in public schools. The proposed wording reads:

> Nothing in this Constitution shall be construed to prohibit individual or group prayer in public schools or other public institutions. No person shall be required by

the United States or by any state to participate in
prayer.[4]

When he announced the proposed amendment, President Reagan
urged a reawakening of "America's religious and moral heart"
and stronger protection of religion from "government
tyranny."[5] The amendment, however, will <u>increase</u> government
intrusion into religious affairs. Since 1962, there have been
four other attempts to overrule the Supreme Court through
constitutional amendments. These were the Becker Amendment in
1964, two Dirksen amendments in the 1960s, and the Wylie
amendment in the early 1970s.

Senator John Danforth of Missouri, an ordained Episcopal
priest, considers government-mandated voluntary prayer a
contradiction in terms. In response to the latest prayer
crusade, Danforth proposed that "voluntary" be defined
correctly: "The term 'voluntary prayer' shall not include any
prayer composed, prescribed, directed, supervised, or organized
by an official employee of a state or local government agency,
including public school principals or teachers."[6]

Q. <u>Is the constitutional amendment the only tactic being used to</u>
   <u>permit prayer in schools?</u>

A. No. Senator Jesse Helms of North Carolina and Representative
   Philip Crane of Illinois have introduced S. 1742, the "Voluntary School Prayer Act." Unlike previous nullification
   attempts which sought to change the Constitution itself, this
   legislation would take the entire issue of prayer in schools
   out of the federal courts' jurisdiction. If enacted, the bill
   would set an alarming precedent in limiting the courts' authority to interpret the Constitution. Although he expressed some
   concern for this danger, Attorney General William French Smith
   has said that the Justice Department would defend the constitutionality of this legislation if necessary.[7] (See "The
   Courts" section.)

   Like the constitutional amendment, the Helms-Crane bill would
   bolster the power of government at the expense of individual
   rights -- hardly in keeping with the conservative tradition.
   Parents would lose their right to sue in federal courts over
   issues of government encroachment of religious freedom. And
   school children would no longer have the freedom to pray as
   they wish in public schools; some government official or

bureaucrat would approve the official prayer for the state or locality and dictate when, where, and how it would be recited.

Q. How have different religious groups reacted to the proposed constitutional amendment?

A. Virtually every major Protestant denomination and Jewish organization has opposed mandatory school prayer for years. Religious leaders worry that government-mandated prayer would restrict religious freedom and trivialize prayer itself. In a formal statement condemning the proposed amendment, major religious groups said that "we are convinced that daily rote recitation of a school-sponsored prayer contributes nothing to the advancement of religion."[8]   Signatories included the Baptist Joint Committee on Public Affairs, the American Jewish Congress, the National Council of the Churches of Christ in the U.S.A., and the Union of American Hebrew Congregations.

At congressional hearings in 1980, then-president of the National Council of Churches Rev. M. William Howard, told legislators, "We believe prayer is too important, too sacred, too intimate to be scheduled or administered by government. It is the responsbility of the family, the home, the religious institution, not the public schools, to provide religious education and experience."[9]

The radical right was jubilant about the proposed constitutional amendment and vowed to press for its ratification. In a one-hour special broadcast on school prayer, aired nationally during primetime, Rev. Jerry Falwell described "how God was kicked out of our schools 20 years ago" and condemned "all the moral and spiritual darkness that is ruining our schools." Viewers were offered bumper stickers that read, "Kids Need to Pray."

Q. What's wrong with a nondenominational prayer?

A. Even though the religious content of school prayer may vary (from Bible readings to a bland blessing), the activity still constitutes a religious ritual mandated by the state. "Neither the fact that the prayer may be denominationally neutral nor the fact that its observance on the part of students is voluntary can serve to free it from the limitations of the Establishment Clause [of the First Amendment]..." wrote Supreme Court Justice Hugo Black in the Engel decision."[10]

Advocates of school prayer take it for granted that the prayer chosen for recitation will not offend their religious convictions. But if religious freedom means anything, everyone's religious convictions must be respected. Would ultra-fundamentalists consent to a "voluntary" reading from the Koran or the teachings of unconventional religious leaders like the Guru Marahaj Ji? No religious denomination has the right to use government to promote its sectarian dogmas, even if they are diluted, disguised, or nondenominational.

Q. Isn't a minute of silence for individual prayers an acceptable compromise?

A. Possibly. The Supreme Court has never ruled on the constitutionality of state laws that allow a period of silent meditation in public schools. Several states have enacted such laws, and the only federal court review of one, a Massachusetts statute, was found constitutional. A period of silent, individual prayer could be a workable solution to the school prayer impasse, but it is not without potential dangers. A deeply religious teacher might easily exploit the opportunity to informally introduce religious discussions into the classroom. Legislators could find, as well, that it is a short step from a period of silent meditation to a period of prayer recitation. In those states determined to make their children pray in school, the "period of silence" may be constitutionally valid but it could easily lead to abuses of students' religious liberties.

Q. But the ban on prayer in schools has fostered the moral decline of American youth! School prayer is essential to our national well-being.

A. Ultra-fundamentalists claim that prayer in public schools plays a decisive role in our national destiny but, of course, they can produce no evidence beyond their own ringing assertions. Rev. James Robison, the nationally syndicated televangelist, ascribes "the assassinations...acceleration of the Vietnam War, escalation of crime, disintegration of families, racial conflict, teenage pregnancies and venereal disease" to the Supreme Court's ban on mandatory school prayer."[11] Bill Bright, head of the Campus Crusade for Christ, told a House subcommittee that a series of "plagues" has afflicted America ever since compulsory prayer was banned:

> I believe that, after God so greatly blessed this nation, the virtual rejection of the Lord from the public schools which had been born in the cradle of the church was especially affronting to him, and that he began immediately to judge and chasten us both for what the action was and forwhat it symbolized about the spiritual direction of our country.[12]

Any participant in public policy debate must meet certain standards of evidence, no matter how religiously motivated the advocacy. By this measure, the "plagues" argument -- that the Court's decisions about school prayer caused national calamities -- fails miserably. Pre-1962 America, when school prayer had a free reign in the public schools, was not exactly an idyllic paradise free from wars, depressions, and social strife. It is also worth noting that at the time of the Court's decisions, only 11 percent of the school systems in the western United States (where Bright and Robison hail from) conducted Bible readings. Only about 2 to 3 percent of all schools conducted devotions.[13] In short, the Supreme Court was not banning an entrenched, widespread American tradition.

And what of the cause-and-effect that moral majoritarians claim for school prayer? Church historian Martin Marty found an effective comeback in humor:

> Why did everything go wrong when everything went wrong? I think that the divorce rate rose shortly after the invention of the Electronic Church. Check the coincidence of the dates. When born-again celebrities started writing born-again autobiographies, teen-age pregnancies increased; and when fundamentalists started writing sex manuals, the Vietnam War accelerated. Didn't you notice the cause-and-effect relation?[14]

Q. Rather than allow religious freedom, the Supreme Court has banned all religion from public schools!

A. This is one of the most common misunderstandings about the Supreme Court rulings. Mandatory religious exercises are prohibited in state facilities (like public schools), but not the study of religion or religious materials. For example, students may and do study the Bible for its ethical, literary, and historical qualities; they can and do study comparative religion; they can and do recite officially approved anthems with declarations of faith in a Deity; and so forth.

Neither the Bible nor moral instruction has been banned from
the schools. Nor is there a ban on students meeting voluntarily for religious reasons after hours. That was the gist of
the 1981 Supreme Court ruling in Widmar v. Vincent, involving
students at the University of Missouri who conducted services
in the state-financed campus facilities.[15]

Q. Congress opens its sessions with prayers, and our coins bear
   the phrase, "In God We Trust." What makes school prayer so
   objectionable?

A. The Supreme Court never intended "to declare unconstitutional
   every vestige...of cooperation or association between religion
   and government," wrote Justice Tom Clark in Schempp.[16] It
   simply wanted to set limits on how far government could intrude
   on an individual's religious freedoms. The Court drew the line
   at mandatory school prayer. The other public displays of
   religious sentiment -- invocations in Congress, slogans on
   coins, military chaplains -- are less intrusive on religious
   liberties and private beliefs of individuals, particularly
   children.

Q. Why shouldn't states or localities have the right to make their
   own decisions on school prayer?

A. Because constitutional freedoms are not subject to state veto.
   All Americans, regardless of their state of residence, are
   entitled to the rights and protections of the Constitution.
   Consider for a moment what state options with regard to school
   prayer could mean. Mormon prayers would likely be recited in
   Salt Lake City; "Hail Marys" would be recited in Baltimore;
   Jewish prayers in Skokie, Illinois; and Baptist prayers in
   Lynchburg, Virginia. The religious minorities in each of these
   cities would obviously be offended by the tyranny of the
   majority religion. Moreover, they would resent and criticize
   the majority religion for its enforced creed. Rather than
   encourage reverence and respect, mandatory school prayer could
   easily provoke hostility toward the majority religion.

QUOTABLE QUOTES

"If we are to stem the tide of lawlessness, drug addiction, and sexual perversion which adversely affect academic performance, we must start with putting God back into our school systems."

> -- Ed McAteer, president of the Religious Roundtable, Family Protection Report, June 1980

"We're in favor of the [constitutional amendment for school prayer] because of its symbolic importance, because it does say to the school children that we recognize the importance of meditation, of communication between a created individual and a creator."

> -- William Billings, president of the National Christian Action Coalition, Education Week, May 12, 1982

"[I]f we ever opened a Moral Majority meeting with prayer, silent or otherwise, we would disintegrate."

> -- Rev. Jerry Falwell, explaining that prayer would offend the ecumenical membership of Moral Majority, Inc., at a meeting of the Religion Newswriters Association, New Orleans, June 12, 1982

"The question cannot be avoided: Whose prayer is it? And all too often it will be either the prayer form of the majority (imposed on the minorities) or a nearly meaningless prayer belonging to no historic tradition. In the latter case, the exercise is likely to be offensive to devout believers of all faiths."

> -- Rev. M. William Howard,
> former president of the
> National Council of Churches

"We believe the purpose of prayer is to praise and petition God, not to serve the secular purpose of creating a moral or ethical atmosphere for public school children."

> -- Rev. John Houck, Lutheran
> Council in the U.S.A.

"It is proper to take alarm at the first experiment on our liberties....Who does not see that the same authority which can establish Christianity, in exclusion of all other Religions, may establish with the same ease any particular sect of Christians, in exclusion of all other sects?"

> -- James Madison,
> The Federalist Papers

"[T]he question is: is public-school prayer apt to serve authentic religion, or is it apt to be mere attitudinizing, a thin gruel of vague religious vocabulary?...According to some polls, more Americans favor prayers in schools than regularly pray in church. Supermarkets sell processed cheese and instant mashed potatoes, so many Americans must like bland substitutes for the real thing. But it is one thing for the nation's palate to tolerate frozen waffles; it is another and more serious thing for the nation's soul to be satisfied with add-water-and-stir religiosity. When government acts as liturgist for a pluralistic society, the result is bound to be a puree that is tasteless, in several senses."

> -- George F. Will, Newsweek,
> June 7, 1982

Sir Thomas More: "What would you do? Cut a great road through
                   the law to get the Devil?"

       Roper: "I'd cut down every law...to do that!"

       More: "Oh, and when the last law was down, and the
                   Devil turned round on you -- where would you
                   hide, Roper, the laws all being flat? This
                   country's planted thick with laws from coast
                   to coast -- man's laws, not God's -- and if
                   you cut them down -- and you're just the man
                   to do it -- do you really think you could
                   stand upright in the winds that would blow?
                   Yes, I'd give the Devil benefit of the law,
                   for my own safety's sake."

                             -- Robert Bolt, in
                                A Man for All Seasons

"Isn't it ironic that folks who quake at the danger of 'secular
humanism' are the very ones pushing for prayer in the public
schools, an ultimate secularization."

                             -- Rev. James M. Dunn,
                                Executive Director,
                                Baptist Joint Committee
                                on Public Affairs

"The best solution is to leave a child's religious instruction
where it belongs, in the home, in the church, in the temple, in
his mind and heart. And when a child learns what prayer is all
about, get him to read Matthew 6:5-8. The passage contains
some marvelously sound advice."

                             -- James J. Kilpatrick,
                                The Washington Post,
                                December 10, 1981

"And when you pray, you must not be like the hypocrites; for
they love to stand and pray in the synogogues and at the street
corners, that they may be seen by men. Truly, I say to you,
they have their reward. But when you pray, go into your room
and shut the door and pray to your Father who is in secret...."

-- Matthew 6:5-6

"Prayer is too important and too private a matter to involve
the government. The Bill of Rights guarantees our freedom of
religion and our freedom from a government that promotes an
established religion. School prayer, when sanctioned by law,
ceases to be voluntary. It is government-mandated religion.
The amendment abridging Americans' sacred First Amendment
rights should not be adopted. It is government compulsion and
we oppose it."

-- Anthony T. Podesta, President,
PEOPLE FOR THE AMERICAN WAY,
May 6, 1982

NOTES: SCHOOL PRAYER

1.   George F. Will, "Opposing Prefab Prayer," Newsweek, June 7, 1982.

2.   Engel v. Vitale, 370 U.S. 421 (1962), Abington v. Schempp, 374 U.S. 203 (1963) and Murray v. Curlett, 374 U.S. 203 (1963).

3.   Engel v. Vitale, at p. 431.

4.   Lou Cannon, "Hill Gets Reagan's Prayer Amendment," The Washington Post, May 18, 1982.

5.   Ibid.

6.   George F. Will, op. cit.

7.   Letter from Attorney General William French Smith to Senator Strom Thurmond, Chairman of the Senate Judiciary Committee, May 6, 1982.

8.   "Statement on Prayer in the Public Schools," May 6, 1982, signed by the American Jewish Congress, the Baptist Joint Committee on Public Affairs, the National Coalition for Public Education and Religious Liberty (PEARL), the National Council of Churches of Christ in the U.S.A., the National Jewish Community Relations Advisory Council, the Synagogue Council of America, and the Union of American Hebrew Congregations.

9.   "Prayer in Public Schools and Buildings -- Federal Court Jurisdiction," Hearings before the House Subcommittee on Courts, Civil Liberties, and the Administration of Justice, [Serial No. 63] July 29, 30, August 19, 21, and September 9, 1980. Rev. Howard has also explained his misgivings about prayer in public schools in a discussion paper for PEOPLE FOR THE AMERICAN WAY, "Whose Prayer? How the School Prayer Amendment Attacks Religious Liberty" (available upon request).

10.   Engel v. Vitale, at p. 430.

11.   House subcommittee hearings, op. cit.

12. Ibid.

13. Richard B. Dierenfield, <u>Religion in American Public
     Schools</u> (Public Affairs Press, 1962), p. 115, cited in
     Martin Marty, "Things Fall Apart," <u>The Christian Century</u>,
     September 10-17, 1980.

14. Martin Marty, "Things Fall Apart," <u>The Christian Century</u>,
     September 10-17, 1980.

15. <u>Widner v. Vincent</u>, Supreme Court of the United States, No.
     80-689, December 8, 1981.

16. <u>Abingdon v. Schempp</u>, op. cit. at p. 225.

FURTHER READING: SCHOOL PRAYER

Americans United for Separation of Church and State, "Why Do
     Religious Bodies Oppose Government Mandated Prayers
     in Public Schools: A Selection of Statements by Some
     of the Major Religious Bodies in the United States."

------ , "Religion in the Public Schools," C. Stanley Lowell
     (Available from 8120 Fenton Street, Silver Spring, MD
     20910).

Baptist Joint Committee on Public Affairs, "Religion in the
     Public School Classroom" (Brochure available from
     200 Maryland Avenue, N.E., Washington, D.C. 20002).

House Judiciary Committee hearings, "Prayer in Public Schools
     and Buildings -- Federal Court Jurisdiction," [Serial
     No. 63] July 29, 30, August 19, 21, and September 9,
     1980.

Howard, Rev. M. William, PEOPLE FOR THE AMERICAN WAY, "Whose
     Prayer? How the School Prayer Amendment Attacks
     Religious Liberty" (Available upon request).

Liberty magazine, November/December 1981.

Supreme Court cases: Engel v. Vitale, 370 U.S. 421 (1962)
                      Abington v. Schempp, 374 U.S. 203 (1963)
                      Murray v. Curlett, 374 U.S. 203 (1963)

RADICAL RIGHT LITERATURE

Dugan, Robert, Jr., "New Hope for School Prayer," Conservative
     Digest, May/June 1980, p. 32.

Leadership Foundation, "How to Bring God Back to America's
     Schools," brochure (Available from The Leadership
     Foundation, 7945 MacArthur Blvd., Cabin John, MD
     20818).

Warren, Rita, and Dick Schneider, Mom, They Won't Let Us
     Pray... (Lincoln, Virginia: Chosen Books, 1975).

Public Policy
Questions

The radical right has demonstrated a special talent for simplifying and exploiting complex public policy issues. Much of its success stems from its skill in defining issues with emotional, religious imagery. The Equal Rights Amendment, for example, is not debated on its merits as a simple guarantee of legal equality but on deceptive emotional grounds that cast it as a satanic anti-Christian attack on "traditional" gender roles. Similarly, the authority of the federal courts to interpret the constitutionality of laws -- a simple fact of our system of government -- is blasted by the radical right as a special form of "secular humanist" tyranny.

There are five major public policy issues -- beyond education -- that radical right groups have transformed into emotional battlefields:

- o The "Pro-Family" Movement. Leaders of this broad-based campaign believe that "traditional" family values can only be restored by limiting the rights of women, children, and gays.

- o The Courts. This drive to strip the federal courts of authority to deal with certain issues could spark a constitutional crisis.

- o The Media. The Coalition for Better Television wants to make TV reflect ultra-fundamentalist not "secular supremacist" values.

- o Foreign and Military Policy. Ultra-fundamentalists believe the Bible gives clear guidance in support of bellicose policies.

o <u>Economics</u>. The Bible holds the answers to contemporary
  macro-economic problems, claims the radical religious
  right.

As in their various education crusades, moral authoritarians
want government policies to endorse their religious dogmas.
Paul Weyrich, the catalyst of so many radical right ventures,
explains it best:

> We are talking about Christianizing America. We are
> talking about simply spreading the gospel in a political
> context. We are in this for the long haul. If we really
> want to turn America around, then we're going to have to
> turn around the legislature. And the only way we can do
> that is for people to be informed and, frankly outraged,
> at what is going on in the nation's capital. Therefore,
> you have to be able to put things in, if you will,
> simplistic, polemical terms. Ultimately, everything can
> be reduced to right and wrong. Everything.

The radical right has taken Weyrich's advice to heart, debasing
serious policymaking into a simple-minded quest for "moral"
vindication. Issues that truly deserve more attention, such as
the stability of the family, the quality of TV programming, and
economic insecurity, are treated through symbolic nostrums
rather than serious reforms. What is perhaps most disturbing
is the radical right's careless disregard for principles that
should govern our public life -- mutual respect and civility,
belief in constitutional processes, and the separation of
church and state.

THE "PRO-FAMILY" MOVEMENT

Q. What is the "pro-family" movement?

A. It is a network of moral authoritarian groups that is pressing
for laws, regulations, and local policies to bolster the
"traditional American family." To a great extent, "pro-family"
activists consider their crusade a backlash against the women's
movement and the values it stands for: equal rights under the
law, reproductive rights, and an end to demeaning attitudes
toward women. "Pro-family" leaders instead call for a return
to "traditional" gender roles for men and women and actively
oppose equal legal protections for women and for homosexuals.
Charging that government and school systems are interfering
with the rearing of children, moral authoritarians work strenu-
ously on behalf of what they call "parents' rights."

By far the most emotional and vigorously fought "pro-family"
campaigns are waged against:

   o the right of women to equality under the law, set forth
      in the Equal Rights Amendment;

   o the right of women to choose whether to terminate their
      pregnancies, as guaranteed by the Supreme Court's 1973
      decision on abortion; and

   o equal civil rights for homosexuals.

The "pro-family" movement also sees numerous threats to "the
family" in public education. Its leaders accuse the schools of
eroding the morality of children by teaching evolution and sex
education, using "humanist" textbooks, and not conducting
mandatory religious devotions.

Q. What do these issues have to do with "the family"?

A. That's the point -- they don't. But the "pro-family" movement
has skillfully manipulated emotional symbols like "the family"
to attract political support. The image of children, too, is
frequently used by moral authoritarians to enlist support for
marginally related issues.

Ultra-fundamentalists use unassailable themes like the family
as "hostages" that they claim will be hurt if their political
remedies are not adopted. For example, Phyllis Schlafly warns
that the traditional American family will wither away if the
ERA is passed: "A direct ramification of national ratification
of ERA would be that women will eventually stop having
children."[1] Equal rights for homosexuals are dangerous,
argues Jerry Falwell, because, "Remember, homosexuals do not
reproduce! They recruit! And many of them are out after my
children and your children."[2]

In the one area where children's welfare is indeed at stake --
public education -- ultra-fundamentalists greatly overstate its
shortcomings. Rev. Tim LaHaye calls modern public education
"the most dangerous single force in a child's life: religiously, sexually, economically, patriotically, and physically."[3] (See Part II, "Education".) Or, alternatively, ultra-
fundamentalists blame unlikely villains (such as the teaching
of evolution) for the problems that afflict public education
today. On issues that do involve women or children, such as
ERA and child abuse laws, they grossly misinterpret and distort
the actual consequences of the policies.

Q. Who are the leading "pro-family" leaders and organizations?

A. The movement does not always march together in lockstep because
its leaders and groups each operate in their own separate uni-
verses. Even so, they generally work closely together on an ad
hoc basis to trade information, mobilize grassroots support, or
lobby a particular bill. The most visible and effective "pro-
family" leaders include:

> o Phyllis Schlafly, the queen mother of the "pro-family"
> movement. Schlafly and her group, the Eagle Forum, are
> largely responsible for defeating the Equal Rights
> Amendment. The Eagle Forum deals with the full array of
> "family" issues, but plans to step up its fight against

"objectionable" textbooks, library books, and school
curricula. Schlafly's "Stop ERA" activists are
expected to rally behind her "Stop Textbook Censorship
Committee."

o Tim and Beverly LaHaye, the energetic authors and
  lecturers. The LaHayes oversee a small empire of "pro-
  family" enterprises -- seminars, radio and TV shows,
  publications, and organizations. They both tour the
  country conducting Family Life Seminars, their family
  counseling program. Tim LaHaye is a luminary in ultra-
  fundamentalist circles as a board member of Moral
  Majority, Inc. He is also the founder of Christian
  Heritage College in San Diego and author of the twin
  treatises, The Battle for the Mind and The Battle
  for the Family, which advise how to live a "Christian"
  life in a "humanist" world.

  For her part, Beverly LaHaye is president of Concerned
  Women for America, a group of 162,000 women who seek a
  moral regeneration in America through "pro-family"
  policies. She also is a board member of the Coalition
  for Better Television.

o Connaught (Connie) Marshner, the movement's top strat-
  egist on Capitol Hill and part of Paul Weyrich's inner
  circle. Marshner heads the Library Court group, an
  informal coalition of "pro-family" leaders who meet
  weekly to plan lobbying tactics on Capitol Hill.
  She is the editor of Family Protection Report and the
  author of Blackboard Tyranny. Conservative Digest has
  described Marshner as the "pivot person in Washington,
  D.C., for the pro-family movement." Marshner was
  appointed in 1982 to the President's Advisory Panel on
  Financing Elementary and Secondary Education.

o Onalee McGraw, an education consultant to the Heritage
  Foundation and editor of the Education Update newsletter. McGraw has authored numerous "pro-family"
  monographs and is one of the movement's leading
  theorists.

o Susan Phillips, a top consultant at the Department of
  Education. Phillips joined the government one month
  after publishing an article in Conservative Digest in

April 1982 about federal funding to "left-leaning
groups" (which include the American Bar Association and
the National Retired Teachers Association). Phillips,
the sister of Howard Phillips, reviews contracts
and grant procedures for the Department of Education.

The "pro-family" movement has many friends in high places in
government. JoAnn Gasper, who edited The Right Woman newsletter for a large and loyal readership, now makes family
policy as deputy assistant secretary for social services policy
at the U.S. Department of Health and Human Services (DHHS).
Also at DHHS is Marjory Mecklenburg, an anti-abortion activist
who now heads the Office of Adolescent Pregnancy Programs.

"Pro-family" activists have a sympathetic ear in government at
the Department of Education as well. Robert Billings, the
Moral Majority's first executive director, is now the chief
liaison officer for the department's ten regional offices. [4]
Dr. C. Everett Koop, a pediatric surgeon appointed U.S. Surgeon
General in 1981, is another influential government offical
whose views, especially on abortion, are applauded by the
"pro-family" movement. [5]

In Congress, many senators and representatives generally
support the "pro-family" agenda. They include Senators Jake
Garn (Utah), Orrin Hatch (Utah), Jesse Helms (North Carolina),
Gordon Humphrey (New Hampshire), Paul Laxalt (Nevada), Roger
Jepsen (Iowa), and Jeremiah Denton (Alabama). In the House,
"pro-family" advocates include Albert Lee Smith (Alabama), Phil
Crane (Illinois), Larry McDonald (Georgia), Henry Hyde (Illi-
nois), Jim Jeffries (Kansas), Bob Walker (Pennsylvania), and
Bob Dornan (California). [6]

Q. What does the "pro-family" movement mean when it talks about
   the "traditional family"?

A. The "reforms" that the "pro-family" movement are seeking are
   intended to bolster a romantic, nostalgic vision of the family
   typified by "Father Knows Best" -- with an authoritarian twist.
   The husband reigns supreme in marriage and the family, the wife
   is submissive and does not work outside the home, and children
   are considered objects of authoritarian discipline and control.
   According to many ultra-fundamentalists, this model derives
   from the Bible; the chain of command runs from God to the
   husband, who in turn has complete authority over his wife and

children. Rus Walton of the Plymouth Rock Foundation laments
the disruptions that the women's rights movement has supposedly
inflicted on the family:

> The real tragedy of the so-called women's rights
> movement is that it fails to restore women to their
> rightful place of authority beside men and seeks to
> put them in competition against men; thus, rather than
> completion, there is conflict.[7]

Any government program, law, or regulation that affects the
"divinely ordained" family arrangement, say ultra-fundamentalists, is a "humanist" intrusion on a family's religious
beliefs and an immoral influence. William Billings, executive
director of the National Christian Action Coalition, sees a
dizzying array of threats to the family:

> Today's society is characterized by 'planned parent-
> hood,' the pill, no-fault divorce, open marriages,
> 'gay rights,' 'palimony,' test-tube babies, women's
> liberation, children's liberation, unisex, day care
> centers, child advocates, and abortion on demand.
> A man is no longer responsible for his family; a
> woman need not honor and obey her husband. God has
> been kicked out, and humanism enthroned.[8]

Paul Weyrich, whose role in founding New Right groups makes him
a preeminent "pro-family" crusader, sees more sinister implications in current social trends. "[F]rom our point of view,
this is really the most significant battle of the age-old
conflict between good and evil, between the forces of God and
forces against God, that we have seen in our country." He
continues:

> We see the anti-family movement as an attempt to prevent
> souls from reaching eternal salvation, and as such we
> feel not just a political commitment to change this
> situation, but a moral and, if you will, a religious
> commitment to battle these forces. I don't mean to be
> simplistic about it, but there is no other way to view
> what is happening, especially if you read, believe in
> and understand Holy Scripture. And I think any other
> interpretation of it misses the point. Among the anti-
> family forces are hard-core socialists who see it as a
> means by which they can attain greater state control.

One of the Communists' chief objectives has always been to break down the traditional family....[9]

In the same vein, Phyllis Schlafly sees a conspiratorial plot by feminists and the federal government to destroy the family. When the government proposed a new benefits formula for Social Security, Schlafly charged, "The Women's Lib Movement and the Federal Bureaucrats have joined in a plan to eliminate the traditional family from our society by making economic survival impossible for the traditional one-income couple where the wife is the homemaker and the husband is the breadwinner."[10]

WOMEN'S RIGHTS

Fueling the "pro-family" crusade is a conviction that women must play a traditional role in marriage and society: diligent homemaker, mandatory mother, and submissive, obedient wife. The very foundations of our society rest upon this ideal for women, says the radical religious right. Equal rights? Career choices? Individual autonomy? These goals are dismissed as unnecessary -- indeed, harmful -- options that erode family stability and cause personal grief. They are often condemned as un-Christian and anti-Biblical. On that basis, the "pro-family" movement would like to restrict the legal rights and social options available to women.

Consider what some leading moral authoritarians have to say about the proper role of men and women in the family:

o Phyllis Schlafly: "I'm a Christian and all good Christians believe that women are special and that God made men to take care of women, to protect them and go to war for them, to help them with their jackets and make sure nobody else messes with them."[11]

o Televangelist James Robison: "Women have great strength, but they are strengths to help the man. A woman's primary purpose in life and marriage is to help her husband succeed, to help him be all God

wants him to be. If a man leads well, a woman is glad
to follow."[12]

o Dr. Charles Stanley, board member of Moral Majority,
  Inc.: "There is a vicious all-out Satanic attack upon
  the American home -- the whole concept of anti-submission and independence....When two people in the family
  become absolutely legally equal, there is no head; both
  become independent of each other and love is
  destroyed."[13]

o Howard Phillips, national director of the Conservative
  Caucus: "It has been a conscious policy of government to
  liberate the wife from the leadership of the husband and
  thus break up the family unit as a unit of government...
  It used to be that in recognition of the family as the
  basic unit of society, we had one family, one vote. And
  we have seen the trend instead to have one person, one
  vote."[14]

o Rev. Pat Robertson, televangelist and head of the
  Christian Broadcasting Network: "I know this is painful
  for the ladies to hear, but if you get married you have
  accepted the headship of a man, your husband....Christ
  is head of the household, and the husband's the head of
  the wife and that's just the way it is....This is the
  way the Bible sets it up."[15]

Everyone is entitled to fashion voluntarily their marriage and
family relationships as they see fit, of course, within laws
that protect the rights of individuals. But moral authoritarians want to legislate their "Christian" ideals of family life
for all Americans, at the expense of individual choice and
equal legal rights. For example, if married couples decide not
to have children, Phyllis Schlafly would like the federal
government to deny them Social Security: "If people decide not
to have children, they should be forced to sign a piece of
paper saying that they will forfeit Social Security benefits.
Even if they have worked all their lives. If they're not
willing to have children...then they shouldn't be entitled to
Social Security."[16]

Q. In what areas does the "pro-family" movement oppose nontraditional rights for women?

A. It is such a multi-pronged attack that it is difficult to
   catalogue the full range of initiatives. But the primary
   vehicles for the attack are Phyllis Schlafly's Stop-ERA drive;
   the Human Life Amendment and other measures that would outlaw
   abortion; and the Family Protection Act.

   The Equal Rights Amendment. The crusade against the ERA has
   wound down since the ERA's defeat in June 1982. Still, the
   battle will continue now that the ERA has been re-introduced.
   So too will misinterpretations about what equal rights means.
   Schlafly argues that the "fundamental error" of ERA "is that it
   will mandate the gender-free, rigid, absolute equality of
   treatment of men and women...."[17] Anti-ERA activists play
   upon fears of an androgynous, unisex society rather than
   address the real issue of equal legal rights for women. Thus,
   Beverly LaHaye charges that if the ERA is ratified, "a few of
   the results would be: 1) Complete integration of the sexes....
   2) Open homosexuality.... and 3) Military service and combat
   duty would be shared equally...."[18]

   Jerry Falwell makes the same threat: "We fear it [ERA] might
   sanction homosexual marriages. We do not believe women belong
   in...the NFL [National Football League]. We believe in the
   superiority of women."[19] He makes the further accusation,
   "I believe the women's liberation movement is mainly staffed
   by a large group of frustrated failures, many of them lesbians,
   and all of them anti-biblical."[20]

   Although the "pro-family" movement sometimes claims to support
   equal rights for women, it refuses to support the ERA. Schlafly
   says the ERA simply duplicates existing federal laws that
   ensure equal rights for women, and thus is unnecessary. Yet
   Schlafly and "pro-family" groups at the same time are trying to
   weaken these very laws. For instance, they want to prevent the
   federal government from protecting the equal rights of girls to
   participate in sports programs and vocational training courses
   that teach high-paying job skills.

   Schlafly's crusade, unable to logically deny a principle as
   basic as equal rights, instead appeals to sexual anxiety.
   Schlafly is especially adept at preying upon such fears: "The
   devil is using one word -- sex -- to take away the rights of

wives and give them to homosexuals. The ERA doesn't give women
rights. It puts sex into the Constitution."[21]

The Abortion Controversy. An equally emotional issue is the
drive to overturn the Supreme Court's 1973 decision establishing the right of women to choose to end their pregnancies. The
issue has polarized much of American society and has become a
symbolic battle for other concerns as well. PEOPLE FOR THE
AMERICAN WAY has limited its work on this divisive issue to the
schemes introduced in the Congress to strip away the jurisdiction of the federal courts from hearing abortion and other
constitutional rights cases.

Beyond court-stripping, however, is the brutal, degrading level
of debate conducted by many moral authoritarians. Two examples:

> o Catholics United for Life: "Please help us talk
>   people out of supporting these murderers for I
>   promise you that even if abortion is made illegal
>   tomorrow, key abortion figures will someday be hunted
>   down like Nazi war criminals and brought to justice for
>   crimes against humanity."[22]
>
> o The Religious Roundtable: "The judgment of God will
>   surely fall on a nation which allows the mass murder
>   of millions of pre-born human beings. For this horrible
>   sin America must reckon with the Holy and Just God of
>   this Universe. Every godly citizen should use his
>   influence to help put a stop to this pervasive curse in
>   our society."[23]

As a uniquely emotional issue, the abortion controversy joins
together diverse radical right factions and provides a basis
for new crusades. For example, the American Life Lobby, headed
by Judie Brown, alerted its members through a special bulletin
(August 10, 1981) that it was "pro-life" to support a bill that
would eliminate the Legal Services Corporation. Brown's
husband, Paul Brown, is executive director of the Life Amendment Political Action Committee.

The abortion issue is frequently used as a vehicle for
unrelated political concerns. The National Pro-Life Political
Action Committee, for example, in 1982 launched a major attack
on Ted Wilson, the mayor of Salt Lake City who was challenging
the incumbent senator, Orrin Hatch. Pro-Life PAC targeted

Wilson not because of his views on abortion -- he is "pro-life" -- but because of his "liberal" views on diverse political issues. Said Peter B. Gemma, Jr., executive director of Pro-Life PAC, "We discovered that a significant number of Utah voters are not aware of the wide philosophical differences between Hatch and Wilson. We plan to correct these misconceptions. Wilson's thinly disguised liberalism will be his Achilles' heel."[24] Why would an anti-abortion PAC try to defeat an anti-abortion candidate? Because Pro-Life PAC wants to use the abortion issue, through which it raised $240,000 in 1981, to advance other ideological concerns.

The Family Protection Act. This proposed legislation brings together in one bill the broadest range of "pro-family" initiatives. Reportedly drafted by Connie Marshner of the Library Court, the bill, S. 1378, starts with the premise that "certain Government policies have....undermined and diminished the viability of the American family." It then sets forth some 31 often dubious and regressive remedies.[24] The bill was originally introduced by Sen. Paul Laxalt (R-Nevada) in 1980 but was re-introduced in 1981 by Roger Jepsen of Iowa and Representative Albert Lee Smith of Alabama, and co-sponsored by Senators Laxalt, Garn and Hatch. The FPA would:

o weaken efforts to prevent wife and child abuse;

o withhold federal funds to purchase public school text-books that fail to "promote the role of women as it has been historically understood";

o permit schools to discriminate against girls in sports and vocational education;

o prohibit the Legal Services Corporation from helping poor women assert their rights in matters of alimony, child support, custody of children and other issues arising out of a divorce;

o permit government-mandated prayer in public schools.

Many of these provisions are also being pushed in separate bills both in Congress and state legislatures. The FPA constitutes the single most comprehensive agenda of the "pro-family" movement. As legislation and a political/cultural symbol, it serves as an inspirational model for the entire movement.

Q. Why do many religious authoritarians attack protections for
   battered women and sexually harassed workers?

A. They regard government-funded shelters for battered women and
   laws protecting abused wives as unnecessary government interference in family affairs. Claiming the Bible gives husbands
   complete authority over their wives, ultra-fundamentalists
   criticize attempts by the state to protect the individual
   rights of a woman in marriage.

   JoAnn Gasper, the former editor of The Right Woman newsletter
   and now deputy assistant secretary for social services policy
   at the Department of Health and Human Services, trivializes the
   very concept of domestic violence. (There are 2.2 million
   reported cases of spouse abuse each year.)[26] Gasper writes
   that it can mean "any form of 'belittling' or 'teasing' or
   'failure to provide warmth' (whatever that may be -- I guess if
   you don't set the electric blanket high enough in the winter)
   or 'excessive yelling.'"[27]

   Sexual harassment is also a problem that most moral authoritarians see no need for government to address. In 1981,
   Senator Orrin Hatch of Utah held hearings to question the value
   of regulations issued by the Equal Employment Opportunity
   Commission to curb sexual harassment in the workplace.[28] In
   her testimony, Phyllis Schlafly asserted that "sexual harassment on the job is not a problem for the virtuous woman, except
   in the rarest of cases."[29] She told the members of the
   Senate Labor Committee, "When a woman walks across the room,
   she speaks with a universal body language that most men
   intuitively understand. Men hardly ever ask sexual favors of
   women from whom the certain answer is 'no.'"

Q. Why do religious authoritarians also want to weaken child abuse
   laws?

A. They claim that such laws are an intrusion of government into
   the family, parents' rights, and the divine authority of a
   husband over his wife and children. In 1981, Moral Majority,
   Inc., of Indiana successfully weakened the state's child abuse
   law.[30] The "reform" was needed, according to Greg Dixon,
   head of the state chapter and national secretary of Moral
   Majority, Inc., because the Bible instructs parents to whip
   their children with a rod. "I am advocating whipping [child-
   ren]. That's a Bible doctrine with fundamentalists....We have

always recognized this [child abuse] law as being a very insidious thing....I said when the bill was passed it would create gestapo agencies all over the state...."[31]   Dixon also cites the property rights of parents as a justification for whipping children: "The state says it owns the child," Dixon said.   "Our position is the parents own the children."[32]   As for the severity of punishment that should be inflicted, Dixon explained, "If you haven't left any marks, you probably haven't whipped your children."[33]

The Mississippi chapter of Moral Majority, Inc., has used the child abuse issue as part of its fundraising effort. A direct mail letter lamented the case of "Timmy," a nine-year-old schoolboy from Terre Haute, Indiana, who allegedly had been seized by the state welfare department without the knowledge of his parents. A local reporter soon discovered that "Timmy's" case was a composite of several cases and that documentation did not substantiate the letter's claims. Karl Falster, the chapter's executive director, nonetheless asserts that there is a "socialistic, communistic and demonically motivated scheme" in the state's welfare department to transform Mississippi children into wards of the state.[34]

Some 400 Mississippi ultra-fundamentalist preachers protested on behalf of Brother Lester Roloff, who was charged with gross physical abuse, negligence and violation of children's rights in his Texas and Mississippi child-care homes. Rev. Greg Dixon of the Indiana Moral Majority came to lend his support. During his trial, Roloff defended himself, "Better a pink bottom than a black soul....We whip 'em with love, and we weep with 'em, and they love us for it."[35]

In his home state, Dixon is so determined to impose his "Christian" notions of child-rearing on other Americans that he demanded that Senator Richard Lugar of Indiana stop distributing a free government booklet, "Your Child From One to Six," which Lugar routinely sent to expectant parents and day care centers. Dixon decried the booklet's advice not to discipline children by spanking or hitting. "That is totally contrary to the scriptures. Everyone is born a sinner."[36] Following Dixon's attack, Senator Lugar's office stopped giving out the booklet except on request.

Strict corporal punishment is the rule in more than 4,500 schools that use the curriculum program provided by Accelerated

Christian Education, Inc. (Jerry Falwell has praised ACE's founder, Rev. Donald Howard, as "the driving force in Christian education today.") Rev. Howard advocates corporal punishment because "...if the child does wrong deliberately and you produce pain in his body and the pain is related to disobedience, then he develops a respect for obedience."[37]

HOMOSEXUAL RIGHTS

To some Americans homosexuality is a sin; to others it is a sickness; to others it is simply a matter of preference. But, the debate about homosexuality should be irrelevant when it comes to constitutional rights; all Americans are entitled to equal protection under the law.

For the radical right, the gay rights movement is considered one of the foremost evils of our time. In sermons and fund-raising letters, gays are said to be engaged in a vast conspiracy to corrupt the morals of American youth and take over the levers of American society. To fight homosexuality, ultra-fundamentalists want to use government to punish "sinners" -- a dangerous concept that should concern all Americans, regardless of their view of homosexuality.

Q. Why do religious authoritarians oppose equal civil rights for homosexuals?

A. Leaders of the radical right see the very existence of homosexuals as a dark menace to American family life, the morals of children, and our national prestige. They complain that guaranteeing equal rights for gays would give the approval of government to a sinful lifestyle. We disagree. Just as the doctrine of church/state separation does not constitute an endorsement of all the religious groups it protects, neither does protection of the rights of homosexuals constitute advocacy of homosexuality. It is simply a civil rights guarantee.

Numerous religious, educational, and professional groups
formally support gay rights. These include the American
Psychiatric Association, the National Education Association,
the American Jewish Congress, and the American Public Health
Association. Some religious denominations and groups that
oppose discrimination based on sexual orientation include the
National Council of Churches, the United Methodist Church, and
the Lutheran Church in America. The statement by the U.S.
National Council of Catholic Bishops is representative of these
groups' attitude: "Homosexuals, like everyone else, should not
suffer from prejudice against their basic human rights. They
have a right to respect, friendship and justice."[38]

Q. What kind of accusations do ultra-fundamentalist leaders make
against homosexuals?

A. Many leaders of the radical religious right have found that
attacking gays is a useful way to raise money and unite their
followers against a scapegoat. Gays are blamed for any decline
in our national greatness, family stability, and the character
of youth. Here is a sampling of some of the charges made by
leading moral monopolists against homosexuals:

> o Televangelist James Robison: "As far as I'm concerned,
> a homosexual is in the same class with a rapist, a bank
> robber, or a murderer."[39]
>
> and: "This past summer [1980], homosexual perverts
> consolidated their power by organizing to control the
> 97th Congress just elected. As a result, we Christians
> may lose our right to preach Christ in freedom; but gays
> will have won the right to seduce our children."[40]
>
> o Rev. Jerry Falwell: "Courts and the laws of our land
> will come to officially legitimatize [sic] perversion
> and perverted acts and the very foundations of moral
> principle upon which this great nation was established
> may soon crumble."[41]
>
> o Dean Wycoff, former head of the Santa Clara County
> chapter of Moral Majority, Inc.: "I agree with capital
> punishment and I believe homosexuality is one of those
> that could be coupled with murder and other sins....It
> would be the government that sits upon this land who
> would be executing the homosexuals."[42]

Homophobia is a pervasive theme in ultra-fundamentalist literature. The underlying premise is that anyone who sins, according to their religious dogma, is not entitled to equal
protection under the law. This authoritarian, mean-spirited
campaign adds to the climate of intolerance and hate in America.
It also has serious personal consequences for men and women who
find themselves victimized at work and in their community.

Q. Some ultra-fundamentalists claim they do not oppose equal
   rights for gays, they just oppose "special rights and
   privileges" for them.

A. Many homophobic leaders like Jerry Falwell have toned down
   their strident attacks on gays in order to gain mainstream
   respectability. Before some audiences they will make moderate
   statements -- while continuing to preach intolerance to their
   own followers. As a result, their public remarks have become
   schizophrenic and contradictory.

   Cal Thomas, communications director for Moral Majority, Inc.,
   and Tim LaHaye, a board member, have both said they oppose
   "witch hunts" against gays.[43] Thomas even said that his
   organization's campaign against homosexuality "does not mean
   that we hate homosexuals or are trying to lock them back in the
   closet or deprive them of the normal civil rights that are
   enjoyed by every other American."[44] The Moral Majority
   Report, echoing this claim, has stated, "While we believe that
   homosexuality is a moral perversion, we are committed to
   guaranteeing the civil rights of homosexuals. We do oppose the
   efforts of homosexuals to obtain special privileges as a
   'bona fide minority'...."[45] Similarly, Falwell has tried to
   temper his harsh remarks by saying, "I love homosexuals as
   souls for whom Christ died, I love homosexuals, but I must hate
   their sin."[46]

   These claims of tolerance are contradicted, however, by many
   continuing attacks. Falwell recently told the Houston
   Chronicle, "I am against giving homosexuals bona fide minority
   status or even recognizing their right to decide who is going
   to rule in the political process."[47] He later told attendees
   at the James Robison Bible Conference that candidates who seek
   support from homosexuals "should be disbarred from running for
   any office."[48] In a direct mail letter that warns of a
   dangerous homosexual onslaught, Falwell's professed love for
   gays is hard to find. "We must stop the homosexuals dead in

their tracks -- before they get one step further towards
warping the minds of our youth!...The enemy is in our camp!
And they are after our most prized possession -- our
children!"[49] Moral Majority, Inc., has even initiated "a
project to investigate, document and expose the gay conspiracy," and has issued a "Special Report" which "exposes" efforts
by gays "to win over our children and to destroy respect and
support for the traditional American family."[50]

Equal civil rights for gays does not give them any "special
privileges." Anti-discrimination bills do not impose any
additional hardships on employers or landlords, nor do they
impose quotas or affirmative action requirements. They would
simply give homosexuals the same legal protections that most
Americans take for granted.

Q. Gay teachers are a threat to school children.

A. The issue that should concern parents is sexual misconduct of
teachers, not their sexual orientation. Under present laws,
teachers can already be dismissed for improper sexual behavior.
Gay rights legislation would not change this fact. At House
hearings for a bill that would prohibit job discrimination
against gays, Dr. Martin Weinberg, director of the Institute
for Sex Research in Bloomington, Indiana, told legislators:

> People do not become homosexual due to role models or
> recruitment. Likewise, no attempts to truly change
> homosexuals into heterosexuals will succeed any better
> than attempts to truly change heterosexuals into homo-
> sexuals. Consequently, withdrawing jobs, services and
> benefits from American citizens who are homosexual will
> never result in fewer homosexuals in America.[51]

An editor of a southern California newspaper said: "If teachers
had such power over children, I would have been a nun years
ago."[52] President Ronald Reagan himself has said, "Whatever
else it is, homosexuality is not a contagious disease like the
measles. Prevailing scientific opinion is that a child's
teachers do not really influence this."[53]

Q. What tactics have ultra-fundamentalist groups used to deny
equal civil rights for homosexuals?

A. Besides repeated anti-gay statements in their literature and public statements, ultra-fundamentalist groups have organized against specific bills that would forbid discrimination against gays. One provision of the Family Protection Act would prevent the Legal Services Corporation from working on cases related to homosexuality.[54] Thus if a tenant were evicted from a rental unit or fired from a job because of allegations of being gay -- no matter what the truth was -- that person might never be able to have his or her day in court.

When the District of Columbia city council wanted to make changes in its sexual assault laws (which included decriminalizing homosexual acts between consenting adults), Moral Majority, Inc., and the National Pro-Family Coalition beseiged Congress asking it to preempt the D.C. government and block the reforms. They succeeded by a vote of 281-118. Moral Majority, Inc., then accused the 118 representatives who had voted to permit the reforms (out of respect for the city's "home rule" charter) of voting in favor of "sodomy." Rep. Arlen Erdahl, a Minnesota Republican who had been among the 118 legislators, blasted the Moral Majority's charges as "slanderous...a distortion of the facts....My vote was for home rule, not for sexual license."[55]

The Gay Bill of Rights, a congressional bill that would forbid discrimination against homosexuals in housing, employment, education, and public accommodations, also provoked exaggerated claims among ultra-fundamentalists. The Christian Voice Moral Government Fund predicted, "Thousands of innocent American children may soon be molested by sex deviates" if Congress enacted the bill. The direct mail letter also warned that the legislation would:

> force every local school to hire practicing homosexuals as teachers, coaches and counselors; force every Christian church to hire a homosexual minister or other church employee; force every family business to hire sodomites....[56]

To achieve a symbolic victory over an inflated threat, the radical right works energetically to deny basic civil rights to many American citizens. It is worth noting that Anita Bryant, who gained national attention from her 1977 "Save Our Children" campaign against gays in Dade County, Florida, had a profound turnabout in her thinking. She told the Ladies Home Journal in 1980, "As for the gays, the church needs to be more loving, unconditionally, and willing to see these people as human beings, to minister to them and try to understand."[57]

John T. (Terry) Dolan, chairman of the powerful National Conservative Political Action Committee, broke ranks with his radical right colleagues in 1982 on the issue of gay rights. He told The Advocate, a national gay magazine, "Sexual preference is irrelevant to political philosophy....If we conservatives believe the government has no right to regulate our economic life, then it certainly has no right to regulate our private life, except to the point where we do harm to each other."[58]

QUOTABLE QUOTES

The Family

"Today the family is being assaulted from without by at least 15 mortal enemies. Homes are being destroyed and children wasted because millions of parents do not even realize that their family's life is under attack....Unconditional war has been declared; antimoral humanism and historic Christianity are in a struggle for survival, with the traditional family at stake."

> -- Rev. Tim LaHaye,
> The Battle for the Family

"Well, let's briefly summarize what we have tried to say....

a) Ninety percent of the mutual tolerations, separations, and divorces are probably due to the failure of the wife to follow the commandments of Scripture.

b) Christian women should submit to their husbands in everything (especially sexual love), except in those things which clearly violate Acts 5:29.

c) Ninety percent of our problems with children are probably the result of a mother who has (1) failed to learn how to really love her man and submit to him, (2) tried to escape staying at home, or (3) hindered her husband in the discipline of the children."

> -- Roy and Elizabeth A. Rood,
> Wife -- 90% of the Fault?
> (the Roods are members of FLAG
> -- Family, Life, America, God)

"We see the antifamily movement as an attempt to prevent souls
from reaching eternal salvation, and as such we feel not just a
political commitment to change this situation, but a moral and,
if you will, a religious commitment to battle these forces....
Among the antifamily forces are hard-core socialists who see it
as a means by which they can attain greater state control. One
of the Communists' chief objectives has always been to break
down the traditional family."

                              -- Paul Weyrich,
                                 Conservative Digest,
                                 May/June 1980

Women's Rights

"Women have great strength, but they are strengths to help the
man. A woman's primary purpose in life and marriage is to help
her husband succeed, to help him be all God wants him to be.
If a man leads well, a woman is glad to follow."

                              -- Rev. James Robison, Texas
                                 Monthly, April 1981

"There is a vicious all-out satanic attack upon the American
home -- the whole concept of anti-submission and independence.
...When two people in the family become absolutely legally
equal, there is no head; both become independent of each other
and love is destroyed."

                              -- Dr. Charles Stanley, board
                                 member of Moral Majority,
                                 Inc., videotape marketed by
                                 First Baptist Church of
                                 Atlanta

"It has been a conscious policy of government to liberate the
wife from the leadership of the husband and thus break up the
family unit of government....It used to be that in recognition
of the family as the basic unit of society, we had one family,
one vote. And we have seen the trend instead to have one
person, one vote."

> -- Howard Phillips, national
> director of the Conservative
> Caucus, The Brooklyn Tablet,
> April 25, 1981

"I know this is painful for the ladies to hear, but if you get
married you have accepted the headship of a man, your
husband....Christ is head of the household, and the husband's
the head of the wife and that's just the way it is....This is
the way the Bible sets it up."

> -- Rev. Pat Robertson, "700 Club"
> broadcast, January 8, 1982

"We fear it [ERA] might sanction homosexual marriages. We do
not believe women belong in...the NFL [National Football
League]. We believe in the superiority of women."

> -- Rev. Jerry Falwell,
> Billings (Montana) Gazette,
> May 15, 1981

Phyllis Schlafly on Women's Rights

"A direct ramification of national ratification of ERA would be
that women will eventually stop having children."

"I'm a Christian and all good Christians believe that women are
special and that God made men to take care of women, to protect
them and go to war for them, to help them with their jackets
and make sure nobody else messes with them."

> -- The Philadelphia News,
> July 2, 1981

"If people decide not to have children, they should be forced
to sign a piece of paper saying that they will forfeit Social
Security benefits. Even if they have worked all their lives.
If they're not willing to have children...then they shouldn't
be entitled to Social Security."

> -- The Philadelphia News,
> July 2, 1981

"The Women's Lib Movement and the Federal Bureaucrats have
joined in a plan to eliminate the traditional family from our
society by making economic survival impossible for the traditional one-income couple where the wife is the homemaker and
the husband is the breadwinner."

> -- The Phyllis Schlafly Report,
> June 1979

[The] "fundamental error [of ERA] "is that it will mandate the
gender-free, rigid, absolute equality of treatment of men and
women...."

> -- The Power of the Positive
> Woman, p. 84

"The devil is using one word -- sex -- to take away the rights
of wives and give them to homosexuals. The ERA doesn't give
women rights. It puts sex into the Constitution."

> -- The Philadelphia News,
> April 22, 1981

"[S]exual harassment on the job is not a problem for the
virtuous woman, except in the rarest of cases....When a woman
walks across the room, she speaks with a universal language
that most men intuitively understand. Men hardly ever ask
sexual favors of women from whom the certain answer is 'no.'"

> -- The Washington Post,
> April 22, 1981

Rev. Jerry Falwell on Equal Rights for Homosexuals

"Remember, homosexuals do not reproduce! They recruit! And
many of them are out after my children and your children."

>   -- Fundraising letter,
>   August 13, 1981

"Courts and the laws of our land will come to officially
legitimatize perversion and perverted acts and the very foundations of moral principle upon which this great nation was
established may soon crumble."

>   -- Fundraising letter,
>   February 15, 1982

"We must stop the homosexuals dead in their tracks -- before
they get one step further towards warping the minds of our
youth!...The enemy is in our camp! And they are after our most
prized possession -- our children!"

>   -- Fundraising letter,
>   April 6, 1981

Other Ultra-Fundamentalists on Homosexuals

"This past summer [1980], homosexual perverts consolidated
their power by organizing to control the 97th Congress just
elected. As a result, we Christians may lose our right to
preach Christ in freedom; but gays have won the right to seduce
our children."

>   -- Rev. James Robison,
>   Fundraising letter,
>   November 1980

"I agree with capital punishment and I believe homosexuality is one of those that could be coupled with murder and other sins....It would be the government that sits upon this land who would be executing homosexuals."

> -- Dean Wycoff, former head of
>   the Santa Clara chapter of
>   Moral Majority, Inc.,
>   TV interview, March 1980

"As far as I'm concerned, a homosexual is in the same class with a rapist, a bank robber, or a murderer."

> -- Rev. James Robison,
>   Texas Monthly, April 1981

"Sexual preference is irrelevant to political philosophy....If we conservatives believe the government has no right to regulate our economic life, then it certainly has no right to regulate our private life, except to the point where we do harm to each other."

> -- John T. (Terry) Dolan,
>   The Advocate,
>   March 16, 1982

Other "Pro-Family" Concerns

"I am advocating whipping [children]. That's a Bible doctrine with fundamentalists....We have always recognized this [child abuse] law as being a very insidious thing....I said when the bill was passed it would create gestapo agencies all over the state...."

> -- Rev. Greg Dixon,
>   national secretary of
>   Moral Majority, Inc.,
>   Penthouse, February 1982

"Our position is the parents own the children."

> -- Rev. Greg Dixon,
> Franklin (Indiana) Daily
> Journal, June 1, 1981

"Better a pink bottom than a black soul....We whip 'em with love, and we weep with 'em, and they love us for it."

> -- Brother Lester Roloff,
> Penthouse, February 1982

[Domestic violence can mean] "any form of 'belittling' or 'teasing' or 'failure to provide warmth' (whatever that may be -- I guess if you don't set the electric blanket high enough in the winter) or 'excessive yelling.'"

> -- JoAnn Gasper, deputy assistant
> secretary for social services
> policy, U.S. Department of
> Health and Human Services,
> Conservative Digest,
> March 1980

"Please help us talk people out of supporting these murderers for I promise you that, even if abortion is made illegal tomorrow, key abortion figures will someday be hunted down like Nazi war criminals and brought to justice for crimes against humanity."

> -- Catholics United for Life,
> press release,
> July 3, 1980

NOTES: THE "PRO-FAMILY" MOVEMENT

1. Greg Walter, "The Divine Mrs. Phyllis," The Philadelphia News, July 2, 1981.

2. Jerry Falwell, fundraising letter, August 13, 1981.

3. Tim LaHaye, The Battle for the Family (Old Tappan, N.J.: Fleming H. Revell Company, 1982).

4. See Charles R. Babcock, "Bob Billings: Christian Right's Inside Man," The Washington Post, March 25, 1982.

5. Burt Schorr, "Choice for Surgeon General Says He's Suited for Post, Defends Stand Against Abortion," The Wall Street Journal, June 19, 1981.

6. "The Pro-Family Movement," Conservative Digest, May/June 1980, pp. 14-24.

7. Rus Walton, FAC-Sheet #16, "Women & 'Equal Rights'" (Marlborough, N.H.: Plymouth Rock Foundation).

8. William Billings, "What It Means to Be 'Pro-Family,'" Family Issues Voting Index (published by Christian Voters' Victory Fund, affiliated with the National Christian Action Coalition, 1980.

9. Conservative Digest, op. cit.

10. Phyllis Schlafly, "Changing Social Security to Hurt the Homemaker," The Phyllis Schlafly Report, June 1979.

11. Greg Walter, "The Divine Mrs. Phyllis," The Philadelphia News, July 2, 1981.

12. William Martin, "God's Angry Man," Texas Monthly, April 1981, p. 224.

13. Dr. Charles Stanley in "Stand Up America" videotape, marketed by the First Baptist Church of Atlanta.

14. "As Others See It," The Brooklyn Tablet, April 25, 1981.

15. Rev. Pat Robertson, "700 Club" broadcast, January 8, 1982.

16. Greg Walter, op. cit.

17. Phyllis Schlafly, The Power of the Positive Woman (New York: Jove/HBJ Books, 1977), p. 84.

18. Beverly LaHaye, fundraising letter, "$1 Million in California, $15 Million Nationwide," Concerned Women of America, undated.

19. Kim Larsen, "Falwell: Brings Back Morality," Billings (Montana) Gazette, May 15, 1981.

20. Jerry Falwell, America Can Be Saved (Murfreesboro, Tennessee: Sword of the Lord Publishers, 1979), p. 36.

21. Greg Walter, op. cit.

22. Catholics United for Life, press release, July 3, 1980.

23. The Religious Roundtable: Issues paper, July 1981.

24. Human Events, July 2, 1982.

25. For more on the Family Protection Act, see Rhonda Brown, "Blueprint for a Moral America," The Nation, May 23, 1981; Frances FitzGerald, "The New Righteousness -- Changing Our Laws, Your Life," Vogue, November 1981, p. 236-7; and Lisa Cronin Wohl, "Can You Protect Your Family from The Family Protection Act?" Ms., April 1981.

26. Study by Dr. Murray A. Straus, Family Violence Research Program, University of New Hampshire, quoted in The New York Times, July 26, 1981. Also J.C. Barden, "New Light on Wife Beatings," The New York Times, August 13, 1981.

27. JoAnn Gasper, "Beating Up on the Family," Conservative Digest, March 1980.

28. Senate Labor Committee hearings, "Sex Discrimination in the Workplace," April 21, 1981.

29. Spencer Rich, "Schlafly: Sex Harassment on Job No Problem for Virtuous Women," The Washington Post, April 22, 1981.

29. Ibid.

30. See Indiana Juvenile Code, P.L. 266, Section 5, Subsection e. See also Nancy Banks, "Spanking Terms Please Only Moral Majority," Hammond (Indiana) Times, July 16, 1981.

31. Michael Disend, "Have You Whipped Your Child Today?" Penthouse, February 1982.

32. Bill Heineke, "Moral Majority Mixes Politics, Religion on Child Rearing, Franklin (Indiana) Daily Journal, June 1, 1981.

33. Ibid.

34. Lea Anne Hester, "Foster 'Timmy' Is An Indiana Boy," Jackson (Mississippi) Clarion-Ledger-News, October 10, 1981.

35. Michael Disend, op. cit.

36. Bill Heineke, "Lugar Stops Distribution of Disputed Child Rearing Booklet," Franklin (Indiana) Daily Journal, August 4, 1981. Also, The New York Times, December 5, 1981.

37. Michael Disend, op. cit.

38. Quoted in Gay Rights National Lobby, "If Your Constituents Ask...About Your Support of Justice for Gays," undated.

39. William Martin, "God's Angry Man," Texas Monthly, April 1981.

40. James Robison, fundraising letter, November 1980.

41. Jerry Falwell, Moral Majority, Inc., fundraising letter, February 15, 1982.

42. Dean Wycoff, TV interview, March 1980.

43. Tim LaHaye, The Battle for the Family (Old Tappan, N.J.: Fleming H. Revell Co., 1982).

44. Cal Thomas address at University of California, Santa
    Barbara, "Religion and Politics: America in the 20th
    Century," January 25, 1982.

45. Moral Majority Report, March 16, 1981.

46. Jerry Falwell, Listen, America! (Garden City, N.Y.:
    Doubleday and Co., 1979), p. 186.

47. Burke Watson, "Falwell: Gays Winning Because 'Moral' Folks
    Are 'Not Committed,'" The Houston Chronicle, February 27,
    1982.

48. Ibid.

49. Jerry Falwell, "Gay Crisis in Minneapolis," fundraising
    letter, April 6, 1981.

50. Jerry Falwell, Moral Majority, Inc., fundraising letter,
    February 15, 1982.

51. Associated Press dispatch, "Gays' Influence on Students
    Debated at House Hearing," Oklahoma City Oklahoman,
    January 28, 1982.

52. Quoted in Gay Rights National Lobby brochure, op. cit.

53. Ibid.

54. S. 1378, The Family Protection Act, Title I, Section 106.

55. "Erdahl Hits the Roof," The Ottawa (Illinois) Daily Times,
    November 28, 1981.

56. Margot Hornblower, "Dying Gay Bill of Rights Stirs Hot
    Debate on Hill," The Washington Post, January 28, 1982.

57. "Anita Bryant's Startling Reversal," Ladies Home Journal,
    December 1980.

58. Larry Bush, "Dolan Apologizes for Anti-Gay Fundraising
    Letters," The Advocate, March 16, 1982. Also, Larry Bush,
    "Homosexuality and the New Right," The Village Voice, March
    20, 1982; and Bill Peterson, "NCPAC's Dolan Quoted As
    Endorsing Gay Rights," The Washington Post, March 18, 1982.

FURTHER READING: THE "PRO-FAMILY" MOVEMENT

Bell, Alan P., Martin S. Weinberg, and Sue Kiefer Hammersmith,
        Sexual Preference: Its Development in Men and Women
        (Bloomington, Indiana: Indiana University Press,
        1981).

Brown, Rhonda, "The Family Protection Act: Blueprint for a
        Moral America," The Nation, May 23, 1981.

Ericson, Edward L., American Freedom and the Radical Right,
        (New York: Frederick Ungar Publishing Co., 1982).

Hacker, Andrew, "Farewell to the Family?" The New York Review
        of Books, March 18, 1982.

Interchange Resource Center, "Unraveling the Right Wing
        Opposition to Women's Equality," 1981.

PEOPLE FOR THE AMERICAN WAY, special report, "The 'Pro-Family'
        Movement's Dangerous Crusade" (Available upon
        request).

Scanzoni, Letha and Virginia Ramey Mollenkott, Is the Homo
        sexual My Neighbor? Another Christian View (San
        Francisco: Harper and Row, 1978).

Shriver, Peggy, "Conflict in the Christian Family: Can You
        Listen to Your Relatives?" Christianity and Crisis,
        October 5, 1981.

Wohl, Lisa Cronin, "Can You Protect Your Family from The Family
        Protection Act?" Ms., April 1981.

RADICAL RIGHT LITERATURE

Falwell, Jerry, Listen, America! (Garden City, N.Y.: Doubleday
        and Co., 1980).

LaHaye, Beverly, "Concerned Women for America" newsletter, June
        1981.

LaHaye, Tim, The Battle for the Family (Old Tappan, N.J.:
          Fleming H. Revell Company, 1982.)

McGraw, Onalee, Family Choice in Education: The New Imperative
          (Washington, D.C.: The Heritage Foundation,
          1978).

"The Pro-Family Movement," Conservative Digest, May/June 1980.

Schlafly, Phyllis, The Power of the Positive Woman (New York:
          Jove/HBJ Books, 1977).

-------- , The Phyllis Schlafly Report (monthly newsletter
          available from the Eagle Forum, Box 618, Alton,
          Illinois 62002).

Walton, Rus, FAC-Sheet #16, "Women & 'Equal Rights'" and
          FAC-Sheet #23, "Women & Civil Authority" (Marlborough,
          N.H.: Plymouth Rock Foundation).

Organizations Concerned with the Rights of Women, Homosexuals, Children and the Family

Alan Guttmacher Institute
300 Park Avenue, S.
New York, NY 10010   212-685-5858

Center for Population Options
2031 Florida Avenue, N.W.
Washington, DC 20009   202-387-5091

Children's Defense Fund
1520 New Hampshire Avenue, N.W.
Washington, DC 20036   202-483-1470

Gay Rights National Lobby
P.O. Box 1892
Washington, DC 20013   202-546-1801

National Abortion Rights Action League
1424 K Street, N.W.
Washington, DC 20005   202-347-7774

National Education Association
1201 16th Street, N.W.
Washington, DC 20036   202-833-4000

National Organization for Women
425 13th Street, N.W., Suite 1048
Washington, DC 20004   202-347-2279

Planned Parenthood Federation of America
810 Seventh Avenue
New York, NY 10019   212-541-7800

Sex Information and Education Council of the United States
84 Fifth Avenue, Suite 407
New York, NY 10011   212-929-2300

THE COURTS

Q. Why does the radical right attack the Supreme Court and the federal courts?

A. Because it disagrees with several key rulings the courts have made in the past 20 years. The most controversial of these issues are:

o school prayer: rulings in 1962 and 1963 that prohibit mandatory religious devotions in public schools; [1]

o school desegregation: a series of decisions since the late 1960s that require busing as a tool to ensure equal educational opportunity; [2]

o abortion: two 1973 rulings that establish the right of women to choose to end their pregnancies. [3]

The radical right also objects to recent court decisions upholding sexual and racial equality in the workplace; environmental protection policies; the rights of defendents, prisoners, aliens, and the mentally ill; and other rulings affecting individual rights guaranteed under the Constitution. Critics say that this pattern of court decisions represents "judicial activism" that goes beyond the courts' constitutional authority. They assert that constitutional rights are not in jeopardy in the above cases; that the courts are making laws, not interpreting them; and that federal judges should be more accountable to popular will.

One federal court decision that incited the radical right to become organized in the first place was a 1971 ruling upholding the denial of tax exemptions to schools that practice racial discrimination. In August 1978, the Internal Revenue Service tried to issue stringent new guidelines for tax exemptions. "That was the spark that set off the powder keg," says Gary L.

249

Jarmin, legislative director for the Christian Voice. "That
was the issue that caused the Christian Right to come into
existence."[4]

Q. How do critics of the courts hope to nullify the courts'
   decisions?

A. Primarily through congressional statutes that would strip the
   Supreme Court, appellate courts, and federal district courts of
   the authority to rule on certain cases (hence the term, "court-
   stripping"). More than 30 different bills are pending in Congress that would prohibit the courts from reviewing school
   desegregation, school prayer, and abortion cases. Sponsors of
   the bills reason that the state courts, who instead would rule
   on such cases, would deliver more favorable verdicts.

Q. Who are the most vocal critics of the federal courts?

A. New Right leaders like Richard Viguerie, Howard Phillips and
   Paul Weyrich frequently rail against the courts, as do Jerry
   Falwell, Pat Robertson, and other ultra-fundamentalists.

   The Free Congress Research and Education Foundation, directed
   by Paul Weyrich, is probably the most influential advocate for
   "judicial reform." In 1981, it issued a collection of essays,
   A Blueprint for Judicial Reform, which tries to lay a theoretical foundation for curbing the courts' power...all in the name
   of the Constitution.[5] "The Constitution has been so perverted
   by the courts, so perverted by government regulations," says
   Paul Weyrich, "it isn't the same Constitution we were talking
   about 20 years ago. I don't want to defend that kind of
   Constitution."[6] Weyrich's Judicial Reform Project charges
   that "many federal judges have used their positions as forums
   to legislate and execute policies and to establish new, pre-
   viously unknown, constitutional 'rights,' which cost government
   and taxpayers millions of dollars."[7]

   In the Senate, the leading backers of court-stripping legislation are John East of North Carolina, Jesse Helms of North
   Carolina, Orrin Hatch of Utah, and J. Bennett Johnston of
   Louisiana. After a long silence on how the administration
   stood with respect to court-stripping bills, Attorney General
   William French Smith delivered his judgment in May 1982 in
   two letters to congressional leaders. Smith warned that
   legislation seeking to limit the power of the Supreme Court

would reduce it to a "position of impotence" within the U.S.
government. But he argued that restrictions on the authority
of lower federal courts would be constitutional.[8] Smith's
statement seemed to find the "Johnston-Helms" anti-busing bill
constitutionally acceptable.

Waging a cruder war of words are religious leaders like Ed
McAteer of the Religious Roundtable and Rus Walton of the
Plymouth Rock Foundation. At a Religious Roundtable "Rally for
Life" held in Dallas on September 3, 1981, a statement was
circulated that attacked federal judges as "selfish elitist
tyrants" who "make war on the American soul."[9] The "Unanimous
Declaration" issued at the rally (which featured as speakers
Jerry Falwell, Phyllis Schlafly, Paul Weyrich, Tim LaHaye, and
Ed McAteer) made a long list of accusations against federal
courts, including:

> These born-again Ayatollahs of Paganism, enrobed as
> federal Judges, with unchecked power, in violation of the
> Constitution, have established their religion of Paganism
> upon us, imposing its barbarisms and corruptions, demand-
> ing the modern materialistic gods of consumerism and
> careerism be sated with children's blood....[10]

Rus Walton, in one of his "FAC-Sheets" (prepared with the help
of John Whitehead, general counsel for Moral Majority, Inc.),
sets forth a patently false understanding of the Constitution:
"...in plain language, the Constitutional place and role
concerning the courts is laid out: Congress is to bridle the
federal courts in their exercise of power."[11] (original
emphasis) Walton goes further to postulate a biblical origin
for the U.S. system of checks and balances.

Q. What's so alarming about shifting the jurisdiction on some
   issues to the states?

A. More than jurisdiction is at stake. Our entire constitutional
   system of government would be profoundly changed by the precedents that any court-stripping bill would set. Constitutional
   scholars warn that court-stripping bills would:

   o undermine the system of checks and balances.
     The framers of the Constitution deliberately divided power
     among three branches of government (the legislative, judi-

cial, and executive) to prevent the abuse of power. The
powers assigned to each branch act as a check and balance
on the other branches. As David Brink, president of the
American Bar Association, explained:

> We have conferred on the executive a role of policy-
> making and administration, on the legislative the
> power to respond with laws to serve changing public
> needs, and on the judicial the interpretation of law
> and the preservation of the rights and liberties
> secured to our citizens by our organic document.[12]

But through court-stripping legislation, Congress is
trying to claim for itself the authority to interpret the
Constitution on selected issues -- a power explicitly
granted to the federal courts. From the experience of
Great Britain, our Founders knew how parliamentary majorities can easily trample on the rights of individuals, so
the framers created an independent judiciary to protect
individual rights. Court-stripping legislation would chip
away at the independent judiciary and profoundly alter the
separation of powers.

o deny federal protection of Americans' constitutional
   rights.
   If individuals can no longer ask federal courts to remedy
   a violation of their rights, the rights themselves are
   worthless. A right is only as good as the remedy. Yet
   court-stripping bills would forbid citizens from seeking
   protection for their constitutional rights through the
   federal courts, and the federal courts would be powerless
   to mandate restitution.

o destroy the uniformity of constitutional rights.
   If court-stripping bills are enacted, the Supreme Court
   would no longer be the "supreme court" on selected constitutional matters. Individual rights that now belong to
   all Americans would vary from state to state. Different
   state courts handing down different constitutional interpretations would produce a hodgepodge of rulings. And all
   Americans would not have "equal protection under the law,"
   as required by the Fourteenth Amendment, for selected
   constitutional rights.

Shifting jurisdiction on some issues to state courts
presents a dilemma for state court judges. Although they
pledge their loyalty to the U.S. Constitution, state
judges would also be empowered to render decisions that
would contradict the U.S. Supreme Court. The Conference
of State Chief Justices has formally stated it does not
want that authority and will continue to uphold the
Constitution and current Supreme Court decisions. The
justices termed the court-stripping bills "a hazardous
experiment with the vulnerable fabric of the nation's
judicial system."[13]

o jeopardize other constitutional rights.
The framers of the Constitution considered constitutional
rights to be basic human rights beyond the power of any
government to abridge. That's why they created a separate
branch of government -- an independent judiciary -- to
protect individual rights from the tyranny of a majority
in Congress or an imperial president. But once the precedent is established that an issue can be removed from
Supreme Court and federal court jurisdiction, then a
simple majority of Congress could in effect rewrite the
Constitution. Any constitutional right would be fair game
-- free speech, free press, religious liberty, and all the
others.

Q. Who are the chief opponents of court-stripping bills?

A. Civil rights and civil liberties groups, educational organizations, labor unions and professional legal associations all
oppose court-stripping legislation. A partial list includes
the United Methodist Church, the American Jewish Congress, the
National Association for the Advancement of Colored People, the
National Education Association, and the AFL-CIO.

The 290,000-member American Bar Association condemned the
proposed bills in a resolution issued in August 1981.[14]
David Brink, president of the ABA, warned that the bills pose
"the most serious constitutional crisis since our great Civil
War" and that they would "convert America into a league of
independent states instead of one nation."[15] Prominent legal
scholars like Yale Law School Professor Robert Bork, USC
Professor Leonard Ratner, Harvard Law School Professor Laurence
H. Tribe and other legal experts spanning the political
spectrum have condemned court-stripping bills.[16]

Even legislators as different in their political views as
Senators Lowell Weicker and Barry Goldwater agree that the
proposed bills would have profound constitutional repercussions.
Said Goldwater: "Whatever our viewpoints may be on the various
social issues as a matter of policy, there are fundamental
principles involving the separation of powers doctrine and the
independence of the courts that must be balanced against our
feelings about busing or whatever the immediate subject
is."[17]

Q. The federal courts aren't accountable to the American people,
   and this nation is a democracy, after all.

A. The courts were not intended by the Constitution to cater to
   popular moods or political majorities; they were meant to
   protect individual rights and render independent judgments that
   stand beyond partisan politics. In Madison's words, "...inde-
   pendent tribunals of justice will consider themselves in a
   peculiar manner the guardian of those rights; they will be an
   impenetrable bulwark against every assumption of power in the
   legislative or executive."[18]

   At root, proponents of court-stripping bills deny several basic
   principles: that genuine constitutional rights are at stake on
   matters of busing, abortion, and school prayer; that the
   constitutional rights of a minority should not be abridged by a
   temporary political majority; and that only an independent
   judiciary can resolve these issues.[19] Rather than acknowledge these central assumptions of the Constitution, moral
   authoritarians instead blame the Supreme Court for "perverting"
   the meaning of the Constitution.

Q. Why shouldn't federal judges be elected?

A. Judges are appointed to life terms to insulate them from
   partisan politics and transient passions. If judges had to
   face re-election, their decisions could be tailored to satisfy
   organized political constituencies and would not be independent, conscientious interpretations of the Constitution.

Q. Why are court-stripping bills an inappropriate way to amend the
   Constitution?

A. Court-stripping proposals are an expedient, backdoor way of
   amending the Constitution with only a 51 percent majority vote

of Congress. They are a vehicle that would let popular
passions and moods of the moment alter our historic national
charter. If popular discontent with any Supreme Court ruling
is great enough, remedies should be pursued through the constitutional amendment process, not through court-stripping legislation. As specified in the Constitution, any amendment must be
approved by two-thirds of both the Senate and the House, and
three-quarters (38) of the state legislatures. It is a slow,
unwieldy process -- for good reasons. The framers of the
Constitution wanted to ensure that any changes in the principles of the U.S. Government were made only if there were widespread and lasting support for them. After all, some profound
principles of self-government and human rights are involved.

Q. Court-stripping bills are constitutional because Article III of
   the Constitution authorizes Congress to regulate the federal
   courts.

A. This provision of the Constitution is a major point of controversy. Article III, Section 2, gives the Supreme Court authority over appellate courts "with such exceptions and under such
   regulations as the Congress shall make." Sponsors of the court-
   stripping bills argue that this provision -- the "exceptions
   and regulations" clause -- allows Congress to define, regulate,
   and limit the jurisdiction of the federal courts.

   The scholarly debate over the "exceptions and regulations"
   clause is too complex to recount here. But the constitutional
   history of this provision is not very illuminating; the few
   legal precedents that do not exist can hardly justify major
   constitutional changes. Many respected scholars argue that
   even if it were agreed that Congress could selectively revoke
   jurisdiction from federal courts, it runs contrary to the
   structure and spirit of the Constitution. As Judge Irving R.
   Kaufman of the U.S. Court of Appeals for the Second Circuit
   notes:

        To assert that the framers, who clearly intended the
        Supreme Court to exercise the power of judicial review,
        also intended to grant Congress plenary authority to
        nullify that power is to charge the framers with a
        baffling self-contradiction. Indeed, the history of the
        exceptions-and-regulations clause suggests that it was
        never intended to carry the heavy constitutional baggage
        with which the bill's supporters are now loading it.[20]

Likewise, the American Bar Association cautions that if
Congress can divest federal courts of their jurisdiction,

> ...then indeed we have a Constitution writ on sand and the
> integrity of our amendment process is eroded. It is
> central to our fundamental Charter that ordinary legisla-
> tion can be changed through ordinary legislation and the
> Constitution only through amendment.[21]

Q. Has Congress tried to curb the federal courts in the past?

A. Many times. But in every case where a showdown was imminent
between Congress and the courts, Congress wisely chose to avert
a constitutional crisis by letting the judiciary fulfill its
assigned role -- to interpret and enforce the Constitution. In
the first part of this century, liberal reformers attacked the
Supreme Court for striking down laws dealing with child labor,
minimum wages, maximum work hours, workers' compensation, and
other occupational issues. One of the most famous attempts to
tamper with the Supreme Court came when Franklin D. Roosevelt
unsuccessfully tried to "pack" the Court with his appointees.
The liberal majority in Congress defied Roosevelt to protect
the Constitution. In the 1950s, there were congressional
attempts to deny court jurisdiction for school desegregation
cases; to have federal judges elected; and to deny First
Amendment rights to political dissidents.[22]

The current campaign against the federal courts is so menacing
because it could well succeed, forcing a major constitutional
crisis. In March 1982, the Senate approved, 57-37, a court-
stripping amendment that would deny federal court jurisdiction
on busing cases.[23] Support for a school prayer bill is also
strong. In November 1981, a symbolic vote on a school prayer
amendment passed the Senate by a vote of 51 to 35.[24] In an
election year, when legislators often succumb to political
pressures on emotional issues, court-stripping legislation
could actually pass Congress. After Attorney General Smith
cautioned congressional leaders to think twice about the
constitutional principles at stake (see footnote 8), some of
the momentum for a school prayer bill may have been diverted
into the constitutional amendment proposed by President Reagan
in May 1982. (See "School Prayer" section.)

What backers of court-stripping bills fail to realize is that
their politically expedient tactics could easily be used

against them in the future by a different partisan majority.
To safeguard constitutional rights over time against shifting
political majorities, the framers of the Constitution, with
shrewd foresight, created an independent judiciary.

QUOTABLE QUOTES

"I'm shocked that federal courts are being used as a tool to undermine religious liberty in America. Some of us have tried to warn our nation for many years that there are those who would use the Constitution to destroy the Constitution. Every effort is being made to crush God-fearing men and women and their ministries. These forces will not be satisfied until they've separated God, decency, and morality from every vestige of American life."

> -- Rev. Greg Dixon, national
>   secretary of Moral Majority,
>   Inc., Hattiesburg, Mississippi,
>   March 2, 1982

"But each of these judges [of the Supreme Court] has extraordinary powers and they influence our lives more than we realize. None of these judges are elected; they are accountable to no one really; they can be impeached but that's rare and they exercise what amounts to a type of dictatorship."

> -- Rev. Pat Robertson,
>   "700 Club" broadcast,
>   October 2, 1981

"The Constitution of the United States, for instance, is a marvelous document for self-government by Christian people. But the minute you turn the document into the hands of non-Christian people and atheistic people they can use it to destroy the very foundation of our society. And that's what's been happening."

> -- Rev. Pat Robertson,
>   "700 Club" broadcast,
>   December 20, 1981

"The rationale of our Constitution is not to be lightly ignored. It was designed to protect individual rights by vesting the Federal courts with the final, binding authority to interpret the fundamental law. The only way to override the Constitution as so interpreted is to amend it."

> -- Irving R. Kaufman, judge of the United States Court of Appeals for the Second Circuit, The New York Times Magazine, September 20, 1981

"We are under a Constitution, but the Constitution is what the judges say it is, and the judiciary is the safeguard of our liberty and of our property under the Constitution."

> -- Chief Justice Charles Evan Hughes

"If we yield to temptation now to lay the lash upon the Court, we are only teaching others how to apply it to ourselves and to the people when the occasion seems to warrant. If we may force the hand of the Court to secure our interpretation of the Constitution, then some succeeding Congress may repeat the process to secure another and a different interpretation and one which may not sound so pleasant in our ears as that for which we now contend."

> -- Senate Judiciary Committee, in report unanimously rejecting President Roosevelt's "court-packing" plan

"If statutory efforts to alter constitutional rights and remedies could be made successful merely by reciting the word 'jurisdiction' the Congress could overrule any court decision and the Constitution would be just a piece of paper."

> -- Then-Senator Walter Mondale, in a 1972 speech opposing an anti-busing amendment to the Higher Education Act

"If, in the opinion of the people, the distribution or modifi-
cation of the constitutional powers be in any particular wrong,
let it be corrected by an amendment in the way which the
Constitution designates. But let there be no change by usurp-
tion; for though this, in one instance, may be the instrument
of good, it is the customary weapon by which free governments
are destroyed."

> -- George Washington in his
> Farewell Address

"We think its [the Supreme Court's] decisions on constitutional
questions should control, not only the particular case decided,
but the general policy of the country, subject to being
disturbed only by amendments of the Constitution as provided in
the instrument itself."

> -- Abraham Lincoln, in response
> to the Dred Scott decision of
> the Supreme Court, which
> declared slaves lacked the
> rights of citizens. Lincoln
> strongly disagreed with the
> decision but supported the
> Court in its authority to
> make its decision.

NOTES: THE COURTS

1. Engel v. Vitale, 370 U.S. 421 (1962), and Abingdon v. Schempp, 370 U.S. 203 (1963).

2. Green v. County School Board, 391 U.S. 430 (1968); Swann v. Charlotte-Mecklenburg Board of Education, 402 U.S. 1 (1971); Keyes v. School District No. 1, Denver, Colorado, 413 U.S. 189 (1973); Columbus Board of Education v. Penick, 443 U.S. 449 (1979).

3. Roe v. Wade, 410 U.S. 113 (1973), and Doe v. Bolton, 410 U.S. 739 (1973).

4. Robert Timberg, "Christian Right to Fight Reagan on Segregated-Schools Tax Bill," The Baltimore Sun, January 27, 1982.

5. Patrick B. McGuigan and Randall R. Rader, editors, A Blueprint for Judicial Reform (Washington, D.C.: The Free Congress Research and Education Foundation, Inc., 1981).

6. Charles R. Babcock, "Justice Doing Something Right...or Left?" The Washington Post, August 24, 1981, p. A7.

7. Annual Report 1981, The Free Congress Research and Education Foundation, Inc., p. 5.

8. Letter to Chairman Peter Rodino of the House Judiciary Committee regarding S. 951 (an anti-busing bill), and letter to Chairman Strom Thurmond of the Senate Judiciary Committee regarding S. 1742, (a school prayer bill). Both letters were dated May 6, 1982.

9. "In Defense of the Constitution: The Unanimous Declaration of the People of America," circulated at a "Right to Life" rally sponsored by the Religious Roundtable, Dallas, Texas, September 4, 1981.

10. Ibid.

11. Rus Walton, FAC-Sheet #19, "Justice & the Courts" (The Plymouth Rock Foundation, P.O. Box 425, Marlborough, NH 03455).

12. David R. Brink, "A Great Partnership in the Organized
     Bar," President's Report to the National Conference of Bar
     Presidents, January 23, 1982. See also, Fred Barbash,
     "ABA Head Sees Crisis for Courts," The Washington Post,
     January 24, 1982.

13. Fred Barbash, "State Justices Reject Sole Power Over
     Social Issues," The Washington Post, February 2, 1982.

14. David R. Brink, op. cit.

15. David R. Brink, op. cit.

16. Irving R. Kaufman, "Congress v. The Court," The New York
     Times Magazine, September 20, 1981. See also, "Constitu-
     tional Restraints on the Judiciary," hearings of the
     Senate Subcommittee on the Constitution, May 20-21, 1981.

17. Barry Goldwater, "Control of Federal Courts Raises Basic
     Questions," Congressional Record, February 9, 1982, p.
     S598. See also, Bill Peterson, "Goldwater to Oppose New
     Social Legislation," The Washington Post, February 10,
     1982.

18. Cited in Archibald Cox, "Don't Overrule the Court,"
     Newsweek, September 28, 1981.

19. See, e.g., William A. Stanmeyer, "Governing the Judici-
     ary," in A Blueprint for Judicial Reform, op. cit.

20. Irving R. Kaufman, op. cit.

21. "Report to the House of Delegates," American Bar Associa-
     tion, Special Committee on Coordination of Federal
     Judicial Improvements, Edward I. Cutler, Chairman, August
     1981.

22. Irving R. Kaufman, op. cit.

23. Steven V. Roberts, "Antibusing Moves Passed By Senate After
     Long Fight," The New York Times, March 3, 1982, p. 1.

24. Steven V. Roberts, "Senate Endorses Prayer Program for
     the Schools," The New York Times, November 17, 1981, p. 1.

FURTHER READING: THE COURTS

American Bar Association, "Report to the House of Delegates,"
        Special Committee on Coordination of Federal Judicial
        Improvements, Edward I. Cutler, Chairman, August
        1981.

American Judicature Society, Judicature, "Limiting Federal
        Court Jurisdiction: Can Congress Do It? Should
        Congress Do It?" Vol. 65, No. 4, October 1981.

Cox, Archibald, "Don't Overrule the Court," Newsweek, September
        28, 1981.

Ericson, Edward L., American Freedom and the Radical Right (New
        York: Frederick Ungar Publishing Co., 1982).

House Judiciary Committee hearings, "Prayer in Public Schools
        and Buildings -- Federal Court Jurisdication,"
        [Serial No. 63] July 29, 30, August 19, 21, and
        September 9, 1980.

Kaufman, Irving R., "Congress v. The Court," The New York Times
        Magazine, September 20, 1981.

Leadership Conference on Civil Rights, "Without Justice: A
        Report on the Conduct of the Justice Department and
        Civil Rights in 1981-1982," February 15, 1982.

PEOPLE FOR THE AMERICAN WAY, "The Crusade Against the Courts:
        An Attack on Our Constitutional Rights," special
        report, April 1982 (Available upon request).

Senate Subcommittee on the Constitution, "Constitutional
        Restraints on the Judiciary," hearings of May 20-21,
        1981.

Trippett, Frank, "Trying to Trim the U.S. Courts," Time,
        September 28, 1981, pp. 93-4.

U.S. Department of Justice, "The Civil Rights Policy of the
        Department of Justice: A Response to the Report of
        the Leadership Conference on Civil Rights," April 3,
        1982.

RADICAL RIGHT LITERATURE

Holt, Earl P., III, "The Supreme Court vs. the Constitution,"
        Human Events, November 28, 1981, pp. 10-12.

McGuigan, Patrick B. and Randall R. Rader, A Blueprint for
        Judicial Reform (Washington, D.C.: The Free Congress
        Research and Education Foundation, 1981).

National Association for Neighborhood Schools, Inc. (Cleveland,
        Ohio) newsletter.

Walton, Rus, FAC-Sheet #19, "Justice & the Courts" (The
        Plymouth Rock Foundation, P.O. Box 425, Marlborough,
        NH   03455).

THE MEDIA

Q. Why does the radical right attack the nation's media?

A. Its leaders denounce the media, especially television, for the values they portray. Although most of the criticisms focus on sex, violence, and profanity -- criticisms that many Americans share -- the radical right harnesses these concerns for their own political purposes. By casting themselves as crusaders for "morality" on television, they have enlisted public support while camouflaging their actual sectarian religious and political motives.

The lead organization in this campaign is the Coalition for Better Television (CBTV), founded on February 2, 1981. The coalition's primary concern is to advance its well-defined political agenda, not any well-accepted notions of "morality" or "better television." To take one example, the head of CBTV, Rev. Donald Wildmon, writes a monthly column in Richard Viguerie's Conservative Digest. In 1982, the coalition has called for a nationwide boycott of NBC-TV and its parent company, RCA. (See below.)

Q. How did the crusade to "clean up" television get started?

A. Rev. Donald Wildmon, a little-known Methodist minister in Tupelo, Mississippi, resigned from his pastorate in 1977 to promote "moral" television programming. The story Wildmon tells is that he tried to watch TV one evening with his family and every channel was broadcasting a show with sex, violence, or profanity. Shocked and outraged, Wildmon founded the National Federation for Decency and labored away in obscurity for four years. Then in 1981, Wildmon gained national attention when Jerry Falwell struck up an alliance with him. With the backing of Moral Majority, Inc., and other political groups, the Coalition for Better Television (CBTV) was launched.[1]

Q. How many organizations belong to the Coalition?

A. Rev. Wildmon was claiming in March 1982 that 1,800 organizations belonged to CBTV,[2] but this number is deceptive because it consists largely of three national groups and their state and local affiliates -- Moral Majority, Inc., the Eagle Forum, and the American Life Lobby. Each group is avowedly political.

The actual size of the coalition has been questioned since a CBS reporter looked into CBTV membership claims in June 1981. Of a sample of 60 organizations and individuals supposedly affiliated with CBTV, 30 percent denied any connection with Wildmon's group.[3] Since then, Wildmon has refused to release a complete list of coalition members.

Q. What kinds of shows does CBTV condemn? Why?

A. Most of the "objectionable" programs are prime-time fare like "Dallas," "Dukes of Hazzard," "Flamingo Road," "Three's Company," and assorted movies. "What we're really trying to do is get 'em to clean up the act some -- I mean explicit scenes, adultery, sexual perversion, incest," says John Hurt, an ally of Wildmon's who runs his own "Clean Up TV" campaign from Joelton, Tennessee.[4] Rev. Wildmon accuses network television of teaching "by design" that "sexual immorality, violence, profanity, vulgarity, etc. [are] values worthy of imitation and emulation."[5]

In its "Battle Plan for 1982," Moral Majority, Inc., asserts, "The [television] industry is riddled with homosexuals and only fierce public, and perhaps, even economic pressure will stop homosexuals' dominance of television."[6] In countless similar attacks, religious authoritarians portray television as a lurid cesspool of unimaginable degeneracy.

These accusations are not only exaggerated but often factually wrong. John Hurt is incorrect: network television does not show "explicit scenes" of adultery, perversion, and incest. The charge that two out of five "Donahue" programs are "sex shows" is false. (Rev. Wildmon later acknowledged that the alleged "sex shows" included a program on breast-feeding and another that featured a celebrity couple who were living together out of wedlock.)[7] Sex is sometimes exploited by network programmers, but the coalition's warnings about video Sodom and Gomorrah are overblown, to say the least.

Although the Coalition for Better Television also condemns TV
violence, it is apparently not a major concern. In the fall
1980 survey of prime-time TV programming, Wildmon's National
Federation for Decency made no mention of the extent of TV violence.   But the NFD did compile some detailed (and dubious)
statistics calculating the number of "skin scenes" in fall 1980
(2,468), "sex incidents per hour" (6.97 average per programming
hour), profane utterances (1,997), and people drinking milk
(187), hot chocolate (12), and alcohol (7,179).   (A brief note
in minuscule type claimed that NFD "is concerned with violence
on television..." but the report made no other mention of the
subject.)[8]

Q. Is "morality" on television really the issue?

A. TV sex, violence, and morality are frequently used as a bait to
capture public attention, which is then switched to the radical
right's political agenda. Richard Viguerie explains the
strategy:

> The networks may beat us, they may after three or four
> years still have their sex and violence on television,
> but in the meantime, Jerry Falwell and others may increase
> their list of supporters by three- or four- or five-fold.
> And we can do something the networks cannot do, which is
> get involved in political campaigns....Even if we go after
> them and lose...we will still win by waging the battle.
> Because we'll bring to our cause maybe five million people
> we don't have now, who will then turn their attention to
> senators and congressmen.[9]

Viguerie's cynical political wisdom has not been lost on the
leaders of the Coalition for Better Television. Nearly all
CBTV executive board members lead other political crusades
that benefit from the anti-television sideshow. Board members
include Phyllis Schlafly, leader of the Eagle Forum; Judie
Brown, director of the American Life Lobby, an anti-abortion
organization; Dr. Ronald S. Godwin, vice president and chief of
operations for Moral Majority, Inc.; Beverly LaHaye, head of
Concerned Women for America and wife of Rev. Tim LaHaye, Moral
Majority, Inc., board member; Lottie Beth-Hobbs, head of the
Pro-Family Forum, a group advocating repressive social legislation; and Rev. Donald Wildmon, founder of the National
Federation for Decency.[10]

The radical religious right has learned that showy displays of moral outrage about television are useful in mobilizing support for their other political ventures. Even though televangelist James Robison is not a member of the CBTV crusade, he finds diatribes against TV useful in raising money: "Tonight, nearly every home in America will have violence, crime, sex, perversion, and filth piped directly into their families' laps." Robison requests a contribution of $25 "to offset Satan's attack."[11] The key to CBTV's success has been to exploit the legitimate complaints many Americans have about television and then to harness that discontent to serve their own narrow political ends.

Q. How can protest against tasteless shows be considered political?

A. Even though religious authoritarians invoke their brand of Christian morality as the basis for their protests, their campaign is a political crusade for influence, publicity, members, and contributions. Their wrath is aimed not only at "jiggle" shows but at serious news and educational programs.

What follows are a few of the sober-minded programs that moral majoritarians have attacked. In each case it is not immorality that they are challenging but the right to express different viewpoints about the way it "ought to be":

   o A TV biography of Margaret Sanger, one of the earliest advocates of birth control and the founder of Planned Parenthood Federation of America. Anti-abortion groups vilify Sanger and Planned Parenthood because of their views and objected to CBS airing the program. Wildmon's NFD was collaborating with the radical right before the CBTV was founded. In July 1980, the American Life Lobby, announced a nationwide boycott of CBS "organized by the National Federation for Decency," Wildmon's group.[12]

   o "Gay Power, Gay Politics." Rev. Wildmon condemned this CBS Reports news documentary as unfit for viewing and lumped it together with two frothy TV movies, "Scruples" and "Anatomy of a Seduction."[13]

   o "Little House on the Prairie." In Beverly LaHaye's organization's newsletter, Concerned Women for America,

a member denounced an episode in which the women of
the village pressed for the right to vote. The member
warned that "some bad values...are being presented in
TV shows which are typically considered 'harmless'....
Women were encouraged by the 'virtuous matron' of the
show, Mrs. Ingalls, to leave their husbands in an
attempt to get their own way, and it works! These are
not the kinds of values and ideas that I want my children to learn towards marriage and that God-given relationship."[14]

o "The Women's Room," the TV adaptation of the book, was
criticized by Rev. Wildmon because "the traditional
role of mother is made fun of and ridiculed."[15]
In a more general vein, Cal Thomas, communications
director for Moral Majority, Inc., asserted, "So
complete has been the emasculation of the American
male on television that it is a wonder we are not
all speaking in falsetto voices."[16]

o Network news and Dan Rather. Wildmon's NFD told
readers of its monthly newspaper: "Researcher Says
Dan Rather Can't Be Trusted." Wildmon accused Rather
of "dishonest journalism" in a story about the problems
of nuclear waste.[17] Rev. Tim LaHaye goes further to
condemn network news: "Not all the fifty or so people
who control network news are committed humanists, but
most of them are....Humanists tend to be liberal in
their world view, while pro-moralists tend to be
conservative."[18]

o "Choice," a TV movie aired in February 1981, was a
drama about a pregnant teenager who considered having
an abortion. Even though the girl eventually decided
not to have an abortion, moral majoritarians objected,
in essence, to the girl even having the opportunity to
make the "right" choice.[19]

Q. How does CBTV judge program content? What are its criteria?

A. Rev. Wildmon claims that CBTV has 4,000 trained volunteers
in 49 states monitoring prime-time television for offensive
content.[20] But he refuses to reveal who any of the volunteers are, how representative they are of the national audience, or the nature of their training. The monitoring forms

that volunteers are instructed to fill out constitute a feeble scientific charade. For instance, if monitors are "left with the opinion that sexual intercourse occurred" -- on screen or off, inside or outside of marriage -- they are instructed to tally it as an objectionable scene.[21] Monitors are also supposed to answer such subjective questions as, "Would viewing the program help promote a better family life?" and "Would the program help build good character in youth and children?"[22]

Wildmon abandoned his scientific pretenses briefly when a four-letter word was uttered on "Saturday Night Live." The penalty? "NBC will be scored double on our monitoring report," Wildmon announced.[23] When one CBTV monitor found 23 "jiggly scenes" in an episode of "Charlie's Angels" and another monitor detected none, Wildmon again threw objectivity to the wind: "I'd just use the higher estimate and not bother with the other one."[24] Wildmon's personal biases are revealed in statements like, "Most television producers are of the Jewish perspective."[25]

By its reliance on bogus survey techniques, unnamed volunteers, secret coalition members, and not-so-hidden political goals, the Coalition for Better Television forfeits any claim to be simply a media reform group.

Q. PEOPLE FOR THE AMERICAN WAY was simply founded to defend network TV and fight the Coalition for Better Television.

A. PEOPLE FOR THE AMERICAN WAY was founded in August 1980, months before the Coalition for Better Television opened its doors in February 1981. Moreover, although concerned about the excesses in CBTV activities, PEOPLE FOR THE AMERICAN WAY deals more broadly with First Amendment issues.

With regard to TV programming, PEOPLE FOR would like to see more diverse, innovative programming rather than the "lowest-common-denominator" approach of the networks. Like any free speech, innovative programming runs the risk of offending some people. That is a risk worth taking in a free society. Moral monopolists, by contrast, want to eliminate any programming that might conflict with their version of "the way it ought to be." That is why CBTV is not really for "better television."

Q. Sex and violence dominate prime-time television. That is what CBTV is trying to eliminate.

A. There is no question that some network television has come to
   rely on tired program formulas, many of which exploit sexual
   innuendo and violence. But this problem stems not from
   "humanist" or immoral network executives, but from the commercial structure of the industry which is obsessed with the
   "bottom line." As Norman Lear explains:

> ...the fires of competition between the networks have
> resulted in an unparalleled and hysterical competition for
> ratings -- which translate to profits. Trapped in this
> ratings war are some very bright TV programming executives
> who wish things were different. I've talked to many of
> them....No one will take the chance with an original and
> innovative idea. When the name of the game is to win
> fast, you don't take chances, you tend toward imita-
> tion.[26]

NBC chairman Grant Tinker agrees: "Our big sin, if one is being
committed, is not the level of sex or violence in shows, but
the lowest-common-denominator phenomenon -- the fact that we're
not producing better shows. I think [Wildmon] is picking on
the wrong evil."[27]

Unfortunately, neither Wildmon nor network television is committed to programming that is truly innovative and experimental
-- programming that would appeal to diverse tastes. The Coalition for Better Television only wants TV to reflect its choices
and would silence viewpoints it disagrees with. Many Americans
will agree with Wildmon that "no other invention in this century has offered such great constructive potential, only to be
used for such selfish purposes."[28] But Wildmon's vision for
television is at least as restrictive and self-serving as the
current programming he attacks.

Long before the emergence of CBTV, such mainline groups as the
Christian Life Commission of the Southern Baptist Convention,
the United Church of Christ, and Action for Children's Television were working to combat problems like sex and violence on
television. Those efforts continue without fanfare.

Q. How does the Coalition for Better Television press its case
   against the networks and advertisers?

A. Through publicity, consumer boycotts, and boycott threats.
   After repeated threats of a boycott in 1981, Wildmon finally

announced a boycott in March 1982 of RCA products and RCA-owned businesses.[29]   (RCA owns NBC-TV.) Curiously, he did not ask his supporters to stop watching NBC programs. In explaining why NBC/RCA was selected for the boycott, Wildmon mentioned numerous programs with sexually suggestive scenes, but he offered no serious monitoring data.

Moreover, it quickly became apparent that sex and violence were simply part of a bigger beef he has with network programming: their "religious discrimination" against Christian characters, values, and culture. He accused NBC of promoting a "secular supremacist" culture and a "make-it-up-as-you-go-along" value system.[30]   All of these accusations were made with scant evidence, and many demands for change had little to do with the "sex, violence, and profanity" attacks that most Americans believe are CBTV's central concerns. For example, the coalition told NBC that "the consumption of beverages should be approximately the same as in real life" and "Commercial ads which pander to sex as a base to sell products should not be aired by RCA/NBC."[31]   CBTV is insisting that the networks act as moral, political guardians for the American people.

Q. Why shouldn't CBTV call a boycott? It's perfectly legal.

A. No one disputes the legality of a consumer boycott. Economic protests have a long and honorable tradition in American politics. But just because a boycott is legal does not make it a desirable or responsible course of action. Hodding Carter III, a media critic and former Assistant Secretary of State, tells how his family's newspaper was targeted for a boycott by organized racists for 15 years. "We decided that the ideas which we expressed were so fundamental to our heritage that, boycott or no boycott, we weren't going to be silenced."[32]

A campaign against tasteless programs -- which many Americans might support -- becomes more ominous when directed against news documentaries and "incorrect" portrayals of women or other groups. Les Brown, editor of the media magazine Channels argues that CBTV:

> has crossed the line of healthy citizen involvement in adopting an action which, though legal, inevitably leads to the silencing of voices and the vanquishing of the creative and journalistic spirit. The coalition intends to clean up television by censoring it.[33]

A case can be made for better, more diverse, innovative TV
programming. A case cannot be made to purge "secular suprema-
cists" from network suites so that one religious sect or political faction can control programming. The CBTV boycott exploits
the widespread desire for better TV in order to suppress other
voices and to advance their own narrow religious/political
orthodoxy.

Q. If a citizen wants to improve the quality of TV programming, is
   a consumer boycott the only answer?

A. No! The Coalition for Better Television uses a boycott threat
   as a first resort, but there are many intermediate strategies
   that responsible media reform groups have developed:

   o Alternative program ratings. A Cambridge (Mass.) firm,
     Television Audience Assessment, Inc., has proposed a
     more sensitive rating system to measure audience satis-
     faction and loyalty and to supplement crude demographic
     data. Such a scale would not only be useful to adver-
     tisers but would also provide TV programmers with a
     more accurate measure of audience reaction.[34]

   o Feedback loops. The same firm also proposes special
     forums for viewers to talk back to the TV networks
     about program content. Programmers could become more
     responsive to audiences through such sessions.[35]

   o Stockholders' resolutions. The United Church of
     Christ's Office of Communications has used this means to
     persuade Kodak not to sponsor violent programs and
     Proctor & Gamble to draft guidelines. The UCC has also
     successfully sought changes in "The Incredible Hulk" and
     "Charlie's Angels" in this manner.[36]

   o Fairness Doctrine or FCC license renewal petitions.
     All broadcast stations must meet certain standards of
     conduct set down by the Federal Communications Commis-
     sion. Citizens who think a station has not met its
     obligations to present both sides of controversial
     issues of public importance can petition the FCC to
     grant air time to respond or, in extreme cases, deny
     renewal of their broadcasting license. Both processes
     are arduous, but certainly no more so than a nationwide
     boycott of dozens of products.

o Publicity. The CBTV has garnered much publicity but
has squandered credibility by making erroneous and
exaggerated claims. By contrast, other citizen groups
like the National PTA have issued annual lists of "ten
best" and "ten worst" programs for family viewing.
Their criteria are not arbitrary, extreme, political,
or based on sectarian religious doctrines. Similarly,
responsible media reform groups like Action for
Children's Television have successfully pressed for
better programming for children.

Q. Besides television, what other media do moral majoritarians
call into question?

A. In November 1981, Moral Majority, Inc., communications director
Cal Thomas singled out the top seven women's magazines for
articles he considered questionable.[37] Thomas pointed to an
article in Woman's Day about amniocentesis (a test that can
spot serious abnormalities in the fetus) and to an interview
with Abigail Van Buren in Family Circle in which she acknowledges her views have changed on some issues over the years --
such as her attitude toward homosexuals. Thomas is also upset
that many women's magazines endorse the Equal Rights Amendment.
The success or failure of CBTV could spur moral majoritarians
to try to regulate the reading habits of the 44 million people
who read the seven top women's magazines.

A boycott of this sort is not far-fetched. Already, the
Pro-Life Action League and other groups are trying to pressure
newspapers to drop Ann Landers for discussing the abortion
issue in her syndicated column.[38] They argue that Ms.
Landers represents "a lethal threat to the unborn" and is
an "ill-informed, secular-minded commentator misleading the
public." Ms. Landers is also condemned for informing her
readers of a poll showing that the majority of Catholics think
abortion should be legal and for commenting on the threatening
mail she's received from "pro-life" activists.

QUOTABLE QUOTES

"Americans drink sixteen times as much water as alcohol, but do you see that reflected on TV?"

> -- Rev. Donald Wildmon,
> New York magazine,
> September 23, 1981

"If you understand the beliefs of a humanist, you will realize how they came to the illogical conclusion that a clean-up TV campaign is censorship. One of the favorite watchwords of humanists is freedom."

> -- Beverly LaHaye,
> Concerned Women for America
> newsletter,
> April 1981

"The networks may beat us, they may after three or four years still have their sex and violence on television, but in the meantime, Jerry Falwell and others may increase their list of supporters by three- or four- or five-fold. And we can do something the networks cannot do, which is get involved in political campaigns....Even if we go after them and lose...we will still win by waging the battle. Because we'll bring to our cause maybe five million people we don't have now, who will then turn their attention to senators and congressmen."

> -- Richard Viguerie,
> The Boston Globe,
> November 22, 1980

"You and I, whether we like it or not, we are opinion makers; we are leaders; the way we go, millions will go with us. We have an obligation to present life not the way it is but the way it ought to be."

> -- Rev. Jerry Falwell, speaking
> to an ABC-TV official,
> Penthouse, March 1981

"Perhaps no one will miss the first program forced off the air
in the name of morality. But the New Right's censorship
crusade will not stop there. What will be the next target? A
production of A Streetcar Named Desire? A documentary on
teenage pregnancy? The news?"

> -- Peggy Charren,
> president of Action
> for Children's Television,
> Channels, June/July 1981

"Recently I watched a movie on television in which one brother
killed another, married his wife, then the son of the murdered
man killed the wrong person thinking it was his uncle; the
daughter of the wrong person went mad and his son decided on
vengeance after she had committed suicide, and the movie ended
with both young men, the mother and the uncle all dead. But
Sir Laurence Olivier played Hamlet so well, I would hesitate to
come out against it."

> -- Rev. Gerald E. Forshey,
> a United Methodist minister,
> quoted in The United Methodist
> Reporter, June 12, 1981

NOTES: THE MEDIA

1. Ron Powers, "The New 'Holy War' Against Sex and Violence,"
    TV Guide, April 18-24, 1981, pp. 6-12.

2. "Boycott of NBC-TV and RCA Urged," The New York Times,
    March 5, 1982.

3. Todd Gitlin, "The New Crusades: How the Fundamentalists
    Tied Up the Networks," American Film, October 1981.

4. Ron Powers, op. cit.

5. Richard Reeves, "'Halt Anti-Christian Bigotry--Or Else':
    The 3 TV Networks Get an Ultimatum from Rev. Wildmon," The
    Chicago Sun-Times, December 10, 1981.

6. "Battle Plan for 1982," Moral Majority, Inc.

7. "Donahue" broadcast, September 29, 1981.

8. "Report of the Fall 1980 Television Monitoring Program of
    the National Federation for Decency," Prime-Time Viewing,
    September 14 - December 5, 1980.

9. David Nyhan, "New Right Preparing for Battle Against Sex,
    Violence on TV," The Boston Globe, November 22, 1980.

10. Conversation with CBTV spokesman, March 2, 1981.

11. James Robison, direct mail solicitation, October 1981.

12. Press release, American Life Lobby, July 3, 1980. Also,
    press release, Elasah Drogin, Catholics United for Life,
    July 7, 1980. Also, An Analysis of the Coalition for
    Better Television: The Issues, the Groups, and the Future,
    Public Issues/Public Policy Group, Hill and Knowlton, Inc.

13. Rev. Donald Wildmon, National Federation for Decency,
    direct mail solicitation (undated: "The enclosed personal-
    ized opinion poll may not look like much of a weapon...").

14. Lori Scheck, Concerned Women for America, June 1981.

15. Rev. Donald Wildmon, direct mail solicitation, op. cit.

16. Cal Thomas, "Do Broadcasters Show America?" _Moral Majority Report_, February 22, 1982.

17. Reed Irvine, "Researcher Says Dan Rather Can't Be Trusted," _The NFD Informer_, September 1981, p. 8, with editor's note by Rev. Donald Wildmon.

18. Tim LaHaye, _The Battle for the Mind_ (Old Tappan, N.J.: Fleming H. Revell Co., 1980), p. 152.

19. "Choice" was the CBS Tuesday Night Movie broadcast on February 10, 1981.

20. William A. Henry III, "Another Kind of Ratings War," _Time_, July 6, 1981, pp. 17-18. Also, Gioia Diliberto, "Sponsors Run for Cover as TV Vigilante Donald Wildmon Decides It's Prime Time for a Boycott," _People_, July 6, 1981.

21. _Time_, July 6, 1981.

22. Coalition for Better Television Monitoring Form.

23. Joel Swerdlow, "The Morality Play for Control Over TV," _The Buffalo Evening News Magazine_, July 5, 1981.

24. Anthony Ramirez, "A Minister's Group Views Sexy TV Fare, Takes Notes on It", _The Wall Street Journal_, November 11, 1978.

25. Gioia Diliberto, op. cit.

26. Norman Lear, "America is Strangling on Its Obsession with the Bottom Line," acceptance speech, William O. Douglas First Amendment Award, Public Counsel, Los Angeles, March 26, 1981.

27. Tony Schwartz, _The New York Times_ syndicated article, "Coalition for Better Television Preparing New Sponsor Boycott, _The Oakland Tribune_, February 1, 1982.

28. Donald E. Wildmon, press statement, Coalition for Better Television press conference, Hyatt Regency Hotel, Washington, D.C., March 4, 1982.

29. Ibid.

30. Ibid. Also, Donald Wildmon, "Media Alert: No Network TV
    Series Shows Anyone with a Meaningful Religious Life,"
    Conservative Digest, December 1981.

31. Ibid.

32. Hodding Carter III, "Viewpoint: Will the Networks Cave?"
    The Wall Street Journal, June 11, 1981.

33. Les Brown, "Overstepping the Delicate Line," Channels,
    June/July 1981.

34. "Audience Attitudes and the Alternative Program Ratings: A
    Preliminary Study," Television Audience Assessment, Inc.,
    1981.

35. Ibid.

36. Ron Powers, op. cit.

37. Ron Powers, commentary on "Morning with Charles Kuralt and
    Diane Sawyer," broadcast, November 6, 1981.

38. Joseph M. Scheidler (Executive Director, Pro-Life Action
    League), "Media Alert: Why Dump Ann Landers," A.L.L. About
    Issues, (American Life Lobby) February 1982.

FURTHER READING: THE MEDIA

Brown, Les, Television: The Business Behind the Box (New York: Harcourt, Brace and Jovanovich, 1971).

Cole, Barry, Television Today (New York: Oxford University Press, 1981).

Gitlin, Todd, "The New Crusades: How the Fundamentalists Tied Up the Networks," American Film, October 1981.

Johnson, Nicholas, How to Talk Back to Your Television Set (Boston: Little, Brown, 1970).

Mankiewicz, Frank and Joel Swerdlow, Remote Control: Television and the Manipulation of American Life (New York: New York Times Books, 1978).

National Citizens Committee for Broadcasting, A Citizen's Primer on the Fairness Doctrine (Washington, D.C., 1982).

Newcomb, Horace, TV: The Most Popular Art (Garden City, N.Y.: Anchor Press, 1974).

Television Information Office. The New Television Pressure Groups: A Perspective on the Drive Against Diversity (TIO, National Association of Broadcasters, 1981).

RADICAL RIGHT LITERATURE

Coakley, Mary Lewis, Rated X: The Moral Case Against Television, (Westport, CT: Arlington House, 1978).

Donnelly, Elaine, One Side Versus the Other Side: A Primer on Access to the Media, Eagle Forum Education and Legal Defense Fund (St. Louis, Missouri: St. Louis Law Printing Co., 1981).

Falwell, Jerry, Listen, America! (Garden City, New York: Doubleday and Co., 1980).

LaHaye, Tim, <u>The Battle for the Family</u> (Old Tappan, N.J.: Fleming
        H. Revell Co., 1982).

Wildmon, Rev. Donald, transcript of "Donahue" broadcast,
        September 29, 1981.

    ------   , "A Rock and Pebbles," speech to the American
        Association of Advertising Agencies," Sun Valley,
        Idaho, October 1, 1981.

    ------   , "A Time for Decision," speech to the National
        Religious Broadcasters, Washington, D.C., February
        10, 1982.

Media Reform Organizations

Action for Children's Television (ACT)
46 Austin Street
Newtonville, MA 02160   617-527-7870

Christian Life Commission of the Southern Baptist Convention
460 James Robertson Parkway
Nashville, TN 37219   615-244-2495

Gray Panther Media Watch
475 Riverside Drive, Room 861
New York, NY 10027   212-870-2715

Media Access Project
1609 Connecticut Avenue, N.W.
Washington, DC 20009   202-232-4300

National Citizens Committee for Broadcasting
1530 P Street, N.W.
Washington, DC 20005   202-462-2520

National Council of Churches
  Communication Commission
475 Riverside Drive
New York, NY 10027   212-870-2567

National PTA TV Action Center
700 North Rush Street   (Illinois residents) 800-942-4266
Chicago, IL 60611   800-323-5177

Office of Communication
  of the United Church of Christ
105 Madison Avenue   212-683-3834
New York, NY 10016   212-683-5656

FOREIGN AND MILITARY POLICY

Q. What is the "Christian" version of U.S. foreign policy that ultra-fundamentalists advocate?

A. They view world events as a real-life morality drama that pits a "Christian America" against "godless communism." Communism is depicted as the incarnation of Satan, which gives a "Christian America" a divine sanction to adopt extreme and violent counter-measures. The familiar argument goes something like this:

> Communism is the enemy of The Lord God. It is the most virulent, most militant anti-Christian system in the world today. It denies God. It persecutes His people. It bans the Bible, forbids parents to teach about Christ, imprisons Christian fathers, forces Christian mothers into slave labor groups, abducts Christian children and rears them in ungodly State institutions. (Rus Walton in his FAC-Sheet newsletter) [1]

In his modern-day version of Martin Luther nailing his 95 theses to the door, Jerry Falwell sets forth his "Ninety-Five Theses for the 1980's."[2] A few of his "Christian" principles for foreign policy include:

10. That this nation serves as the only barrier to world-wide Communistic occupation.

11. That because of this, we are obligated to remain strong to assure our own liberty and to protect the very concept of freedom itself.

12. That any attempt to weaken our defense systems is both an act of treason and a crime against the remaining free nations in the world's community.

13. That all able-bodied U.S. male citizens are obligated
    to fight to the death, if necessary, to defend the
    flag.

The ultra-fundamentalist passion for military matters may be
due in part to the role of military imagery in their brand of
Christian belief. As Frances FitzGerald has noted with regard
to Falwell:

> [I]t is the military analogy that is so central to
> [Falwell's] view of the church and its role in the world.
> "The local church is an organized army equipped for
> battle, ready to charge the enemy," he has said. "The
> Sunday school is the attacking squad." And elsewhere,
> "The church should be a disciplined, charging army....
> Christians, like slaves and soldiers, ask no
> questions."[3]

The military motifs can go to extremes. A guest columnist in
James Robison's magazine, for example, once told readers that a
strong national defense would require "multi-megaton prayer
power from the Christians of this country."[4]

Q. How do ultra-fundamentalists steer around Bible passages that
   tell Christians to love their enemies and to beat swords into
   plowshares?

A. Through a selective reading of the Bible and some complex
   theological interpretations. Ultra-fundamentalists give a
   novel interpretation to the oft-quoted passages:

> And they shall beat their swords into plowshares, and
> their spears into pruning-hooks; nation shall not lift up
> sword against nation, neither shall they learn war any-
> more. (Isaiah 2:4)

> But I say unto you, Love your enemies, bless them that
> curse you, do good to them that hate you, and pray for
> them which despitefully use you, and persecute you.
> (Matthew 5:44)

Rus Walton, a tireless booster for a "Christian nation,"
disposes of these passages by pointing out, "We must not
confuse our love for our personal enemies with love for the

enemies of God." He warns that "God's people are not to be
yoked in any way with God's enemies (Ex. 23:32; Deut. 7:2; II
Cor. 6:14). To do so is to make 'a covenant with death and
with hell'...."[5]

In the same manner, Falwell claims that the Bible supports an
aggressive U.S. military policy: "Jesus was not a sissy. He
was not a pacifist."[6] Falwell also asserts that the U.S.
government (condemned as an agent of Satan in other contexts)
is divinely blessed to mete out punishment to Satan:

> The bearing of the sword by the government is correct and
> proper. Nowhere in the Bible is there a rebuke for the
> bearing of armaments...the role of government is to
> minister justice and to protect the rights of its citizens
> by being a terror to evildoers within and without the
> nation.[7]

For many other ultra-fundamentalist leaders like James Robison,
Pat Robertson, and Tim LaHaye, saber-rattling is seen as a
reliable, desirable tool in U.S. diplomacy.

Q. Are ultra-fundamentalists alarmed by the threat of nuclear war?

A. They are troubled but not terrified. They usually discuss
   nuclear warfare in terms of an apocalyptic end of the world,
   based on their reading of biblical prophecy. According to
   their theology, the world will soon experience seven years of
   great suffering and tribulation and will witness the rise of
   the Anti-Christ. In a fiery Battle of Armageddon, which will
   pit the satanic Soviet Union against Israel, the Christian
   legions will defeat the forces of darkness. Following this
   apocalypse, Christ will reign over the earth for 1,000 years
   until the Final Judgment.[8]

In this scenario, nuclear war is considered almost inevitable.
Indeed, because it is regarded as a prelude to the Second
Coming of Christ, some ultra-fundamentalists almost seem to
welcome a nuclear holocaust. Speculation about the end of
human history has such a lurid fascination for ultra-fundamentalists that a small cottage industry has emerged to generate a
steady stream of doomsday books. Perhaps the most famous of
these is Hal Lindsay's The Late, Great Planet Earth, which has
sold millions of copies. But Rev. Tim LaHaye has written his
own interpretations of biblical prophecy, The Beginning of the

End and Revelation: Illustrated and Made Plain.[9]

Rev. James Robison is also unperturbed by the prospect of a
nuclear holocaust. At a revival meeting in Memphis, Robison
said he doesn't care if all the Soviet warheads are aimed at
his house. "I think I could walk right through a nuclear
strike and not even smell of smoke if God's got a plan for my
life." Robison, who has been invited to the White House
several times, says, "I don't think we'll be destroyed in the
first strike. I think we'll be humbled. I believe there'll be
enough of us left to rally the church to preach revival
throughout the world."[10]

Numerous obscure authors like Jim McKeever have published their
own renditions of the last days of the world. McKeever's
Christians Will Go Through the Tribulation, and How to Prepare
for It, reads like a survivalist handbook, instructing readers
how to survive a nuclear attack and other catastrophes of the
coming tribulation. McKeever writes:

> A little preparation will go a long way towards helping
> you stay alive. A package of garbage bags at the office,
> a very inexpensive shelter in your home, some stored water
> -- simple things such as these do not take much money at
> all. Storing up a little bit of water and purchasing some
> fire extinguishers are good steps to begin with. The main
> thing is to pray about this matter and to do whatever God
> leads you to do. It is very possible that He wants you to
> survive World War III and to share the precious story of
> Christ with non-Christians who also survive.[11]

McKeever muses, "Most Christians fear death, which is very
strange. I believe that what Red Harper said, right after the
first atomic bomb was dropped, epitomizes what we should feel.
I heard him say, 'This here atomic bomb don't bother me at all.
It would just be BOOM, hello Lord!' Death is simply stepping
out of this messed up world into a beautiful eternity with our
Lord."[12]

Perhaps the "Christian survivalists" represent only a small
portion of moral authoritarians, but there is a consensus that
U.S. foreign and military policies are instruments of God's
will. "God expects nations that acknowledge Him to prepare to
defend themselves against external enemies," says Jim Cox, who
argues a militaristic "Christian case for defense." "God gives

the victory, but His people must prepare for their defense," he admonishes.[13]   Phyllis Schlafly, who prides herself on being "pro-life," considers the atomic bomb "a marvelous gift that was given to our country by a wise God."[14]   As for unilateral disarmament, televangelist James Robison says it "goes directly against the Bible."[15]

Q. What do other religious groups say about the nuclear arms race?

A. Most mainline religious groups have opposed the arms race and nuclear weapons for decades. Recently, a groundswell of religious activism has given the issue new urgency. Roman Catholic bishops have been perhaps the most outspoken religious leaders, but most major Protestant and Jewish organizations have also issued strongly worded statements deploring the use of nuclear weapons. These include the United Presbyterian Church in the United States; the American Baptist Churches; the Unitarian Universalist Association; the National Council of Churches; the World Council of Churches; and many others.[16]

The statement issued by the American Baptists is typical of the substance and tone of resolutions issued by other religious groups. They declared: "The presence of nuclear weapons and the willingness to use them is a direct affront to our Christian beliefs and commitment....We can find no justification in Scripture or tradition for the use of such weapons which would unleash uncontrolled devastation on the human community."[17]

Dr. Billy Graham has also come to renounce his hardline militaristic stance in favor of nuclear disarmament: "The present insanity of the global arms race, if continued, will lead inevitably to a conflagration so great that Auschwitz will seem like a minor rehearsal."[18] He conceded, "I am not a pacifist and I don't believe in unilateral disarmament," but he stressed, "I do believe in the destruction of nuclear weapons. As long as any of these weapons exist there is a danger...."[19]

Q. What policies do religious authoritarians seek towards Latin America?

A. Until recently, ultra-fundamentalists considered the Panama Canal Treaties as the most controversial U.S.-Latin American issue. The treaties, blasted as a "giveaway" of U.S. territory

and assets, were eventually ratified by the Senate in 1979.
But, as Richard Viguerie pointed out at the time, the Panama
Canal controversy served a more pragmatic political purpose:

> It's an issue the conservatives can't lose on. If we lose
> the vote in the Senate, we will have had the issue for
> eight or nine months. We will have rallied many new
> people to our cause. We will have given our supporters an
> issue, a cause to work for.[20]

As for the current unrest in Central America, the radical
right again postulates the "domino theory," in which nonaligned
Third World nations will supposedly fall to communism if the
U.S. does not intervene. Howard Phillips of the Conservative
Caucus predicts that "if our State Department permits [El
Salvador's] economic policies to continue, then next to fall
will be Honduras and Guatemala and in a couple of years, we'll
be fighting guerrillas on our own territory."[21] Robert
Billings, the founder of Moral Majority, Inc., in 1980 praised
Guatemala for its "freedom of expression, freedom of mission-
aries, few government restrictions," even though the nation's
right-wing dictatorship was in the midst of a civil war with
left-wing guerrillas.[22]

These and other foreign policy concerns are commonly portrayed
as "Christian" and even family issues. The Christian Voice in
its 1981 review of Congressional votes claimed that U.S. aid to
El Salvador and Zimbabwe were among "12 key moral/family
issues." Similarly, as part of his religio-political
manifesto, "Ninety-Five Theses for the 1980's," Rev. Falwell
believes it is a "Christian" imperative for the U.S. to "help
friendly nations" such as South Korea and South Africa (Thesis
25).

Q. How do ultra-fundamentalists regard African nations and the
United Nations?

A. Most ultra-fundamentalist leaders disapprove of Third World
nationalism and the efforts of black majorities to govern
themselves. Rev. Jerry Falwell condemned the recent change of
power in Rhodesia, saying, "The recent election of Comrade
Mugabe, the new Marxist dictator of that country, may well have
ended any opportunity of genuine Christian witness there."[23]
As for the apartheid government of South Africa, Falwell views
the black unrest in that country as the stirrings of a

communist takeover: "Undoubtedly, the next target of communist conquest will be the Republic of South Africa. The many Christian believers of that great nation need our prayers that their doors remain open to the Gospel. If we are not careful, the United States will be next."[24]

Because it is a forum that allows Third World countries to express their foreign policy views, the United Nations is another target of many ultra-fundamentalists. In Thesis 27 of his "Ninety-Five Theses for the 1980's," Rev. Falwell asserts, "[W]hile we support all genuine efforts for world peace in the community of nations, we nevertheless express little confidence in the United Nations to achieve this because of past failures and the anti-American philosophies displayed by that organization."[25]

QUOTABLE QUOTES

"Jordan is a little pipsqueak country. They haven't got any
money, they haven't got any people, they haven't got any
land....They've got no oil, they've got no strategic importance
whatsoever....I mean, I love the people, but the reality is,
they're nothing."

> -- Rev. Pat Robertson,
> "700 Club" broadcast,
> November 4, 1981

"I think I could walk right through a nuclear strike and not
even smell of smoke if God's got a plan for my life....I
believe there'll be enough of us left to rally the church to
preach the revival throughout the world."

> -- Rev. James Robison,
> Memphis Commercial Appeal
> April 10, 1982

[The atomic bomb is] "a marvelous gift that was given to our
country by a wise God."

> -- Phyllis Schlafly,
> The Boston Globe,
> July 15, 1982

"Most Christians fear death, which is very strange. I believe
that what Red Harper said, right after the first atomic bomb
was dropped, epitomizes what we should feel. I heard him say,
'This here atomic bomb don't bother me at all. It would just
be BOOM, hello Lord!' Death is simply stepping out of this
messed up world into a beautiful eternity with our Lord."

> -- Jim McKeever, author of
> Christians Will Go Through The
> Tribulation, and How to
> Prepare for It

"I knew that Iran was going to fall, and that when it did, it
would fall into the Soviet orbit....It says so in the Bible.
Those are the kinds of insights you're not going to get, say
from Dan Rather."

> -- Rev. Pat Robertson
> The Wall Street Journal
> September 11, 1981

"It was a mistake to identify the Kingdom of God with the
American way of life. I've come to see that other cultures
have their own way that may be of just as great a value....I've
come to understand there are no simplistic answers to the
exceedingly complicated problems we face as a country -- and as
a planet."

> -- Billy Graham, Parade magazine,
> February 1, 1981

"The presence of nuclear weapons and the willingness to use
them is a direct affront to our Christian beliefs and
commitment....We can find no justification in Scripture or
tradition for the use of such weapons which would unleash
uncontrolled devastation on the human community."

> -- "To Proclaim Peace: Religious
> Statements on the Arms Race"

Rev. Jerry Falwell on Foreign and Military Policy

"Jesus was not a sissy. He was not a pacifist."

-- The Washington Star,
   July 3, 1980

"The bearing of the sword by the government is correct and proper. Nowhere in the Bible is there a rebuke for the bearing of armaments...the role of government is to minister justice and to protect the rights of its citizens by being a terror to evildoers within and without the nation."

-- Listen, America!, p. 98

"The recent election of Comrade Mugabe, the new Marxist dictator of that country, may well have ended any opportunity of genuine Christian witness there."

-- Listen, America!, p. 256

"[W]hile we support all genuine efforts for world peace in the community of nations, we nevertheless express little confidence in the United Nations to achieve this because of past failures and the anti-American philosophies displayed by that organization."

-- Thesis 27 of Rev. Falwell's
   "Ninety-Five Theses for the
   1980's,"

NOTES: FOREIGN AND MILITARY POLICY

1. Rus Walton, FAC-Sheet #21, "Making Covenants With God's Enemies."

2. Jerry Falwell, "Ninety-Five Theses for the 1980's."

3. Frances FitzGerald, "A Disciplined, Charging Army," The New Yorker, May 18, 1981.

4. Jim Cox, "A Christian Case for Defense," Life's Answer (magazine of James Robison Evangelical Association), October 1981, pp. 10-11.

5. Rus Walton, op. cit.

6. Lisa Myers, "Falwell Strives for Role as Political Kingmaker," The Washington Star, July 3, 1980.

7. Jerry Falwell, Listen, America! (Garden City, N.Y.: Doubleday and Co., 1979), p. 98.

8. William Martin, "Waiting for the End," The Atlantic Monthly, June 1982, pp. 31-7. See also, James L. Franklin, "The Religious Right and the New Apocalypse," The Boston Globe, May 2, 1982.

9. Tim LaHaye, The Beginning of the End (Wheaton, Illinois: Tyndale House Publishers, Inc., 1972). Also, Tim LaHaye, Revelation: Illustrated and Made Plain (Grand Rapids, Michigan: Zondervan Publishing House, 1973).

10. Michael Clark, "Revival or Nukes is Robison's Choice," Memphis Commercial Appeal, April 10, 1982. For Rev. Robison's vision of the end of history, see Kenneth L. Woodward, "This Way to Armageddon," Newsweek, July 5, 1982.

11. Jim McKeever, Christians Will Go Through the Tribulation, And How to Prepare for It (Medford, Oregon: Omega Publications, 1978), p. 135.

12. Ibid., p. 294.

13. Jim Cox, op. cit.

14. Susan Page, "That Schlafly Touch," The Boston Globe, July 15, 1980.

15. Harry Cook, "Is the Country Doomed?" The Detroit Free Press, October 24, 1981.

16. John Donaghy, editor, "To Proclaim Peace: Religious Statements on the Arms Race" (Available from the Fellowship of Reconciliation, Disarmament Program, Box 271, Nyack, N.Y. 10960, for $1).

17. Ibid. See also, Charles Austin, "2 Major Protestant Churches Call for an End to Arms Race," The New York Times, December 18, 1981.

18. "A Change of Heart: Billy Graham on the Nuclear Arms Race," Sojourners, August 1979, pp. 12-14.

19. Marguerite Michaels, "Billy Graham: America is Not God's Only Kingdom," Parade magazine, February 1, 1981, pp. 5-8.

20. William J. Lanouette, "The Panama Canal Treaties -- Playing in Peoria and in the Senate," National Journal, October 8, 1977, p. 1560.

21. Harry Covert, "Will Guatemala Fall Next in Central America?" Moral Majority Report, May 1, 1980, p. 4.

22. Ibid.

23. Jerry Falwell, Listen, America! (Garden City, New York: Doubleday and Co., 1979), p. 256.

24. Ibid.

25. Jerry Falwell, "Ninety-Five Theses for the 1980's."

ECONOMICS

Q. Is there an ultra-fundamentalist approach to economic issues?

A. Yes. For the radical religious right, economic matters do not
inspire the same sort of emotional enthusiasm as, say, the
"pro-family" movement or educational issues. Nonetheless,
ultra-fundamentalists hold strong convictions about unregulated
markets, labor-management relations, social aid programs, and
the Social Security system. It is an article of faith for
ultra-fundamentalists that "Bible principles of ethics are the
standard of economics," in the words of Dr. Gary North, founder
of the Institute for Christian Economics.[1]

Jerry Falwell's economic positions provide a good illustration.
"The free enterprise system is clearly outlined in the Book of
Proverbs in the Bible," says Falwell in his classic, Listen,
America! "Jesus Christ made it clear that the work ethic was
part of His plan for man. Ownership of property is biblical.
Competition in business is biblical. Ambitious and successful
business management is clearly outlined as a part of God's plan
for His People."[2] Falwell approvingly quotes secular commen-
tators like Milton Friedman, William Simon, Senator Jesse
Helms, and Margaret Thatcher in Listen, America![3] Other
ultra-fundamentalists make leaps of theological interpretation
to condemn the levels of taxation, the Social Security system,
the end of the gold standard, regulations to protect the
environment and people's health and safety, and social aid
programs.[4]

Q. What is "Christian economics"?

A. A handful of ultra-fundamentalists have tried to create a new
academic discipline by joining biblical ethics with economics.
The godfather of this effort is Dr. Gary North, who founded the
Institute for Christian Economics in 1976 after ten years of
doing such work. North's economic theory holds that the

government is God's rival and, thus, government-managed economic decision making is godless and fallible. The "free market," by contrast, is regarded as the natural, divine plan. "Christian economics" claims different premises from secular theories:

> Man is not God; God is not impotent, irrelevant, or silent; men are responsible for their actions, both before other men (the market) and God; societies are responsible for enforcing the moral laws of God, and those that refuse eventually suffer economic losses (or worse), etc....[5]

Richard Viguerie's Conservative Digest explains why such a chasm separates traditional and Christian economics:

> The trouble with Christian economics is that econ-omists are repulsed by the very thought of religion having any influence over the analytic principles of economics; Christians are repulsed by the idea that they are religiously responsible for adhering to these economic rules and regulations.[6]

"Christian economists" do not blame national economic woes on crop failures, trade imbalances, or other complexities because these are regarded as symptoms of a deeper problem: the sinful-ness of the American people. Our nation's economic salvation thus depends on our religious salvation. Says Falwell: "When we as a country again acknowledge God as our creator and Jesus Christ as the Savior of mankind, we will be able to turn this nation around economically as well as in every other way."[7]

Q. How well-developed is "Christian economic theory"?

A. Not very. The economic literature of "Christian economics" resembles a patchwork quilt. Different advocates advance arguments that are variously crude or sophisticated, folksy or abstract, strictly biblical or somewhat secular. They want "to convince the liberal-leaning evangelicals of the biblical nature of the free market system."[8]

To meet this task, several self-styled "Christian economists" pore over the Bible looking for divine guidance on contemporary economic problems. Gary North dispenses his economic advice in several bimonthly newsletters, especially in Christian Recon-struction and Bible Economics Today.[9] Another "Christian

economist," Rus Walton, makes his own creative interpretations
of the Bible in his newsletter, FAC-Sheet.[10]   ("FAC" stands
for "Fundamentals for American Christians.")   Walton is the
founder of the Plymouth Rock Foundation and a stalwart in
the crusade to make America a "Christian nation."

Q. Do capitalism and Christianity go hand in hand?

A. Most ultra-fundamentalists believe that the U.S. economic
system is divinely ordained, while economic systems that
involve government planning or regulation are pagan, atheistic systems.   The choice, says Biblical Economics Today,
is between our "Judeo-Christian economic heritage" and
"atheistic regimented collectivism."[11]   The newsletter
explains that "American prosperity has really been a by-
product of the moral principles under which we produce and
exchange goods and services.   The strategy of those who
would weaken our nation is to weaken our faith in our
principles."[12]

Rus Walton agrees, adding, "That should be no surprise.   When
we walk in the light of The Lord, we prosper; when we stray
from the way, things go sour."[13]   William C. Wagner, chairman
of a Bible-based investment seminar and director of financial
planning for William R. Bright's Great Commission Foundation
(Bright is founder and president of Campus Crusade for Christ),
asserts, "The Bible -- the inerrant word of God -- is the
undisputed book on financial success.   There are some 500
verses in the Bible on prayer, but there are 2,000 on money
and possessions."[14]

Q. Why do many leaders of the radical religious right condemn the
Social Security system?

A. There is a spectrum of reasons.   Some ultra-fundamentalists
agree with the secular New Right that the financial structure
and social aid goals of Social Security should be changed.
But other moral majoritarians focus instead on the "ethical"
problems of Social Security: that it violates the Bible and
contributes to the decline of the traditional family.

The Heritage Foundation has denounced the "welfare principles"
of the Social Security system, that it pays "substantial un-
earned benefits to those generally not considered needy."[15]
The Heritage Foundation also complains about the progressive

structure of the benefit formula, which returns a higher portion of wages to the poor than to the rich. Many New Right groups want to make Social Security a voluntary system run partly or completely by private industry.

Phyllis Schlafly is also a vocal critic of Social Security, but from a different angle. When the Department of Health, Education and Welfare (now Health and Human Services) proposed changes in 1979 that would equalize the benefits formula, Schlafly blasted it as "the women's lib plan to drive all wives and mothers out of the home by placing financial penalties on the traditional family unit."[16] She reasoned that because the regulations would make wives shoulder a more equal burden of Social Security payments, there would be a "built-in incentive to the wife to divorce her husband rather than stay married...."[17]

Schlafly sees the Social Security system primarily as an instrument to reinforce the traditional family and male/female gender roles. Not only should it be used to bolster marriages, says Schlafly, but it should be used to punish those who choose not to have children:

> If people decide not to have children, they should be forced to sign a piece of paper saying that they will forfeit Social Security benefits. Even if they have worked all their lives. If they're not willing to have children...then they shouldn't be entitled to Social Security.[18]

Probably the most extreme complaints against the Social Security system are made by biblical literalists like Rus Walton, who consider it "an example of disobedience to God's law regarding the family, the care of the elderly, and 'welfare' programs. Through OSAI (Old Age and Survivors' Insurance), there has been an attempt to shirk personal and family responsibilities and transfer them to the State; that won't work." (original emphasis)[19]

Rev. R.J. Rushdoony, writing in televangelist James Robison's monthly magazine, tells readers that no Christian in the Continental Army applied for a federal pension because of I Timothy 5:8: "But if any provide not for his own, and specially for those of his house, he hath denied the faith, and is worse than an infidel."[20] Rev. Rushdoony, who is a member

of the Board of Governors of the Council for National Policy,
advises modern-day Christians to be wary of the "sinful" Social
Security system:

> Clearly, failure to provide for one's needy kin is a
> fearful offense in the sight of God. The Social Security
> system is a welcome fact for all such sinners, who are
> readier to see this tax increase than to care for their
> parents. [21]

Presumably, Walton, Rushdoony, and their followers would like
to see the Social Security system abolished entirely -- for
biblical reasons -- but it is a proposal unlikely to sit well
with millions of elderly Americans who may not hold the same
religious convictions.

Q. What do ultra-fundamentalists say about various government
   programs?

A. Consistent with their belief that economic fortunes are dic-
   tated by moral character, ultra-fundamentalists have little
   sympathy for the unemployed. They consider unemployment
   insurance and other government programs as wasteful payments to
   idlers. Falwell assures us that his sense of Christian charity
   extends to the sick and elderly, but not to the

> lazy, trifling bunch lined up in unemployment offices
> who would not work in a pieshop eating the holes out of
> donuts....My edict for them is, Let them starve. [22]

Falwell also compares the situation of the unemployed to two
spoiled dogs a friend once gave him. The dogs, who were
accustomed to meat, refused at first to eat the Purina he set
out for them. "But after four days, they did! And if we let
these bums get hungry enough, they will find a job and they
will go to work and become productive citizens."[23]

The radical right condemns a variety of federal programs:

   o Community programs. In its April 1982 issue, Conservative
     Digest unleashed a full-scale attack on dozens of federal
     community programs and called on Congress and the Presi-
     dent to "de-fund the Left." Among the 175 "left-leaning"
     groups that the magazine targeted were the American Bar
     Association, the National Retired Teachers Association,

the Center for Independent Living, and the Audubon Society.
Said Richard Viguerie, publisher of Conservative Digest,
"Federal funding of these groups is like an ugly cancer
growing inside our government. Cosmetic surgery --
trimming a little bit away here and there -- just won't
work. If any is left, it will continue to grow until it
poisons the whole system and destroys it. Only radical
surgery can remove it once and for all."[24]

o Worker safety and health: "I think we ought to take the
shackles off [business] and get rid of outfits like OSHA,"
said Jerry Falwell. "We're making it so difficult to make
money that there are no jobs anymore. Businessmen have
lost their incentive. I don't think a guy who makes a lot
of money should pay more taxes than a guy who makes a
little."[25]

o Minimum wage laws: "Why the drastic increase in unemployment among non-white teenagers?" asks Rus Walton. His
answer: "By far the greatest cause has been the Federal
minimum wage laws....One of the most helpful things we
could do would be repeal the minimum wage laws. Get
government out of the wage-setting business and let
minimum wages seek their own level."[26]

o Legal Services Corporation. The Conservative Caucus,
headed by Howard Phillips, spearheaded a drive in 1981 to
abolish the Legal Services Corporation (LSC), the government-funded program that provides legal assistance to the
poor. In its report, "Missionaries for Liberalism: Uncle
Sam's Established Church," the Conservative Caucus accuses
the LSC of "illegal lobbying activities" by employees who
"have used their mandates to represent the poor in a way
which may be antithetical to the interests of the larger
portion of their clients."[27] When serving in the Nixon
administration, Phillips sought to abolish the Office of
Economic Opportunity, the federal agency that coordinated
funding of several community services programs.

QUOTABLE QUOTES

[How can U.S. economic problems be solved?] "There's the biblical way and the way we ought to do it, and that is to declare a year of Jubilee and cancel all the debts."

> -- Rev. Pat Robertson,
> "700 Club" broadcast,
> December 28, 1981

"The Bible -- the inerrant word of God -- is the indisputed book on financial success. There are some 500 verses in the Bible on prayer, but there are over 2,000 on money and possessions."

> -- William C. Wagner,
> financial associate of
> William R. Bright, founder
> and president of Campus
> Crusade for Christ,
> The Los Angeles Times,
> June 1, 1981

"Man is not God; God is not impotent, irrelevant or silent; men are responsible for their actions, both before other men (the market) and God; societies are responsible for enforcing the moral laws of God, and those that refuse eventually suffer economic losses (or worse)...."

> -- Gary North,
> founder of the Institute
> for Christian Economics,
> Conservative Digest,
> November 1981

"If people decide not to have children, they should be forced to sign a piece of paper saying that they will forfeit Social Security benefits. Even if they have worked all their lives. If they're not willing to have children...then they shouldn't be entitled to Social Security."

> -- Phyllis Schlafly,
> The Philadelphia News
> July 2, 1981

Rev. Jerry Falwell and "Christian Economics"

"When we as a country again acknowledge God as our creator and
Jesus Christ as the Savior of mankind, we will be able to turn
this nation around economically as well as in every other way."

-- Listen, America!, p. 81

"Jesus Christ made it clear that the work ethic was part of his
plan for man. Ownership of property is biblical. Competition
in business is biblical. Ambitious and successful business
management is clearly outlined as a part of God's plan for His
people."

-- Listen, America!, p. 13

"There is not an unemployment problem in this country. People
today are looking for a position, not a job. They can make
more money by doing nothing. Well, this world doesn't owe
anybody anything -- not work or anything."

-- Speech to Word of Life Inn
and Camp, June 19, 1981,
Ticonderoga (N.Y.) Sentinel,
June 30, 1981

"I believe we should care for the sick and those who cannot
work. But I will tell you what I don't believe in: I don't
believe we ought to feed that lazy, trifling bunch lined up in
unemployment offices who would not work in a pieshop eating the
holes out of donuts...."

-- America Can Be Saved, p. 35

[Material wealth] "is God's way of blessing people who put Him
first."

-- Newsweek, September 15, 1980

"I think we ought to take the shackles off [business] and get
rid of outfits like OSHA. We're making it so difficult to make
money that there are no jobs anymore. Businessmen have lost
their incentive. I don't think a guy who makes a lot of money
should pay more taxes than a guy who makes a little."

-- The Atlanta Constitution,
August 23, 1980

NOTES: ECONOMICS

1. Gary North, "What is the ICE?" (undated).

2. Jerry Falwell, Listen, America! (Garden City, N.Y.:
    Doubleday and Co., 1980), p. 13.

3. Ibid. See especially the chapter, "A Look At Our
    Government Today," pp. 69-81.

4. See, e.g., Rus Walton, FAC-Sheet #1, "Debts and Deficits";
    FAC-Sheet #2, "Inflation"; FAC-Sheet #3, "The Cost of
    Government"; FAC-Sheet #9, "Value-Added Taxation"; and
    FAC-Sheet #25, "Money, Morality and God." See also Jerry
    Falwell, Listen, America!, passim.

5. "Christian Economics? Yes, and Gary North's Institute
    Will Tell You All About It," Conservative Digest, November
    1981, p. 40.

6. Ibid.

7. Jerry Falwell, Listen, America!, p. 81.

8. Gary North, "What is the ICE?" (undated).

9. Christian Reconstruction is published six times a year,
    alternating with Biblical Economics Today. Both are
    available free upon request from the Institute for
    Christian Economics, P.O. Box 6116, Tyler, TX 75711.

10. FAC-Sheet is published by the Plymouth Rock Foundation,
    P.O. Box 425, Marlborough, NH 03455.

11. D.P. Diffine, "Christianity and Capitalism: Friends or
    Foes?" Biblical Economics Today, December/January 1982.

12. Ibid.

13. Rus Walton, One Nation Under God (Washington, D.C.:
    Third Century Publishers, 1975).

14. Russell Chandler, "God as Capitalist: Seminar Promotes
    Religion and Riches," The Los Angeles Times, June 1, 1981.

15. United Press International dispatch, "Voluntary Social Security Urged by Conservative Group," The Washington Post, January 4, 1982.

16. Phyllis Schlafly, "Changing Social Security to Hurt the Homemaker," The Phyllis Schlafly Report, June 1979.

17. Ibid.

18. Walter Greg, "The Divine Mrs. Phyllis," The Philadelphia News, July 2, 1981.

19. Rus Walton, FAC-Sheet #22, "Social Security, the Family & the Elderly" (newsletter of the Plymouth Rock Foundation).

20. R.J. Rushdoony, "Social (In)Security," Life's Answer, October 1981, pp. 4-5.

21. Ibid.

22. Jerry Falwell, America Can Be Saved (Murfreesboro, Tennessee: Sword of the Lord Publishers, 1979), p. 35.

23. Ibid., p. 36.

24. Michael E. Hammond, "Missionaries for Liberalism: Uncle Sam's Established Church" (Vienna, Virginia: The Conservative Caucus, 1981).

25. Jim Auchmutey, "The Gospel According to Falwell, The Atlanta Constitution, August 23, 1980.

26. Rus Walton, One Nation Under God, p. 143.

BOOKS INTO ASHES

By Kurt Vonnegut

My novel Slaughterhouse-Five was actually burned in a
furnace by a school janitor in Drake, North Dakota, on instructions from the school committee there, and the school board made
public statements about the unwholesomeness of the book. Even
by the standards of Queen Victoria, the only offensive line in
the entire novel in this: "Get out of the road, you dumb
m(___)." This is spoken by an American antitank gunner to an
unarmed American chaplain's assistant during the Battle of the
Bulge in Europe in December 1944, the largest single defeat of
American arms (the confederacy excluded) in history. The
chaplain's assistant had attracted enemy fire.

So on November 16, 1973, I wrote as follows to Charles
McCarthy of Drake, North Dakota:

Dear Mr. McCarthy:

I am writing to you in your capacity as chairman of the
Drake School Board. I am among those American writers
whose books have been destroyed in the now famous furnace
of your school.

Certain members of your community have suggested that my
work is evil. This is extraordinarily insulting to me.
The news from Drake indicates to me that books and writers
are very unreal to you people. I am writing this letter
to let you know how real I am.

I want you to know, too, that my publisher and I have done
absolutely nothing to exploit the disgusting news from

Drake. We are not clapping each other on the back,
crowing about all the books we will sell because of the
news. We have declined to go on television, have written
no fiery letters to editorial pages, have granted no
lengthy interviews. We are angered and sickened and
saddened. And no copies of this letter have been sent to
anybody else. You now hold the only copy in your hands.
It is a strictly private letter from me to the people of
Drake, who have done so much to damage my reputation in
the eyes of their children and then in the eyes of the
world. Do you have the courage and ordinary decency to
show this letter to the people, or will it, too, be con-
signed to the fires of your furnace?

I gather from what I read in the papers and hear on
television that you imagine me, and some other writers,
too, as being sort of ratlike people who enjoy making
money from poisoning the minds of young people. I am
in fact a large, strong person, fifty-one years old, who
did a lot of farm work as a boy, who is good with tools.
I have raised six children, three my own and three adopted.
They have all turned out well. Two of them are farmers.
I am a combat infantry veteran from World War II, and
hold a Purple Heart. I have earned whatever I own by hard
work. I have never been arrested or sued for anything.
I am so much trusted with young people and by young people
that I have served on the faculties of the University of
Iowa, Harvard, and the City College of New York. Every
year I receive at least a dozen invitations to be commence-
ment speaker at colleges and high schools. My books are
probably more widely used in schools than those of any
other living American fiction writer.

If you were to bother to read my books, to behave as
educated persons would, you would learn that they are not
sexy, and do not argue in favor of wildness of any kind.
They beg that people be kinder and more responsible than
they often are. It is true that some of the characters
speak coarsely. That is because people speak coarsely in
real life. Especially soldiers and hardworking men speak
coarsely, and even our most sheltered children know that.
And we know, too, that those words really don't damage
children much. They didn't damage us when we were young.
It was evil deeds and lying that hurt us.

After I have said all this, I am sure you are still ready to respond, in effect, "Yes, yes -- but it still remains our right and our responsibility to decide what books our children are going to be made to read in our community." This is surely so.   But it is also true that if you exercise that right and fulfill that responsibility in an ignorant, harsh, un-American manner, then people are entitled to call you bad citizens and fools.   Even your own children are entitled to call you that.

I read in the newspaper that your community is mystified by the outcry from all over the country about what you have done.   Well, you have discovered that Drake is a part of American civilization, and your fellow Americans can't stand it that you have behaved in such an uncivilized way. Perhaps you will learn from this that books are sacred to free men for very good reasons, and that wars have been fought against nations which hate books and burn them. If you are an American, you must allow all ideas to circulate freely in your community, not merely your own.

If you and your board are now determined to show that you in fact have wisdom and maturity when you exercise your powers over the education of your young, then you should acknowledge that it was a rotton lesson you taught young people in a free society when you denounced and then burned books -- books you hadn't even read.   You should also resolve to expose your children to all sorts of opinions and information, in order that they will be better equipped to make decisions and to survive.

Again: you have insulted me, and I am a good citizen, and I am very real.

*

That was seven years ago.   There has so far been no reply. At this very moment, as I write in New York City, Slaughter-house-Five has been banned from school libraries not fifty miles from here (on Long Island).   A legal battle begun several years ago rages on.   The school board in question has found lawyers eager to attack the First Amendment tooth and nail. There is never a shortage anywhere of lawyers eager to attack the First Amendment, as though it were nothing more than a clause in a lease from a crooked slumlord.

LIBRARY BILL OF RIGHTS

The American Library Association affirms that all libraries are forums for information and ideas, and that the following basic policies should guide their services.

1. Books and other library resources should be provided for the interest, information, and enlightenment of all people of the community the library serves. Materials should not be excluded because of the origin, background, or views of those contributing to their creation.

2. Libraries should provide materials and information presenting all points of view on current and historical issues. Materials should not be proscribed or removed because of partisan or doctrinal disapproval.

3. Libraries should challenge censorship in the fulfillment of their responsibility to provide information and enlightenment.

4. Libraries should cooperate with all persons and groups concerned with resisting abridgment of free expression and free access to ideas.

5. A person's right to use a library should not be denied or abridged because of origin, age, background, or views.

6. Libraries which make exhibit spaces and meeting rooms available to the public they serve should make such facilities available on an equitable basis, regardless of the beliefs or affiliations of individuals or groups requesting their use.

Adopted June 18, 1948.
Amended February 2, 1967, and January 23, 1980, by the ALA Council.

WHERE WE STAND:
THE EVANGELICAL RIGHT

American Jewish Congress

There is a mood developing in some quarters of American
life that is deeply disquieting.

For the most part it has been engendered by the scurrilous
accusations and violent rhetoric wielded by the Evangelical
Right during recent political campaigns. Imperious and self-
righteous, this new mood is contradictory of the traditionally
open, inclusive character of the American people. It is the
inevitable result of the deliberate manipulation of fear and
suspicion as a political program - fear, especially, of the
risks and diversity inherent in democracy and freedom. The
solution to uncertainty proposed by the Evangelical Right is to
wall us within the limits of the religious doctrine, to straight-
jacket our minds, to require that we subordinate our differing
views to their version of religious truth.

Under our constitutional system, religious spokesmen have
the right to urge and advocate political positions. Religious
groups have a natural and legitimate interest in the quality of
public life and their political advocacy does not infringe upon
the constitutional requirement of separation of Church and
State. But the methods adopted by the Evangelical Right to
advance its views are divisive and destructive: they are deeply
offensive to the principles of democracy if not to its laws.

The device used by the Evangelical Right to intimidate and
suppress difference is to claim for itself an absolute moral
and political rectitude allegedly validated by the Bible and
confirmed by Revelation: a rectitude so perfect and complete as
to preclude all possibility of reputable disagreement. They
not only claim that they represent a moral majority but act as
if they possess a moral monopoly. In their terms, expression
of disagreement is not only evidence of lack of wisdom, it is
proof of lack of virtue.

We reject those claims and those who make them. We deplore
their willingness to wield religious commitment as an instrument
of political coercion, their use of fundamentalist piety as the

principle measure of political competence, their readiness to
invoke Divine authority -- and thus trivialize Divine sanction
-- for every minute, ephemeral political issue which they find
of current interest. We deplore their efforts to intimidate
where they cannot persuade, to bully by using the size of their
electronic congregations and to threaten political reprisal by
the proliferation of their "hit lists." We deplore, finally,
their efforts to play upon and abuse the apprehension and
emotional vulnerabilty that so often accompany genuine spiritual search. These tactics of the Evangelical Right have
degraded our national political discourse.

Fortunately, these excesses have come under increasingly
critical scrutiny by analysts and observers cutting across the
political spectrum, including most recently the president of
Yale University and even such conservative spokesmen as Senator
Barry Goldwater. We join a call to revitalize and rehabilitate
the political process. This would require blunt disclosure and
identification of Evangelical Right spokesmen as entrepreneurs
of politics rather than as disinterested purveyors of exalted
truths. It requires the exclusion from permissible political
debate of slander of a candidate's moral qualifications because
his political judgments fail to conform to someone else's
sectarian specifications; and finally it calls for our own
renewed and diligent efforts to reinforce those areas of personal and public freedom that have been targeted for destruction by the strategists of the New Right.

We are mindful that many leaders and spokesmen for the
Evangelical Right vigorously defend and support the State of
Israel. We acknowledge and welcome that support, but this
consideration is irrelevant to our assessment of their domestic
programs. The damage done by their efforts to curtail domestic
freedom is not made less by the soundness of their views on
Israel. Although we welcome their support for Israel this will
in no way cause us to mitigate or modify our opposition to the
many policies and practices of the Evangelical Right with which
we disagree.

That opposition, however, will not be availing unless it
extends beyond merely documenting the excesses of the Evangelical Right and developing a counter-rhetoric. It must include a
more rigorous and forceful assertion of our traditional concerns, both in the public forum and, when necessary, in the
courts.

The way to confront the New Right is to challenge it on
the issues -- on such issues as support for the separation of
Church and State and protection of the public school classroom;
support of the Equal Rights Amendment and the right of women to
choose to have an abortion; support for human rights and opposition to all oppressive governments; support for the right to
dissent and opposition to censorship; support for compassionate
social welfare legislation and opposition to discrimination and
poverty -- and in short, by aggressive advocacy of the classic
agenda of democracy.

We are encouraged by the knowledge that there are many
others, including the majority of evangelicals in this country,
who are equally disturbed by the electoral depredations of the
Right and with whom we can find common cause. The Evangelical
Right is a recent political phenomenon and may prove to be a
brief one. Certainly, in retrospect, its early boast of total
effectiveness must be dismissed as grossly inflated.

The American people have been notoriously impatient with
zealots, single-truth fanatics of all types, and especially with
those who would preempt the right to personal decision making.
It is inconceivable that a nation so insistent upon new possibility, so adamantly independent, will long countenance the
erosion of the pluralistic tradition that has made our country
so extraordinary and so strong.

This statement was drafted by Phil Baum, associate national
director of the American Jewish Congress. It was adopted
as a resolution by the National Governing Council of the
Congress on October 4, 1981.

THE SEARCH FOR "NEW RULES"

Remarks by Anthony T. Podesta
to the
Religion Newswriters Association
June 12, 1982

"All modern American literature comes from one book by
Mark Twain called Huckleberry Finn," according to Ernest
Hemingway. Hemingway said, "It's the best book we've had.
All American writing comes from that." Hemingway's literary
judgment is intriguing -- and even a little ominous -- because
once again Huckleberry Finn is under attack by censorship
crusaders. Are we destroying our own best accomplishments?

So I took Huckleberry Finn off the shelf to re-read and
came across some themes that seem terribly relevant to the
troubles we face as a nation today. The most arresting image
was of Huck and Jim floating down the Mississippi on the raft.
As a white boy and an escaped slave, Huck and Jim were very
different people. But Huck realized that on the tiny raft, he
and Jim had to learn a basic code of behavior. As Huck
explains:

> What you want, above all things, on a raft, is for
> everybody to be satisfied, and feel right and kind
> toward the others.

Mark Twain was clearly writing about the challenges we
face as a nation in fulfilling the American Dream. Like Huck
and Jim, the American people come from very different backgrounds. We have different religious beliefs, different ethnic
traditions, different colored skin. But on a crowded raft, it
is very important that everybody be satisfied, and feel right
and kind toward the others.

Make no mistake, it is a difficult proposition. But if
we are going to get along as a diverse people, there have to
be some rules for governing ourselves. Some of the rules are
legal, constitutional rules. Others are moral, ethical and
cultural values and traditions. What's important is that we
agree on the rules and abide by them. In so doing, we enhance
the possibilities that we can have peace and harmony on our
crowded little raft.

Some of the rules that govern life in America are in flux.
There is a debate as to what personal rules should govern
people's lives and what constitutional rules should govern our
national life. The proliferation of "lifestyles" is almost as
great as the proliferation of constitutional amendments.
Pollster Daniel Yankelovich has identified this trend in his
book, The New Rules. He argues that Americans no longer abide
by the values that governed the post-war generation, but they
have not yet crystallized "the new rules."

Women, blacks, and other minorities have fought toward
equal civil rights with their fellow rafters, but some segments
of our society still refuse to accept this fact. We cannot go
back to the bygone era when bigotry was pervasive, sex discrimination was the rule, and political conformity was enforced by
congressional witch hunts.

If we will not go back to the world of "Father Knows
Best," what lies ahead? What "new rules" or social covenant
can we formulate to help everybody be satisfied and feel right
and kind toward the others? For the moment, we are stranded
between the "no more" and the "not yet" with no obvious consensus.

The guidance we need, I submit, will come from the "rules"
of constitutional democracy and the ethical values that derive
from religious teachings. These two value systems are at the
core of the American experience. Especially in times of great
change and upheaval, the Constitution and religious faith have
given Americans strength and guidance.

It does a disservice to reduce either democracy or religion to a mere "set of rules" because they are, of course, much
more. They are living traditions that guide our daily lives.
More importantly, their common values bind us together as a
people. Our search for "the new rules," therefore, should
begin with the traditions of religion and constitutional
democracy.

PEOPLE FOR THE AMERICAN WAY has embarked upon such a
search. We believe that our covenant as a nation is embodied
in the Constitution and the Bill of Rights, which lay out
fundamental rules for self-government. But the strength of
this covenant is grounded in the everyday work of countless
social institutions: public schools, civic groups, families,

synagogues and churches. These institutions are equally
important to our national well-being. If churches and schools
and families are not stable and secure -- if they cannot create
the bonds of community -- then our many cherished democratic
freedoms are jeopardized as well.

The question before us is how to rejuvenate these institutions. How can we stabilize our families amidst skyrocketing
divorce and unemployment rates? How can public education
prepare our children for the diverse challenges of life in a
pluralistic, democratic society? How can our churches provide
moral guidance and strengthen our communities? Finding answers
to these questions will strengthen our constitutional democracy....

If our children are to grow up respecting their fellow
citizens on our crowded raft, they must learn to respect the
rules of constitutional democracy. The First Amendment freedoms of speech and religion, the separation of church and
state, and equal protection under the law -- these are constitutional "rules" that help our diverse citizenry get along
together. They unite us despite our many, many differences.

Americans have not always enjoyed the harmony that these
principles help produce. Dissenters like Roger Williams were
banished for their religious convictions and Quakers suffered
jail, whipping, banishment and even death. Until 1775, the
Puritan colonies forced all citizens to pay a compulsory religious tax, even if they disagreed with Puritan religious
beliefs. Pennsylvania wrote into its constitution a religious
oath excluding non-Christians from officeholding. Nine of the
original thirteen states at one time had an official state
religion.

Ironically, it was the state of Virginia, even in
Lynchburg, that banished Roman Catholics and banned Baptists.
But it was in Madison's and Jefferson's Virginia that the
statute on Religious Liberty was enacted and served as a
precursor to the First Amendment and Article VI.

Contemporary Americans too easily forget what ugly conflicts have been avoided because of our nation's constitutional
guarantees. Now that the First Amendment is 191 years old, we
must not forget that it was enacted for the purpose of protecting freedom of conscience and religious liberty, and still

today serves that purpose. Many Americans forget James Madison's far-sighted plea before the Virginia House of Delegates that "the same authority which could establish Christianity in exclusion of all other religions, could establish any particular sect of Christians in exclusion of all other sects."

Government must not be the captive of any sectarian religious view. One of the greatest advances in the history of civil society and religious freedom is the doctrine of church/ state separation. Rev. Falwell shows little respect for this tradition, when he writes that "America is a Christian Nation," and demands a "Christian Bill of Rights."

Another ultra-fundamentalist leader does not see the Constitution as a shared national heritage, but as the exclusive possession of his particular Christian denomination. Rev. Pat Robertson tells his national TV audience that the Constitution is "a marvelous document for self-government by Christian people." But he warns that "the minute you turn the document into the hands of non-Christian and atheist people, they can use it to destroy the very foundations of our society -- and that's what's been happening."

PEOPLE FOR THE AMERICAN WAY has joined the discussion over values that can bind us together. We must remember that in a culture that too often worships the newest fad and discards the faded, all the old rules are not necessarily bad and not all the new ones are necessarily good. But it is important, as we sort through the old and struggle with the new, that we distinguish between, on the one hand, rules which are private values we choose freely to govern our own personal lives, and on the other hand, the public rules that govern all of us as the law of the land.

Two old rules are, we think, self-evidently good and mutually interdependent: pluralistic religious liberty and constitutional democracy. So, while we must respect the personal values of those who live their lives by the old rules, we must also respect our proud heritage of religious liberty and freedom of conscience that prohibits us from imposing sectarian doctrine onto public institutions.

As today we discuss new rules, we must keep in mind that the oldest rule of American society is freedom -- freedom of thought and speech and freedom of belief and worship. That oldest rule is why many of our ancestors came here and what our founders fought for and built 200 years ago. We must not change that rule!

Above all, we should try to heed the truth stated so well by Abraham Lincoln: "I am concerned to know not whether the Lord is on my side, but whether I am on the Lord's side." If we keep President Lincoln's concern in mind, our prospects will be greater for all of us on this raft to be satisfied and feel right and kind toward the others.

THE OLD RIGHT IN THE NEW 80's

Rev. Charles V. Bergstrom
Executive Director, Department of Governmental Affairs,
Lutheran Council in the United States

Member, Board of Directors, People For The American Way

April 1981

It needs to be stated clearly that churches, nonprofit
organizations, and individuals have every right to speak to the
government. This of course includes both right-wing fundamentalists and left-wing activists. However, it also needs to be
said that all those who teach or say "Lord, Lord" do not always
speak a good biblical theology. Sometimes they may even tell
false stories about their goals and activities. In his recent
article in Context, Martin Marty suggests that right-wing
religious groups should neither be taken too seriously nor too
lightly. Their strength should be neither underestimated nor
overestimated.

All of us are aware of the rise of the so-called "electronic church." TV preachers like Pat Robertson of the "700
Club," Jim Bakker of the "PTL Club," and Jerry Falwell of the
"Old Time Gospel Hour" have become household names in some
parts of the country. Generally fundamentalist in approach,
such TV personalities have focused on the "moral problems" of
the nation. Their list of "moral issues" ranges from school
prayer to abortion, from defense spending to homosexuality.
Increasingly, their solutions to these "moral dilemmas" have
taken the form of right-wing political positions. Thus, they
are described in the media as the "religious New Right" because
of their combining of evangelism with governmental lobbying.

Originally, the leading figures in the electronic church
rejected any involvement in politics and condemned other
religious groups for their excursions into this area. But in
recent years many have begun to speak openly of the need for
political action on the part of what they say are truly "born-
again" Christians. Best known and most active is the Moral
Majority organized by Jerry Falwell, a Baptist preacher from
Virginia. Actually, there are several related but separately

incorporated Moral Majorities. One is a registered lobbying group; another's stated purpose is educational; yet a third is a political action committee which is allowed to make campaign contributions to political candidates. Claiming 72,000 pastors -- the Moral Majority has semi-autonomous chapters in individual states. The Moral Majority also claims to have registered three million new voters who, it maintains, were instrumental in electing candidates who will "vote right" on its list of moral issues.

In letters to his extensive network, Jerry Falwell writes that God has given him a "divine mandate" to speak to government and to carry out the work of the Moral Majority. One example is a "Christian Bill of Rights" which he advocates -- while at the same time preaching that he does not support the concept of a "Christian" republic. The Christian Bill of Rights outlines in detail so-called Christian positions on such issues as school prayer and abortion -- positions which he contends should be legislated in many cases.

Jewish leaders have expressed (legitimate) concern about this Christian Bill of Rights. The document seems to hold that this nation will be properly governed only when it has adopted legislation and regulations that express the moral and theological beliefs of its drafters. A view like that leads precisely to the notion of a Christian State that Falwell says he disavows. For that reason noted evangelical Stanley Mooneyham, head of World Vision, writes that he is "as scared of any evangelical power block as of any other. World power in religious hands -- Islamic or Christian -- has hardened into more than one inquisition. That God has saved us from the hands of zealous or misguided saints is all that has saved us at times."

Groups such as the Moral Majority understand the United States as "God's chosen people" and discuss American history in glowing, but highly selective, terms. They often talk about the "good old days" in contrast to the terrible days of present immorality. Wealth and success are the expected rewards for "good" people. A "moral America" will become powerful again. However, the past realities of such evils as slavery and the oppression of Native Americans -- events which are also part of our history -- are conveniently ignored. Their rhetoric reintroduces an emphasis on states' rights as a way to escape federal regulation in areas where they would be free.

Black leaders have shared with us their deep concern about
this rhetoric. Behind the appeal for states' rights we need to
recognize the potential for institutional racism. In the days
before federal civil rights legislation, state governments were
not seen as paragons of racial justice. Today we are exper-
iencing a resurgence of such groups as the Klu Klux Klan and
the American Nazi Party. While we imply no linkage, we must be
sensitive to the concerns of minority groups in society. We
need to join them in acknowledging past and present injustices
and in building a just and equitable society.

Some of the tactics of groups associated with the religious New Right cause us concern also. Instances of direct
deception, biased discussion of issues, attacks on the morality
of those who disagree on political issues, and the development
of "hit lists" targeting such candidates for defeat -- all of
which our office has observed firsthand -- conflict with the
Christian Gospel these groups claim to profess....

Openness and clarity are needed if the public is construc-
tively to debate policy positions or specific pieces of legislation and regulations. This challenge needs to be given not
only to The Christian Voice and other groups of the religious
right, but to all those -- left or right -- who involve themselves in the governmental decision-making process.

Most important, the religious right wing is strangely
silent about the basic issues of poverty and the needs for
justice; their moral lists generally do not include such
concerns. A biblical, evangelical Christianity, faithful to
the New Testament and the Old Testament, cannot be silent these
days about the inequities and the hurts which may be alleviated
with the help of the government acting with support of the
church. Furthermore, the religious New Right fails to discern
the issues which really cry out for Christian attention. As
evangelical Senator Mark Hatfield of Oregon writes, the gri-
evous sins of our society are militarism and materialism -- not
the ratifying of the Taiwan treaty or the supporting of the
Equal Rights Amendment, however much we may disagree on the
specifics of those decisions....

In one of his TV programs prior to the presidential
election, Southern Baptist Bill Moyers explored the relationship between some evangelical leaders and their supporters. He
ended with harsh words for religious leaders who follow the

conservative line and in turn try to persuade others to follow
it too. Moyers said,

> They're being misled, these people, by manipulators of
> politics, masquerading as messengers of heaven...The same
> Jerry Falwell who claims a divine mandate to go right into
> the halls of Congress and fight for laws that would save
> America is caught lying in public about a meeting he had
> with President Carter...Some majority, some morality!

The born-again Christian preachers who operate in close
relationship with political action leaders have often succumbed
to rhetoric which has little to do with basic Christian faith
or morality. The terms used -- "success," "winning," "attacking," "targeting," and "intimidating" -- are political terms.
Preachers are certainly free to use them, but when they do they
ought not baptize their excoriations as evangelical or as
religious advocacy....

Parishioners need to be informed on how church bodies
arrive at collective decisions on major social issues. They
need to be helped to distinguish between legitimate advocacy
and an uncritical mixing of religion and politics. A recent
statement by the leaders of the Lutheran Council member
churches might help:

> Lutheran churches support pluralism and freedom of all
> people in the political process in the United States, and
> maintain that pushing for total agreement on moral issues
> is not the same as advocating for legislation which will
> enhance the common good. "Religious grounds" should not
> be used as the exclusive yardstick for determining the
> quality of candidates for political office. We strongly
> discourage members of Lutheran churches from joining or
> supporting movements which confuse church-government rela-
> tions and distort the church's advocacy mission in the
> political world. We support parish pastors and church
> leaders who do not endorse such movements.

In many of the radio and television appearances that I
have made, those doing the interviewing asked, "Why don't the
mainline churches provide the media with programs to give a
platform for some of their great preachers on social justice?"
That indeed may be one of the things we have to do. However,
all of us need to make sure that our efforts in the advocacy

for justice are based on a deeper motivation than outdoing the
present day religious entertainers.

God's world is not intrinsically evil, we Lutherans hold,
but is the arena where his love and the ministry of the church
are carried out. Secular is not automatically the equivalent
of godless, nor the mere application of religious terms
guarantee of the holiness of the enterprise. As the churches
and their members strive for justice in the world, they need
not label their political position as "Christian" or "moral" to
justify what they do. Yes, there are passages of Scripture to
support this concept of ministry: "I was hungry, and you gave
me food; I was thirsty, and you gave me drink; I was a
stranger, and you welcomed me; I was naked, and you clothed me;
I was sick and you visited me." The ministry of advocacy --
side by side with other ministries of advocacy -- side by side
with other ministries of the church -- attempts to respond to
these needs as we strive for justice in the world. That is
really evangelical.

So what the media began to call the New Right turns out to
be not so new after all. It is in fact the old conservatism in
the new eighties. How long it will continue to be a force in
American politics no one can guess. But we need not doubt that
a patient, persistent ministry of advocacy on behalf of justice
for all, expecially the poor and the oppressed, will be needed,
perhaps now more than before. In the long run such ministry
carries more power than any that may glitter self-righteously
under the glare of TV lights.

Rev. Bergstrom's remarks are excerpted here with permission
from the April 1981 issue of LCA Partners, the monthly magazine
of the Lutheran Council of America.

REMARKS TO

Temple Emanu-El, San Francisco
September 24, 1981

Eileen R. Growald

Member, National Advisory Council of
People For The American Way

Fundamentalist movements are nothing new in America.
According to Sidney Ahlstrom, author of The Religious History
of the American People, the first era began in 1896 when a
group of evangelical ministers, primarily Baptist and Presbyterian, became convinced that the United States and the whole
Christian world was "sinking so deeply and so decisively into
apostasy and heresy that it could only mean the approach of the
last days."

Obviously, these predictions were not fulfilled but the
onset of World War I caused a revival in the form of apocalyptic warnings. In the 1920's, fundamentalists refined their
fears to the effect that modern modes of life and thinking,
right down to social dancing, were going to doom the world.

In the 1950's, the McCarthy era's fundamentalists found
new reasons for acerbic homilies. They focused their targets
on Communism as the precursor of Satan who would end civilization by destroying the American family.

By the 1970's, an interesting reversal took hold. No
longer were preachers blaming society for ruining the family.
Instead, they blamed the breakdown of the family for the
spawning of Communism. Preachers James Robison and Jerry
Falwell claimed the onset of feminism, pornography and militant
homosexuality to be the snake in the eaves of American homes.
And with these decrees in 1979 came the dawning of the self-
named "Moral Majority."

Jerry Falwell, the founder and self-appointed President of
the Moral Majority, is a Baptist minister from Lynchburg,
Virginia. He, like many other small town preachers, has a

regular congregation. The difference between Jerry Falwell and
other preachers is he not only tells people how to <u>live</u>, but
how to <u>vote</u>. He speaks of his political objectives in terms of
a "holy war," of a battle between the forces of good and evil.
The crux of the battle is humanism versus Christianity but the
ammunition spreads far beyond....

The issue of censorship has drawn equal attention from the
press. Though the Moral Majority has been credited with much
of the hullabaloo, there are in fact numerous other organizations and individuals involved. Most of them, such as Paul
Weyrich's Committee for Survival of a Free Congress, the
Heritage Foundation and others are devoted strictly to promoting political candidates who they deem morally fit for office.
But many others, like Phyllis Schlafly of The Eagle Forum, have
joined Falwell in censorship of books and movies.

The issue has become so pronounced now that volumes of
Shakespeare, Steinbeck, Salinger and other well-known authors
have been stolen from library shelves and burned in the name of
"morality". Even dictionaries have been confiscated because of
the use of the word "bed" as a verb. And a few moments of
embarrassment occurred when an evangelist professor at Indiana
University confiscated a book entitled <u>Making It With Mademoi-</u>
<u>selle</u>, only to discover later that it contained merely dress
patterns for girls!

On any of these issues Falwell and his fellow evangelists
speak out in apocalyptic hyperbole. Their audiences are
scathed in the cauldron of their accusations and people emerge
either as converted saints or condemned sinners.

One questions the attraction of such admonitions. Why do
these people have such a large following, if not in numbers at
least in dollars? In the words of Joan Jones, a Democrat and a
member of Lynchburg, Virginia's state legislature, "These are
disquieting times for the average person. To have someone like
Jerry around, who creates an identity for them, is very comfort-
ing." Many of the followers are blue collar workers hard hit
by the past decade of inflation and the Reagan administration's
recent budget cuts. They are people who, as described by news
commentator John Salisbury, feel "frustrated in their personal
goals and achievements, frustrated by their lack of community
recognition, who feel the desparate need to belong, to be a

part of something, and the bigger the better."

The problem is, their leaders are false, and in telling
what is right they are getting rich by being wrong....

It is the fact of this religious intolerance which has
driven television producer Norman Lear out of the studio and
into the public. In September, 1980, Lear founded a group
called People For The American Way. Its purpose was to
counteract the religious intolerance of the Moral Majority and
other groups of the New Religious Right. Through media campaigns, lectures and informative mailings he has already
gathered a prestigious national board of advisors and thousands
of new members every week.

Lear believes that the religious New Right:

Is more than just old-fashioned evangelism. It is a
well financed ($150 million raised last year), highly
coordinated, computerized campaign not just to preach
their faith and their politics -- which they have the
right to do -- but an attempt to impose their political
and moral beliefs on the rest of us....

The New Religious Right professes to be concerned with the
family unit, the threat of communism and the multi-faceted
corruption in our society today. In fact, what they are really
preaching is intolerance, narrowness, bigotry and fanaticism.
They have the right to state their opinions but they do not
have the right to tell others they are sinners if they don't
agree.

Without tolerance there can be no diversity. And without
diversity our country cannot be.